Spectacular Listening

Spectacular Listening

Music and Disability in the Digital Age

BYRD McDANIEL

OXFORD
UNIVERSITY PRESS

Oxford University Press is a department of the University of Oxford. It furthers
the University's objective of excellence in research, scholarship, and education
by publishing worldwide. Oxford is a registered trade mark of Oxford University
Press in the UK and certain other countries.

Published in the United States of America by Oxford University Press
198 Madison Avenue, New York, NY 10016, United States of America.

© Oxford University Press 2024

All rights reserved. No part of this publication may be reproduced, stored in
a retrieval system, or transmitted, in any form or by any means, without the
prior permission in writing of Oxford University Press, or as expressly permitted
by law, by license, or under terms agreed with the appropriate reproduction
rights organization. Inquiries concerning reproduction outside the scope of the
above should be sent to the Rights Department, Oxford University Press, at the
address above.

You must not circulate this work in any other form
and you must impose this same condition on any acquirer.

Library of Congress Cataloging-in-Publication Data
Names: McDaniel, Byrd, author.
Title: Spectacular listening : music and disability in the digital age /
Byrd McDaniel.
Description: New York : Oxford University Press, 2024. |
Includes bibliographical references and index.
Identifiers: LCCN 2023038542 (print) | LCCN 2023038543 (ebook) |
ISBN 9780197620465 (paperback) | ISBN 9780197620458 (hardback) |
ISBN 9780197620489 (epub)
Subjects: LCSH: Music—Social aspects. | Sociology of disability. |
Listening—Social aspects. | Air guitar. | Lip sync. | Discrimination
against people with disabilities.
Classification: LCC ML3916 .M379 2024 (print) | LCC ML3916 (ebook) |
DDC 780.87—dc23/eng/20230913
LC record available at https://lccn.loc.gov/2023038542
LC ebook record available at https://lccn.loc.gov/2023038543

DOI: 10.1093/oso/9780197620458.001.0001

Paperback printed by Marquis Book Printing, Canada
Hardback printed by Bridgeport National Bindery, Inc., United States of America

Contents

List of Figures	vii
Preface	ix
Acknowledgments	xxi

Introduction: Listening as an Expressive Act	1
Defining Disability and Normalcy	4
Normal Listening	7
Against Normal Listening	15
Scope and Methods	18
Outline of the Book	23

1. Use Your Illusion: Disability Masquerade in the US Air Guitar
Championships	25
Methods	28
Overview of Air Guitar	30
Disclosure and Masquerade	33
Shreddy Boop	35
Damaged	38
Cindairella	43
Kara	48
Giant Junk	51
Conclusion	54

2. Fluent Circulation: Lip Syncing from musical.ly to TikTok to
YouTube	58
Methods	61
Defining musical.ly	64
Defining the Disability Community on musical.ly	67
Musicking on musical.ly	74
ASL In-Groups	78
Conclusion	82

3. Tactical Reactions: Toward a Crip Music Criticism
	86
Methods	89
The Broad Context of Reactions	91
The Tactical Reactions of Disabled Creators	96
Mobilizing Chain Reactions	104
Conclusion	111

vi CONTENTS

4. Accessible Listening: Podcasts as Audible Models   113
  What Is a Podcast?   114
  What Is the Point of Listening?   116
  Methods   117
  Listening as Exchange   122
  Listening Technologies   126
  Listening Through Others   130
  Podcasting as Accessible   135

  Conclusion: When Spectacular Becomes Standard   139
  The Sharing Imperative   140
  Syncing Out Loud   146
  Marginal Practices   152
  Performing Listening   157

Notes   161
Bibliography   177
Index   189

Figures

I.1 Tiger Claw with replica. Photo credit: Dan LaFever. 7

I.2 "Another Car Ride with Motoki." Motoki Maxted. Screenshot by the author on July 17, 2022. 15

1.1 Professair at Hard Rock Café in Boston. Photo credit: Clara Schwager. 26

1.2 Shreddy at Dark Horse. Photo credit: author. 35

1.3 Damaged at Dark Horse. Photo credit: author. 39

1.4 Cindairella in Lawrence. Photo credit: Whitney Young. 43

1.5 Kara Portrait. Photo credit: Lenny Gotter. 47

2.1 Ariel Rebecca Martin. "Musical.ly Tutorial Part #2 Making Duets!:) | Baby Ariel." Screenshot by the author on July 17, 2022. 62

2.2 Keenan Cahill. "Teenage Dream (Keenan Cahill)." Screenshot by the author on July 17, 2022. 67

2.3 Eliza Caws "GLITCHY MUSICAL.LY TUTORIAL // Tips and tricks [Eliza Caws]." Screenshot by the author on July 17, 2022. 76

2.4 Shaheem Sanchez. "Pills & Automobiles—Chris Brown (in Sign Language)." Screenshot by the author on July 17, 2022. 81

3.1 Anthony Fantano. "Danny Brown—XXX ALBUM REVIEW." Screenshot by the author on July 17, 2022. 87

3.2 America's Got Talent. "America's Got Talent 2019 WINNER KODI LEE Auditions And Performances | Got Talent Global." Screenshot by the author on July 17, 2022. 105

3.3 Stephanie Bethany. "An Autistic's Thoughts on Kodi Lee (AGT Golden Buzzer)." Screenshot by the author on July 17, 2022. 110

4.1 Power Not Pity. Podcast Thumbnail. 119

4.2 Reid My Mind. Podcast Thumbnail. 120

4.3 Disability Visibility. Podcast Thumbnail. 121

C.1 Social Repose. "BILLIE EILISH REACTED TO MY COVER II Billie Eilish Watches Fan Covers on YouTube | Glamour." Screenshot by the author on July 17, 2022. 144

viii FIGURES

C.2 Ford Foundation. "(Audio Described) Political participation & disability, ft Alice Wong, #CripTheVote." 150

C.3 Marquina in Oulu. Photo credit: author. 155

C.4 Air guitarists play "Free Bird." Photo credit: author. 157

Preface

My grandfather's final moments occurred in a nursing home. Under lockdown due to COVID-19, the facility administrators prevented guests from visiting patients. My family spent many hours wondering about his quality of life, since he couldn't speak to us due to dementia. After a period of time, the staff permitted us to crack the window six inches. Given this new opportunity, we would crouch outside in a flowerbed in the hot sun, crooking our necks to fit our mouths right in the opening of the window. We would speak to him. He was mostly unresponsive, but we continued to try to make contact.

My family eventually found a solution, which became a ritual. We would situate a Bluetooth speaker on the windowsill. Using our phones, we would play a Spotify playlist through the crack in the window. The playlist consisted of songs that reminded him of his youth and World War II—"Over There," "Fly Me to the Moon," and "Summertime." We had to pick a version with prominent vocals. When the music would play, he became animated, awakening from his stillness. He would actually sing some of the words. While lying on his bed, he would use his arms to make circles, air conducting with the music. At a certain level, he must have known we were present there too, making the music possible, but he did not always acknowledge us, at least not in any consistent way. But his expressive listening gave us the visual feedback we so desired, confirming a connection with us through the music.

I was writing this book during this time, researching practices that transform listening into a theatrical act. I became interested in listening as a performance. My grandfather's example felt like a strange yet apt instance of theatrical listening, in which listening becomes something that may be witnessed by others. To witness someone else listening can awaken powerful forms of listening in oneself. We found ourselves listening to the music *as he might listen*, in order to select music that would resonate with him. Our technologies—speakers and platforms—became technologies through which we could connect with him.

In the pages that follow, I focus on performance practices that take these everyday acts of listening and elevate them into performance genres. These performance genres have traditions, practitioners, histories, and aesthetics. As strange and superficial as they may seem, the case studies in this book stem from some of the more mundane listening acts that occur in everyday life. I hope that they call upon you to think about these mundane acts, as you marvel at the spectacular ones.

The pandemic has heightened the stakes for the themes that appear here. Millions of people around the world have died, including many musicians and music lovers. Those who survived COVID-19, with or without getting the virus, live with its consequences still, in ways that compound preexisting global inequalities and health disparities.

The pandemic provided an impetus for public discussions about health, trauma, care, and accessibility, but these conversations had been happening for a long time within disability circles in many online spaces. Building on the powerful legacy of disability activism that drew upon protest in physical spaces (from the 504 Sit In to the Capitol Crawl), a loose network of online activists had been actively advancing disability justice via social media. For example, in 2016, three activists—Andrew Pulrang, Gregg Beratan, and Alice Wong—founded #CripTheVote, in order to challenge the erasure of disability in presidential elections in the United States. Following the election of President Trump, activists staged a digital march to accompany the in-person Women's March.[1] People continued to mobilize in public spaces to protest injustice and support Black Lives Matter, and organizations like the Harriet Tubman Collective, founded in 2016, released materials that emphasize ableism as an inherent quality of white supremacy.[2]

Online spaces also became opportunities for more dynamic discussions of everyday life with disability. Twitter, TikTok, Facebook, and Instagram developed subcultures for disabled creators to share their art and themselves. Hashtags helped organize discussions. Keah Brown writes about creating the viral hashtag #DisabledAndCute in 2017, which honored the fact that "in this black and disabled body, [she], too, deserved joy."[3] Dawn Gibson formed "Spoonie Chat" as an opportunity for people on Twitter and Facebook to discuss chronic illness and invisible disabilities.[4] Digital platforms enabled folks to call out ableism of public figures,[5] and these spaces also enabled public figures—many musicians—to open up about their bodies in new ways.

While disability activism online flourished due to the exigencies of the pandemic, music scenes also began to increasingly move online, increasing their accessibility to remote and physically dispersed audiences. During the early moments of the lockdowns, folks began circulating public singing across social media. Inspired by Europeans singing from their balconies during quarantine, two Chicagoans organized a singalong to "Livin' on a Prayer" by Bon Jovi in a Facebook event called "Chicago-Wide Sing-a-Long," in which over 8,000 people participated. They sang collectively in public spaces, synchronized through their organizing on Facebook, and they circulated their music across various platforms online. In New York City, some residents collectively sang "Yellow Submarine" and "Lean On Me," while others took to Frank Sinatra to celebrate essential workers. Similar events followed in cities across the country. On YouTube, Twitch, Instagram, and many music apps, musicians found create ways to stage live performances on digital platforms—from the celebrity-studded Verzuz webcast series to the countless karaoke performances in spaces like Smule. Some live venues closed and never came back. Many venues made livestreaming a key component of all live performances.

In short, the pandemic reveals how interwoven physical and digital spheres have become. One can hardly think of a protest without an online component, although that was not true in the recent past. And all online activity points back to the physical bodies and contexts that make digital cultures possible.

I wrote this book in this way to recognize the interwoven nature of physical and digital spheres.[6] In my opening example, I present a combination of a physical platform (a window sill) and a digital platform (Spotify), along with the speaker, Bluetooth, the physical space of the room, and the people connected across these technologies. In my case studies, I seek to offer a similar approach, which weaves together the physical and digital realms that encompass performances of listening.

US Air Guitar represents a hybrid online and offline case study, although the pandemic has rapidly changed the scene. US Air Guitar has traditionally been a live music scene that takes place in various physical spaces, all of which is made possible by online organizing. Competitors compete in live music events, where they gesturally represent rock solos using elaborate choreographies. Each live event occurs as a result of logistics, rehearsing, planning, and audio editing, all of which takes place online. Air guitarists use Facebook to stay in touch with the community. They use digital audio workstations to edit clips for performances. They livestream events via Periscope, and they use Twitter to live tweet results.

The pandemic has pushed US Air Guitar more online. US Air Guitar has proven adaptable. In recent years, they have begun staging exclusively online events, one of which I judged remotely from an office building in downtown Providence. Air guitarists now perform on Twitch and Instagram. They've used their competitions as opportunities to promote vaccination and social distancing. Their competition was even featured on ESPN, giving them an ability to broadcast their sport to a wide audience.

Compared to the case studies that follow, US Air Guitar also represents an older, historical performance genre. Participants tend to be middle aged. Many have families and children. So the scene stands in stark contrast with the contemporary, youth-oriented practices in Chapters 2 and 3. Contemporary air guitarists tend to look back to the rock heroes of the past, so nostalgia appears as an implicit quality of these performances. Air guitar competitions have taken place at least since the late 1970s, and their contemporary manifestations involve many people who came of age in the 1970s and 1980s. But air guitar has also been incredibly influential in contemporary gestural popular music practices today—dances, video games, and embodied movements on digital music apps. While air guitar may be nostalgic, the impulse to pantomime to popular music has novel new iterations.

In my chapter on US Air Guitar, I emphasize the personal dimensions of the practice, particularly performers who seek creative outlets to explore their disabilities and identities. As my subsequent case studies expand in scale and scope, I begin with a chapter about these personal stories in order to emphasize how these performance practices involve complex people who want to share aspects of their impairments with audiences in covert and overt ways. My decision to focus on disability disclosure stemmed from the fact that air guitar quite literally transforms something invisible into something visible.

The act of disclosure has always been a feature of life with disability,[7] but the pandemic has created a context where acts of disclosure have become more commonplace. Public disclosures of coronavirus test results have become a performance genre. In the early days of the pandemic many celebrities publicly announced their diagnoses, such as Idris Elba, Tom Hanks, and Brooke Baldwin.[8] Today these acts of announcing a positive COVID test appear quite common, almost routine and unmentionable. The act of coming out with a positive diagnosis echoes the HIV/AIDS crisis, yet we should be hesitant to make comparisons in the current moment.[9] But there are nonetheless lessons from these past crises that pertain to our current situation. In particular, epidemics and pandemics bring about deserving and undeserving victims. Some become heroic survivors; others become demonized

PREFACE xiii

populations. Indeed, as I discuss in the conclusion for Chapter 1, the act of sharing can bring about a sense of validation or be a painful reminder of one's vulnerability.

The next chapter presents an online, youth-oriented version of the exact same kinds of pantomime practices as air guitar, and I foreground the theme of circulation within the musical.ly community. While researching air guitar, I found many online practices that engaged in a very similar set of techniques, adapting popular music clips for new performances. Online performers would edit the music, choreograph gestures to animate sounds, and circulate these sounds within online spaces. At the time of my research, musical.ly was ascendant with shocking numbers of daily active users. So I set out to examine the ways that musical.ly enabled performers to use their phones as both an object for performance, as well as a device to record performances to share with others. I recognized that a focus exclusively within the app would only tell one part of the story, which is why I include the gestures that happen outside of the screen and feed the content on the platform.

Rather than dwell on the personal questions as with US Air Guitar, I decided to examine the community as a whole, in order to trace the factors that help performers congeal as a particular cohesive subculture. In distinction to practices that might have formal membership (e.g., a music organization or a Facebook group), musical.ly users were connected in much more diffuse ways, so I theorize fluent circulation as a way of explaining how people can be connected through common approaches to the app.

While researching the app, I realized that my explanation of musical.ly would quickly need to have multiple dimensions and encompass other platforms. The gestures on musical.ly seemed to travel into and emerge out of other apps, as well as tutorials on YouTube. I sought to explain how YouTube serves as the backbone of musical.ly in many ways, as a place to store content, reflect on the practice, and compile videos into thematic series. While doing this research, musical.ly was acquired by ByteDance and became part of TikTok. So I also gathered that musical.ly would soon be historical, as a phase in the development of a much larger platform that now boasts over a billion users.

During the pandemic, TikTok flourished. In the initial days of the pandemic, creators were forced inside,[10] and this social isolation led to abundant content about diagnoses and social distancing. TikTok became a platform for public health officials, doctors, political campaigns, disabled activists, pro-vaccination efforts, anti-vaccination efforts, and many creative music makers. In the early days of the pandemic, screen time rose 18 percent to an average of five hours and forty minutes per day,[11] which means higher engagement from followers but also more competition for attention, and Instagram and Facebook Live doubled their view counts. Twitch reported record streaming on the platform.[12]

Every minor example that I emphasize on musical.ly seems to have spawned an entire subculture on TikTok, although questions about community cohesion remain. While I did not think of this way at the time, I came to retrospectively regard musical.ly as a critical foundation for TikTok. I hope my chapter documents some of the early experiments among disabled creators, whose work has now become part of established disability subcultures online. Indeed, musical.ly felt transient and somewhat fleeting during my research, and the disappearance of the platform gives me a sense that defining this ephemerality can be an important contribution of my chapter. How does a community hold together in the constantly disruptive flux of digital innovation?

My third case study—reaction videos—centers a practice that feels distinctly sui generis on the internet *and* traditional in the long history of music reception. A longtime reader of music reviews, I had come to appreciate written reviews as a valuable way to find new music, and my growing understanding of disability studies led me to feel like that many of these reviews offered an extremely narrow idea of both listening and musical works. Music reviews, in the style found in *Rolling Stone* or *Pitchfork*, often survey new releases, in ways that completely bracket questions of how one uses the body to engage with recorded sounds. The object of these reviews feels like a given and listening seems straightforward, almost always ear-based.

I encountered reaction videos on YouTube as part of my broader research on digital cultures, and I found them to be quite familiar as music reviews, although they offered completely different evaluative criteria. Similar to written reviews, they examine music for aesthetic qualities and artist identities, but they also prioritize how music feels, presenting these feelings as a performance in the act of listening. They perform listening as a way of evaluating musical excellence.

So in Chapter 3, I examine reactions among creators, including a wide range of reactions that involve filming feelings about popular media. Sometimes these videos include in-the-moment listening; sometimes they involve reflection after the fact. In this case study, I am less concerned with drawing clear parameters around reaction videos with a specific definition, and I am more so invested in presenting reactions as common feature of online circulation of media. In these videos, people place faith in the fact that embodied performances are the best way to convey an evaluation of popular media.

After writing the chapter, I came to see reactions as part of much larger trend in popular culture. I started this work when reactions were somewhat niche and nascent trend, and now reactions have become a standard business practice. Many media companies have used the format to launch new products or build hype around an artist. For example, they may pay influencers to react to their products or create a reaction series. Musicians and labels pay people to react to their new songs. Some creators told me that they sometimes get paid to retract bad reactions.

During the pandemic, numerous influencers filmed themselves reacting to getting COVID. For example, on one YouTube channel, I find a video of a man and a woman who appear in a car on their way to get tested for coronavirus in a drive-through Los Angeles testing site.[13] These two partners sit with their Instagram-famous dog, in the back seat of the car. The woman mentions a chronic illness, which puts her in an at-risk group for virus complications, and the video reveals a litany of symptoms that have led her to believe she will test positive: no taste, no sense of smell, migraine, hard to take deep breaths, and so on. Also having multiple symptoms, the man decides not to seek out a test, believing that his wife's diagnosis would be enough confirmation for the both of them. They wait in line and narrate their experience for viewers. They vacillate between jokes and a resigned acceptance of the situation, but they keep filming, taking viewers step by step in this process. As they wait in the car, they see a bee on the windshield. They react to skateboarders in defiance of social distancing. They finally manage to get a test. The woman swabs her cheeks and the roof of her mouth, as instructed. The end of the video cuts to few days later, when the two are at home. She receives confirmation over the phone that she does indeed have the virus. The video ends with the man cautioning viewers to stay inside at all costs.

Initially YouTube took an explicit stance against people profiting from coronavirus-related content.[14] YouTube halted monetization of videos about the coronavirus as a result of its "sensitive events" policy, which prevents ads from being associated with videos about horrific events (mass shootings, terrorist attacks, etc.). Eventually YouTube CEO Susan Wojcicki announced a decision to resume the monetization of coronavirus videos for "a limited number of channels," including those related to various news organizations and those of creators who participate in a "self-certification system" (basically, a kind of rewards system for creators who accurately identify and label their content).[15] Despite these easing restrictions, some creators took an explicit stance against profiting from their coronavirus disclosures, while others continued to turn their plight with the coronavirus into media for others to watch.

From a certain vantage point, these COVID reaction videos operate as a kind of brand-awareness play for creators, producing an opportunity to expand their audience through gaining more subscribers. Their coronavirus videos might not be monetized, but the recommendation algorithm may push a subsequent video that is. Even if they don't monetize a particular video, they still benefit from the attention the video receives. They share this in common with major news outlets, whose ratings have surged since the dawn of the social-distancing era.[16] A crisis can be good for business. These acts of sharing relate to what I call the "sharing imperative" in my conclusion, in which people come to see sharing as a source of empowerment.

"Reactions" also captures a broader aesthetic that has come to represent emotionally charged online interactions. While researching reaction videos, I would view cable news networks, in which hosts would ask politicians to react to media clips, such as the January 6th Capitol riots or the war in Ukraine. These reactions ideally would create additional chain reactions, as people reacted to those initial reactions. When I would watch protests, I would see protesters try to get a reaction from others, as a form of provocation, and these reactions would become popular media that would circulate online. When I went online, I would see posts that proved popular primarily because they were so polarizing. So my chapter on reaction videos aims to evaluate how reactions online influence music reception in particular, while offering insights that apply to a wide range of reactive content.

I added a final chapter on podcasts in order to emphasize critical perspectives on disability advocacy. The pandemic has elevated so many public figures as well as a whole cadre of COVID influencers.[17] Some of these influencers have promoted testing, masking, and vaccinations, and others have risen to popularity out of opposition to all of these things. COVID-19 has produced new opportunities for influencers of many varieties, including fashion influencers and home-fitness instructors.[18] Many have leveraged their fame for personal and financial gain. Some online personalities, for example, tried to use their influence to secure COVID tests at a time of scarcity, and some used their financial resources to socially isolate in picturesque locations around the world, as a sort of privileged vacation from society.[19]

In contrast to some of the privileged folks who used privileges to secure resources, I offer a final case study that elevates influential perspectives, particularly from those who have long been trying to raise awareness about health disparities and disabilities. For example, ADAPT continued to organize grassroots movements to challenge the widespread illness and death among disabled folks during the pandemic. In their public statement, they write in September 2021: "ADAPT members created the Lives Worth Life social media campaign in early 2020 to bring attention to the fact that disabled and aging people in nursing homes, institutions and other congregate settings were dying at alarming rates. These settings were COVID-19 cluster sites, resulting in the deaths of 70,000 people, 40% of the total COVID-19 deaths."[20] In terms of stories and narratives, Alice Wong, who I feature in Chapter 4, continued to put out podcast episodes on topics that make these issues personal, such as "Black Doctors with Disabilities," "Coronavirus and Disaster Planning with Germán Luis Parodi and Valerie Novack," and "Coronavirus and Spirituality with Eliot Kukla." In ways personal and general, these examples represent important perspective on how the pandemic impacts disabled communities.

In my final case study, I also wanted to highlight the unique role of audio media in telling these stories, particularly for the ways that audio can persuade people to listen. The pandemic called upon so many to ask for more, better, and deeper listening. But these calls for listening often felt like platitudes without attention to the actual accessibility issues revolving around listening itself. I often found myself wondering what exactly listening sounds like.

So in Chapter 4, I demonstrate how audio media can train us to listen to future audio media. Much music scholarship dwells exclusively on music, and I add this case study to emphasize how non-music forms of sound media can influence all forms of sound media. My interest in non-music sound media came in part from a brief period of working at NPR in Washington DC, where I saw people craft events into audio stories. I witnessed famous radio personalities create their personas through audio editing, as they planned scripts, rehearsed their vocalizations, and recorded stories in the booth. I discovered how audio media can provide a particular point of view—the auditory equivalent of the gaze.[21]

xviii PREFACE

So I center podcasters who do this for the disability community, as they model the ways that people might listen. I also present a chapter that emphasizes three particularly prominent disability advocates, in order to have this book honor their work. Throughout the book, I make decisions about anonymity and giving people credit through direct acknowledgment, depending on the circumstance and the arrangement with an individual. In this final chapter, I hope to give a signal boost to these podcasters to support their work.

I also hope to sharpen the importance of podcasts as form of DIY media, although the status of podcasting has been rapidly changing into a much more professional enterprise. The podcasting industry developed significantly in the course of writing this book. Much like YouTube and TikTok, podcasting exists in an extremely wide spectrum today—from DIY versions that embrace low-tech aesthetics to high-polish output that comes from major news organizations. Podcasting appeals to people due to a low barrier of entry and widespread distribution, but these factors make podcasting extremely variable, offering a platform for all kinds of political ideologies. My final case study emphasizes the important cultural work of podcasters who tell stories about disability by people with disabilities.

* * *

Given the rapid changes occurring in digital cultures across my case studies, I decided to focus on general themes that would apply across and beyond these examples, rather than dwell too much on extensive technical analyses of affordances, algorithms, or platform design. All of these elements appear in the pages that follow, but my goal is to have the ideas in this book live beyond these particular manifestations, offering universal questions about belonging, acceptance, and protest. I offer ideas that can transcend some of the particulars of these platforms, while also attending to some of the peculiarities that make them notable at a particular moment in time.

One element that unites these case studies is that they all pertain to relatively public arenas—platforms, digital or physical spaces, apps, and formats. I frequently refer to people as "activists" or doing "activism" within these spaces. My use of this word intends to honor the work of people who engage in labor for the sake of a broader community's benefit, particularly the disabled community. Chapters 3 and 4 present many people who embody activism in a more traditional sense. In Chapters 1 and 2, the activist dimensions may seem more ambiguous. In many instances across these various sites and scenes, people work to change public perceptions about disability and sometimes their own, and this kind of work hold an important place alongside other forms of activism, including those focused on rights, economics, policy, or politics.

Performing bodies remain at the center of this work, as agents of change and vehicles for arguments. Activism can take the form of political speech and discourse, and people often colloquialize activism as "conversations" that need to take place between various groups. I do not want to diminish these forms of discourse, but I also emphasize the ways that the body can dialogue with other bodies through performance, as well as through using technologies. I show how bodies can do activism, even if and a when a person might not have the language to participate in another way. This emphasis may seem entirely unsurprising to many music scholars, most of whom know how powerfully musical bodies can make political arguments, but the argument may seem a bit foreign to other scholars, for whom verbal and textual arguments may be the norm.

While disability remains the point of emphasis here, I share in the core mission of so many disability-justice scholars, captured in the words of Eli Clare's preface to *Exile and Pride*: "I want nondisabled progressive activists to add disability to their political agenda. And at the same time I want disability activists to abandon their single-issue politics and strategies."[22] I aim to entwine disability activism with these other movements, in order to advance conversations that consider disability as an essential part of discussions about race, sex, gender, ethnicity, and class.

The pandemic reveals that disability needs to be a consistent part of public consciousness, as well as the fact that the arts offer critical resources in times of need. My case studies offer perspective on the intersection of the arts and disability, as people work to present listening as a creative act. Their consumption of art, in times of crises and pleasure, becomes the source material for new performances. In my conclusion, I consider what happens when spectacular listening becomes standard, which resonates with many of the vast changes brought about by the recent years. These final thoughts revolve around the idea that the remarkable aspects of spectacular listening may soon become part of the fabric of our daily lives—the impulse to share/disclose, the desire to be in sync with popular music clips, and the need for marginal practices that can agitate systems of oppression.

Acknowledgments

I am deeply indebted to many incredible people who shaped this project.

I have been so fortunate to have guidance and feedback from a large community of friends and scholars, who have given me perspective and endurance in this project. Thank you to all of those who shared a panel with me, read my drafts, and engaged with my ideas. I also thank my students, who always test my ideas and expand my horizons.

I thank my sage and patient editor, Norm Hirschy, whose steadfast support and enthusiasm for this work proved invaluable in the many steps along the way. I also thank Ris Harp, Egle Zigaite, Rebecca Cain, Brady McNamara, Zoe Barham, Dharuman Bheeman, the production team at Newgen Knowledge Works, and the many others at Oxford University Press who helped this book become a reality.

I thank the wonderful folks at Trinity University and especially Stephen Fields, Jinli He, Ginger Wu, Claudia Stokes, Betsy Winakur Tontiplaphol, and David Rando. In your respective ways, you gave me an incredible foundation, which ignited a fascination with language that appears throughout these pages.

I am immensely grateful to the brilliant people at the University of Alabama, including Edward Tang, Michael Innis-Jiménez, and Stacy Morgan. I want to extend a special thanks to Jolene Hubbs, who helped me link language with culture, and Eric Weisbard, who gave me the tools to think about music critically and creatively. Thank you to these folks and many others for helping me gain my footing as a scholar.

My many thoughtful friends and colleagues at Brown University profoundly shaped my project, and I want to extend a deep sense of gratitude to Joshua Tucker, Marc Perlman, Rebecca Schneider, Paja Faudree, Bill Simmons, Betsey Biggs, Erik Deluca, Dana Gooley, Sydney Skybetter, and VK Preston. I am particularly appreciative to Kiri Miller for her persistent support as this project transformed from idea to research to dissertation to book. My insights are deeply indebted to her field-leading work.

I would also like to especially thank Will Cheng, Robin James, Kaleb Goldschmitt, Sydney Hutchinson, David Locke, Nick Seaver, Daniel Strong

xxii ACKNOWLEDGMENTS

Godfrey, Vanessa Ryan, Dale Chapman, Brittnay L. Proctor, Stephanie Jenkins, Stephanie Doktor, Jasmine Johnson, Francesca Inglese, Laura Stokes, Jenn Vieira, Sheila Hogg, Mary Rego, Paula Harper, Kate Galloway and Katherine Meizel. I also want to thank a particular community of scholars who I had the fortune of knowing in my PhD program: Cora Johnson-Roberson, Kathleen Haughey, Esther Kurtz, Jamie Corbett, Louis Wenger, Luis Achondo, Violet Cavicchi, and Melody Chapin. In quite distinct ways, this group helped me shape my initial ideas for this project through countless conversations in classrooms and outside. A special thank you goes to my thought partner Paul Renfro, who read many drafts and always helped sharpen my ideas.

My work on this book project was dramatically disrupted by the pandemic, and I had the fortune of joining the Fox Center for Humanistic Inquiry, which offered a critical refuge for me in a time of great need. The opportunity to be a postdoctoral fellow in the Fox Center bolstered my motivation to complete this project and provided a community of support at a pivotal time. I thank Walter Melion, Keith Anthony, Colette Barlow, and Amy Erbil.

A few other opportunities shaped my work in a significant way. My initial interest in popular music pantomime was bolstered by the kind folks at the Association for Recorded Sound Collections, who gave me a grant to do experimental research at Middle Tennessee State University at the Center for Popular Music. My conversations with the wonderful people at the center helped me orient myself to a history of listening and performing, and the interesting things in between. I want to thank my phenomenal colleagues who I taught alongside at Northeastern University and Tufts University. In addition, the creative coworkers at the Rhode Island School of Design influenced many of the ways I thought about creative practice as research. I recognize the privilege to work and teach in these schools and universities, and I remain deeply grateful to my colleagues who made these jobs feel worthwhile and engaging.

I want to give thanks to all of those whose insights appear in these pages, in the form of quotes, interviews, conversations, emails, citations, and musical performances. I want to especially thank the many delightfully strange people in US and World Air Guitar communities. These air guitarists opened up a way of thinking about musical listening that shines through all of my other case studies.

Finally, my family was instrumental in my work—Kathy McDaniel, Jay McDaniel, Matthew McDaniel, Lisa McDaniel, Mark Schwager, Patricia

Flanagan, Zach Schwager, Jessica Schwager, Hannah Schwager, Mike Caruso, and many extended family members. Thank you for your unceasing support, patience, and wisdom. I thank my ancestors as well.

Most importantly, my life partner Clara Schwager deserves so much thanks. Creative thinker, motivator, spiritual guide, common-sense examiner. Clara has taught me so much and been essential in the development of this book.

Thank you to all of you and so many more. This book represents your collective wisdom, which I have been honored to receive.

Introduction

Listening as an Expressive Act

Among the incredible performers I have met in my life, one friend stands out. The period between 2006 and 2008 represented the height of his craft. Garnering somewhat of a following in select circles in San Antonio, he would typically play in Wal-Mart parking lots in his car. He delivered amazing performances—dexterous, daring, impassioned, improvisational, and precise. Performances usually began with him in the driver's seat, and he would casually shuffle through a binder of CDs. He would pull one out, spin the face of the CD against his shirt to remove dust particles, and put it in the CD player. As the music started playing, he would adjust the volume, such that it felt a bit too loud—just slightly over the threshold of comfort. He would try to pick music somewhat at odds with the prevailing taste of his passengers: Katy Perry, the Eagles, or Brad Paisley. He wanted to offend our sensibilities, so anything that created a sense of tension would do the trick. As the song began playing, he would ease into his performance with a little narration, commenting on the idiosyncratic lyrics or the conventions of the genre. This would intensify our investment in the song. He would begin to sing along, while subtly fingering and tapping imaginary instruments. When the song reached a climax, he would unleash a dramatic and unrestrained one-man air-band performance. Breaking a sweat, he would throw his arms into the air, nailing every drum fill, guitar note, lyric, and pantomime. People would stare into the car with awe. We laughed and felt disarmed by his vulnerability, as his performances called on us to witness his experience of listening in his body.

In our everyday lives, the performance of listening appears in dramatic and mundane ways. Here are a few more examples. A teenager blares her homemade beats on a car sound system, which rattles the windows of nearby cars. At a nursing home, a woman moves her walker to the croon of Perry Cuomo on the radio, displaying her mobility to her friends. With his headphones plugged in, a man raps Lauryn Hill's hardest bars out loud at a bus

Spectacular Listening. Byrd McDaniel, Oxford University Press. © Oxford University Press 2024.
DOI: 10.1093/oso/9780197620458.003.0001

stop. While recording a podcast, a host vocalizes his surprise at the new Fiona Apple album so others can hear his excitement.

I call this phenomenon *spectacular listening*. Spectacular listening can be defined as the performance of music consumption, where people translate private reception into a public display of skilled interpretation. Listening becomes the subject of a performance. Spectacular implies spectacle, which I use in the most expansive sense of the term. In this project, spectacle involves causing a scene, commanding attention, and evoking awe. Spectacle is not simply visual but also auditory. The spectacular performances in this book can be ostentatious, flamboyant, pretentious, and sincere.

I focus on four ethnographic case studies that organize these spectacular listening activities into distinctive performance genres: (1) the US Air Guitar Championships; (2) lip syncing on musical.ly, TikTok, and YouTube; (3) popular music reaction videos on YouTube; and (4) podcasts as sonic art. In four different but related ways, these practices stage listening as the subject of musical performances, aligning pre-recorded media with new bodily acts. All of these genres bridge online and offline spaces, revealing the way digital worlds increasingly incentivize the performance of listening as an empowering act of consumption.

Listening is hardly, if ever, private. Contemporary digital platforms actively encourage people to share their consumption with others. Think of TikTok or Instagram, which enable users to bundle pre-recorded sounds and bodily movements. Think of Spotify, which makes listening habits public by default. We can share our listening on social media, and we can also have our listening be shared without our awareness. We can search for music online, and those searches can follow us as suggestions across our digital worlds. We can listen to music on our devices, and they can listen to us. Whether speaking of leaky online networks or attention-hungry music streaming platforms,[1] our musical listening always generates traces, data, and evidence far beyond the moment of consumption.

The performers featured in this project exploit the fact that listening can never be fully private. They exhibit, disclose, and even delight in the taboos of turning private listening into something public. They dramatize the experience of listening, in order to hail others as spectators in exaggerated representations of the listening experience. They take the imperative to share our listening and embrace it as ethos.

The disruption of listening norms may be a playful exercise for some, but for others the challenge comes as part of a broader opposition to ableism, which revolves around a set of universal ideas about the senses, bodies, and musical meaning. The idea that people can and should listen to music in particular ways often implies a set of universal qualities about listeners, which marginalizes and erases disability. Although an abundance of popular music centers disabled artists and musical themes, disability seems to disappear from music histories, criticism, and pedagogy. Listening has proliferated as a topic in academic research, and yet so many works simply assume all bodies under consideration share some normative set of features. How many books about listening do not mention disability and yet dwell on questions about the body and identity? This book centers the perspective of disabled folks on their own terms, while calling attention to the norms that haunt dominant ideas of musical reception.

Listening involves the entire body, and thus bodily difference matters in the act of music interpretation. Consistent with the work of Jean-Luc Nancy, I define listening as a reach toward meaning, which involves using the entire body, to generate understanding or awareness from musical performances.[2] As Pauline Oliveros reminds us, listening involves "mechanics of the ear, skin, bones, meridians, fluids, and other organs and tissues of the body."[3] Performers in this project use their entire bodies to listen—ears, eyes, limbs, bones, muscles, gestures, movements, props, assistive devices, and delivery technologies. They reveal how bodily difference can enhance how one listens.

The case studies in this book exemplify the ways that spectacular listening can challenge what I call "normal listening." Following the work of Joseph Straus,[4] I use this introduction to outline "normal listening," the dominant and privileged mode of listening in our contemporary musical institutions, technologies, and discourse in the United States. Normal listening is ableist and also typical. In the case studies that follow, I draw upon the works of scholars in disability and crip traditions, in order to emphasize how spectacular listening can challenge dominant ideas about musicality, virtuosity, skill, and reception.

Not all forms of spectacular listening challenge ableism. Some people may translate private listening into a public display of skilled interpretation, in a way that reinforces the privilege of non-disabled bodies. I select case studies in this book that use spectacular listening to do something important— challenge the ableist assumptions that undergird common ideas about listening. My goal is the same as that of the many people featured in this project when they step onstage or in front of their cameras. I show how spectacular performances of listening can expose normal listening as a narrow and

4 SPECTACULAR LISTENING

privileged construct, putting in its a place a wider variety of ways of understanding popular music.

Defining Disability and Normalcy

Any discussion of musical ability must account for the broader cultural system that shapes ideas about norms, abilities, and disabilities. In order to understand how spectacular listening can challenge normal listening, I first want to describe the norms that undergird a pernicious ableism in a non-musical context in the United States.

Dominant ideas about disability tend to depict it as an ahistorical, biologically determined condition that impacts individuals in tragic yet isolated ways. Such a perspective organizes a majority of bodies together as normal, while segregating others as too different to be accommodated or accepted as such. Contemporary ideas of disability emerge from specific historical developments in the nineteenth century. Lennard Davis, for example, describes the rise of concepts like "norm" and "normal," which emerge out of a combination of statistics and shifting political ideologies.[5] Davis describes how the word "normal," a lack of deviation from a particular standard, enters European languages around 1840. Ellen Samuels describes how these nineteenth-century trends entwine with identity, as people begin to think of disability as always visible and binary (one is disabled or not disabled, rather than disabled in a particular situation).[6] These ideas about disability crystallized into laws, medical systems, political systems, immigration policies, and countless other de jure and de facto forms of exclusion for people. The medical model of disability, in particular, emerged out of these ideas of disability as an unwanted deviation from a norm, which should be corrected and/or cured. Disabled people have suffered discrimination, segregation, sterilizations, incarceration, and death, and ideas about disability undergird broader belief systems about who deserves to be a member of our communities and on what terms.

Beyond legally and medically enforced oppression, discrimination toward people with disabilities appears in all kinds of social ways that can be ambiguous and obvious: a preference for non-disabled bodies, pity or discomfort at disability, ideas that disability makes for a diminished life, inspirational narratives that celebrate people who escape their disabilities, euphemisms that hide disability, and the association of disability with

INTRODUCTION 5

unwanted personality traits (think of villains in films always marked with visible disabilities or criticisms of reviled political figures using ableist slurs).[7] Indeed, the oppression of many groups historically rested on arguments that depicted them as not normal—flawed, deficient, deviant, overly emotional, physically weak, mentally feeble, unintelligent, irrational, and incapable.[8] Disability scholars have described different dimensions of these norms as the "hegemony of normalcy," "compulsory able-bodiedness," "compulsory able-mindedness," and simply "ableism."[9] I use "ableism" throughout this book, adopting Fiona Kumari Campbell's definition as:

[A] network of beliefs, processes and practices that produces a particular kind of self and body (the corporeal standard) that is projected as perfect, species-typical and therefore essential and fully human. Disability then, is cast as a diminished state of being human.[10]

This definition captures the way in which ableism fundamentally draws a line between bodies deemed typical and those otherwise, creating a sense of diminished life in the latter category.

The social model of disability emerged as an alternative to the medical model. The social model acknowledges that disability, in ways similar to race, gender, and sexuality, arises as a social construction in a given society.[11] In their built environments and cultural assumptions, societies organize around ideas of what bodies should be capable of doing. The social model of disability differentiates impairments from disabilities. An impairment names a particular aspect of one's body (e.g., having one hand), while disability names the condition produced by an environment that renders that impairment as an impediment to access or full participation (e.g., a musical instrument that requires two hands). In other words, the social model emphasizes the constructed nature of disability identity, much like people might argue for the constructedness of gender or race.

The recognition that society should accommodate disability as a part of life has generated significant yet imperfect gains for disabled folks. Disability activists in the 1970s paved the way for a full Disability Rights Movement in the 1980s, leading to achievements such as the Americans with Disabilities Act (1990), ADA Amendments Act (2008), Web Content Accessibility Guidelines (1999), and the emergence of disability studies as a distinct field.[12] Scholars and activists have pushed and pushed beyond the social model of disability, considering many dimensions disability as lived experience and

6 SPECTACULAR LISTENING

identity.[13] A recurring idea in much of this work is that legal activism can never fully succeed without cultural activism. Building on the work of Eve Sedgwick, Rosemarie Garland-Thomson argues that "disability studies should become a universalizing discourse" in the style of queer theory, since disability is involved in "structuring a wide range of thought, language, and perception that might not be explicitly articulated as 'disability.'"[14]

In what follows, I define disability as any stigmatized bodily difference that falls beyond the categories of race, ethnicity, gender, sexuality, and class, while acknowledging that all discussions of disability must keep in mind its inextricable link to these other categories. I draw upon the disability justice framework put forth by *Sins Invalid*, who emphasize how ableism undergirds colonialism, carcerality, racism, sexism, and gender-based discrimination.[15]

My approach brings together folks who variously consider themselves disabled, crip, impaired, and non-disabled. I model this approach on the work of Alison Kafer, who argues that disability can function as a "collective affinity":

> Collective affinities in terms of disability could encompass everyone from people with learning disabilities to those with chronic illnesses, from people with mobility impairments to those with HIV/AIDS, from people with sensory impairments to those with mental illness. People within each of these categories can all be discussed in terms of disability politics, not because of any essential similarities among them, but because all have been labeled as disabled or sick and have faced discrimination as a result.[16]

I gather perspectives from people across a wide spectrum of bodily differences and sound practices. Rather than focus on musical activities explicitly designed around disability, I demonstrate the presence of disability in non-disability-centered performances that people dismiss as trivial or peripheral to serious musical performances, in order to show how these practices are actually sites where a collective affinity can mobilize in surprising ways.

I use the terms "disabled people," "people with disabilities," and "crip" throughout this text. In instances in which I am describing someone, I use the terms that they prefer. For many, "people with disabilities" puts the person before the disability, in what folks refer to as "people-first language." For others, the term "disabled people" can emphasize disability as a source of pride, rather than something that should be concealed. People refer to this as "identity-first language."[17] "Crip" is a term reclaimed by disability activists to assert disability as an affirmative identity, and crip implies a more oppositional stance to the oppressive norms that organize society.[18] I use these terms to honor multiple ways of thinking. In occasional instances, I reference terms that have been historically used to oppress disabled people, in order to emphasize how pervasive ableist language and ideology can be.

Normal Listening

I sat in my living room, staring into my laptop screen at Tiger Claw, who sat in his living room in San Francisco. His face—obscured by a large tiger mask that he wore during multiple interviews—took up most of the screen, with shelves of air guitar books and air guitar competition memorabilia in the background. "I've been playing air guitar since 1979," he told me. He gave

Figure I.1 Tiger Claw with replica. Photo credit: Dan LaFever. Email consent attached.

i. Tiger Claw appears in a red wrestling singlet with tattoos appearing on his shoulders. He wears an orange mask with tiger stripes, which covers the top half of his face. He holds a figurine, which is a replica of himself that features the same mask, a red shirt, and zebra-striped pants.

8   SPECTACULAR LISTENING

a robust laugh but quickly switched back to a serious register. "I've been to hundreds of concerts in the past thirty years . . . And I've always stood on the right side to understand what guitarists are doing. And they're right-handed, and I'm left-handed. So it's perfect. It's like a mirror. I can find all of those notes on the [air] fretboard." We continued talking, and the topic shifted to the way his stroke, which happened ten years ago, affects his air guitar playing. "I have my own mobility issues that I deal with. That alone makes me worried about falling. I worry about tripping. I don't have two legs; I have one and a half. I don't have two hands; I have one and a half. The stroke affected the right side of my brain, so I walk with a limp and with a cane." A combination of life-threatening complications from a stroke, seizure, and double pneumonia led him to rethink the capabilities of his body regarding air guitar playing, and he began to focus on technical precision with his arms and fingers rather than using his legs and torso. "I can do jazz. I can air guitar to classical," he explained. "The key is synchronicity."

A white middle-aged man, Tiger Claw regularly performs as part of US Air Guitar competitions, and his performances stem from his everyday listening practices. When he takes the stage to perform air guitar, he offers an exaggerated version of his everyday approach to musical listening. He presents listening as a form of skilled interpretation, which has evolved along with changes in his body.

Listening is a learned technique of the body.[19] Much of the way we listen comes from socialization. In what follows, I differentiate listening from hearing. I refer to hearing as a sensory capability, involving an ability to detect sounds with the ears. I define listening as an active process of reaching for meaning with the entire body.[20] This process can involve perception with the ears but does not exclusively involve the ears. Listening involves the wide range of ways that we may perceive musical sounds, using a combination of the senses, gestures, and conceptual engagement. Much like we might think of looking, staring, or the gaze as a power-laden visual technique for interacting with the world, I follow the works of scholars who present listening in the same way. Judith Becker defines a "habitus of listening," which refers to "an inclination, a disposition to listen with a particular kind of focus, to expect to experience particular kinds of emotion, to move with certain stylized gestures, and to interpret the meaning of the sounds and one's emotional responses to the musical event in somewhat (never totally) predictable ways."[21] Listening, in other words, imposes certain expectations and a kind of focus onto the sonic experience. The performance of listening—the subject of this book—translates this process of perception into a performance for others, in a way that elevates aspects of this interpretive process.

While listening can be incredibly varied across musical styles and cultures, I argue that pervasive ideas about listening permeate music industries, pedagogy, criticism, journalism, technologies, and discourse. These pervasive ideas can be called normal listening, as an ableist set of beliefs about listening. Normal listening is rarely acknowledged as such, but it constitutes what we might call the dominant regime of listening in the United States. Normal listening is both idealized (the way people *ought* to listen) and naturalized (the way people *do* listen). Indeed, this is why "normal listening" seems to many to be simply "listening," in some neutral, natural, and universal sense of the word.[22] My approach denaturalizes these ideas of listening, in order to call attention to alternative ways of engaging with music.

I define normal listening as having three elements: (1) an emphasis on ear-based engagement and contemplation, (2) a concept of sound as a bounded object for critical analysis, and (3) a celebration of meaningful listening as capable of being written or described through words. These norms do not describe how most people listen, much like all norms represent idealizations of everyday life. These norms *do* describe how people often think about listening.

In what follows in this section, I cannot give an exhaustive explanation of how people have listened for the past two hundred years, but I hope to highlight how normal listening evolved to revolve around these three characteristics in particular spheres. My goal is to offer a few critical developments that explain why "listening" connotes a particular type of engagement with sounds in a contemporary United States context.

The origins of normal listening can be traced, in part, to the Enlightenment, which eventually created a context for listening to become linked to scientific inquiry of sonic objects. While prevailing histories of the Enlightenment emphasize occularcentrism, where vision becomes the preeminent sense for rational inquiry and critical distance, Jonathan Sterne describes the way that hearing followed suit in the nineteenth and early twentieth centuries. In *The Audible Past*, Sterne describes how cultural ideas informed technological innovations, which linked hearing with "logic, analytic thought, industry, capitalism, individualism, and mastery."[23] Researchers and scholars began isolating hearing as a discrete sense, and they also began thinking of sounds as bounded objects, capable of capture and analysis. This relationship created what Sterne calls an "audile technique," or a mode of listening

10 SPECTACULAR LISTENING

that connects hearing with a detached examination of sound as an isolated object.

The dominance of these audile techniques has always been threatened with alternatives. Veit Erlmann argues, "reason's autocratic status as the center of all modern virtues" has been "constantly threatened with implosion," particularly by notions of "resonance."[24] In other words, the idea of critical distance for rational scientific inquiry always exists in tension with the subjectivity of sensory perception. As human beings, our critical distance is always plagued by our subjective experience of stimuli or objects under consideration. The tension—between critical distance and subjective experience—is worth noting as a historical debate, simply because it foreshadows contemporary tension between spectacular listening and normal listening. Normal listening often strives for critical distance; spectacular listening prioritizes the resonance of music in and with the body.

In the nineteenth and early twentieth centuries, theories of musical listening, from critics and philosophers, mirror some of these ideas about listening as connected to mastery and expertise. Tracing a historical lineage in the ideas of Eduard Hanslick, Edmund Gurney, David Prall, and Monroe C. Beardsley, Theodore Gracyk demonstrates how influential thinkers in the history of Western art music and theory have often idealized listening as a high-minded, intellectual, and contemplative activity, which aims for an "exclusive focus" on particular elements of a given piece of music in order to evaluate formal structures.[25] According to Gracyk, these individuals had many points of disagreement, but their ideas culminate in concepts of listening that prioritize: (1) "conscious knowledge about music" rooted in "disciplined listening," and (2) a listening style that emphasizes "a limited object within the total aural experience" and (3) directs people to "tonal structures."[26] Ultimately, these ideas about listening privilege mastery as rooted in honed listening skills. In ways that complement these ideas, perhaps most famously, Theodor Adorno would eventually advocate for "expert listening" that can be "fully conscious" and "defined by entirely adequate hearing," where the "ear thinks along with what it hears."[27] In their own respective ways, many historical figures have elevated listening as a skilled act of interpretation, which requires training and focused attention on a relationship between musical elements. Importantly, these expert skills revolve around privileged forms of music, as well as narrow ideas of bodily variation (if and when the body matters at all).

Listening, as a form of mastery, comes from many places, and structural listening offers another example. The act of listening to music in

INTRODUCTION   11

order to evaluate musical structures has been historicized as structural listening. Rose Subotnik traces this form of listening to the final phases of the Enlightenment and, more specifically, German philosophical traditions, such as the works of Immanuel Kant on aesthetic pleasure and judgment.[28] This line of thinking brought forth a view of musical works as structurally autonomous and the highest form of art. The goal of listening should be to discover the internal relationships in a cohesive musical work. Subotnik argues that, somewhat counterintuitively, structural listening actually deemphasizes engagement with sounds, instead emphasizing analysis of a written score or contemplative evaluation of elements in a piece.[29] Andrew Dell'Antonio puts this succinctly: "[T]he written score is seen (!) as having more integrity than any sonic realization of the musical work."[30] In other words, the act of structural listening becomes so removed from the experiential dimensions of a musical performance, such that a listener can just conceptually consider structures within a piece rather than attend to the bodily experience of music at all. Structural listening continues to be a major flashpoint in music research, and the listening technique that Subotnik identifies perfectly encapsulates the preference for serious contemplation, which emerges from a consideration of objective elements of a piece—rather than the subjective experience of listening. These techniques of sophisticated listening privilege mastery, in a way that excludes marginal practices that might approach music differently.

These theories of listening also entwine with historical and systemic forms of pression, including racist, sexist, and ableist ideas of musical value. These privileged modes of musical listening mastery have functioned in a way that finds Western art music to be superior, aligning idealized listening with white, Eurocentric music in increasingly elite circles. For example, normal listening impacted how white settlers heard Indigenous musical traditions. Hillel Schwartz writes of a fascination with the ear in the early twentieth century as a "bodyguard, herald, explorer, and confidant,"[31] and early ethnographers often transcribed and recorded Indigenous musical performances, applying ideas of Western music theory to their music in order to translate them into colonialist paradigms. Dylan Robinson describes "hungry listening" of settlers as a form of domination and control.[32] Such a perspective also informed the way white listeners heard Black sonic practices, leading Jennifer Lynn Stoever to theorize the "listening ear" an "ideological filter" that "represents a historical aggregate of normative American listening practices."[33] Hearing folks have also imposed a silence on

12 SPECTACULAR LISTENING

d/Deaf listeners and musical traditions. Despite a long history of music and artistic expression, d/Deaf education around the turn of the century revolved around assimilating d/Deaf culture into hearing cultures, as part of a broader shift toward oralism.[34] In her description of American Sign Language, Jeanette Jones describes why the idea of ear-based listening cuts against d/Deaf musical traditions:

> In ASL there are signs to describe how a person listens. Typically, a hearing person will LISTEN-EARS; the ears are the primary mode of receiving communication. To create this sign, the Bent-3 handshape is placed by the ears along with a motion that indicates the receiving of sound. By contrast, a Deaf person will LISTEN-EYES, using the same handshape placed by the eyes. This handshape indicates the reception of information; the position of the handshape will indicate the part of the body through which the communication is received.[35]

Jones' work reveals how conceptions of listening as exclusively ear-based represent only a small portion of the actual listening acts that people engage in. Indeed, all of these examples indicate how normal listening revolves around particularly exclusive ideas of musical listening, which mirror broader social forms of oppression.

Cultural ideas about listening have also been formalized in music institutions and technologies, often prioritizing a sense of control, mastery, and consumption of masterworks. In both public and private spaces, the act of controlling sound has been a pervasive goal of sound design. In the *Soundscape of Modernity*, Emily Thompson writes about the ways scientists and engineers in the early twentieth century worked toward controlling sound through technological mediation, essentially abandoning architectural acoustics of spaces in favor of speakers that produced more controllable listening experiences for live audiences.[36] She writes:

> A fundamental compulsion to control the behavior of sound drove technological developments in architectural acoustics, and this imperative stimulated auditors to listen more critically, to determine whether that control had been accomplished . . . control was a means by which to exercise choice in a market filled with aural commodities; it allowed producers and consumers alike to identify what constituted "good sound," and to evaluate whether particular products achieved it.

INTRODUCTION 13

Later in the twentieth century, private listening devices have reproduced this control for the individual. Despite their indebtedness to hearing aids, mobile listening devices—from the Walkman to the iPod—have reinforced idealized forms of serious listening that privilege sound as a bounded object, even while they simultaneously enable the possibilities for new styles of listening completely at odds with this approach.[37] The file and delivery formats—from 45s to cassette tapes to MP3s—use standardized ideas of normal human cognition, which reduce bodily variance through assumptions about perception (e.g., perceptual coding or compression).[38]

Normal listening is also deeply rooted in the ways that people analyze popular music today, whether as critics or scholars. An implied listener exists in any and every analysis of a musical work. In conference paper presentations, music seminars, articles, and monographs, scholars will often reproduce these ideas of normal listening. One common way that this takes place involves scholars reading complexity into popular music works imagined to be primitive and simple, in order to show how the work does, after all, have complexity that does not conform to Western art music models of complexity. They may use Western staff notion or semiotics to make this claim. They may draw attention to chord structure or timbre. But these analyses often regard listening as straightforward, and they often dwell on ear-based modes of listening, focusing on an ear-based engagement with a bounded object (a song or composition) and bracketing discussions of file formats, listening devices, and bodily perception of vibrations. A quick survey of music reviews online will reveal that almost all authors writing for mainstream publications imagine that listeners are non-disabled with entirely normative hearing and bodies, and they often imagine that listening to a recording involves engaging with abstract element of the musical work (a sound file), rather than focusing on any devices used to make that work accessible to the listener.

Music pedagogy also reproduces ideas of normative listening. In music-appreciation courses, for example, educators make many decisions about listening that implicitly inform their instruction. They teach students which zones of their body should be relevant to listening, often exclusively emphasizing the ears and the conscious mind. They model techniques for listening and how listening can be shared with others, usually through verbal descriptions of elements that one heard in a given recording or piece. In progressive versions of these seminars, teachers may attempt to expand the selections typically featured in a musical-appreciation seminar, giving

14 SPECTACULAR LISTENING

students a wide range of examples from around the world, but they often leave the idea of listening as unexamined. Hillel Schwartz writes: "[T]he sounds people hear may change, and their reactions to those sounds do change, but how people hear remains the same."[39] Indeed, a history of the senses tends to disappear from these conversations. Dylan Robinson writes, "For those with the opportunity to be disciplined through formal music education in Western art music, the ear is thus 'civilized' into 'higher listening' forms of recognition and identification," which "orient the ear toward identifying standardized features and types."[40] Such an approach maintains a possessive investment in normal listening, reinforcing the supremacy of the prevailing disciplinary knowledge of music.

The core tenets of normal listening are pervasive in the ways many people interact and think about music recordings. In his work on music and disability, Joseph Straus summarizes this normal listening into a kind of exaggerated scenario:

> Normal hearing involves a listener alone in a room, listening to recorded sounds: nothing to see, nothing to touch, no opportunity to move, no active participation (playing or singing), and above all, no intervention or assistance from anyone else. Normal listening is a solitary activity, something each person does alone in the privacy of his or her own individual, autonomous mind. This prevalent idea of hearing as a solitary activity expresses deep-seated Western, and especially American, ideas of autonomy, individuality, independence, and self-sufficiency.[41]

While Straus' description of normal listening may seem like a caricature, this long history of norms undergirds the idea of listening in this way. Of course, listening in such a way would be relatively impossible for anyone, but Straus captures the dominant ways that people think about listening, which stem from their inherited ideas of the ideal relationship between people and musical works. Straus emphasizes how these ideas inherently favor non-disabled listeners, primarily through reserving the definition of listening itself for a quite narrow set of techniques of the body.

Normal listening crystalizes in a wide range of historical ideas and practices, and the core assumptions of normal listening are pervasive in our pedagogy, technologies, aesthetics, and institutions. To summarize, normal listening revolves around three values: (1) ear-based engagement for contemplation, (2) sound as a bounded object, and (3) meaningful listening as capable of being described. Understanding these underlying ideas of normal listening can help explain why alternatives can seem so funny, strange, or subversive. Each of these normal listening characteristics may not always and forever be ableist, but they have historically existed in aggregate as a collection of listening norms that has marginalized many alternative ways of engaging with sounds.

Against Normal Listening

Before the rise of TikTok in the United States in the mid-teens of the 2000s, Motoki Maxted captivated audiences on YouTube with viral lip-syncing performances, such as "Car Rides with Motoki," "Christmas Car Ride with Motoki," and "Another Car Ride with Motoki."[42] With over 45 million views on these three videos collectively, Motoki appears in each one in the car with his mom, as he thumbs through the radio dial in search of a good song. As each song comes on, he dramatically lip syncs to the music as an almost involuntary response, while his mother sits beside him with a stoic look on her face. In my conversation with him, he elaborated on this approach: "I'll listen

Figure I.2 "Another Car Ride with Motoki." Motoki Maxted. Screenshot by the author on July 17, 2022.

i. Motoki appears in the car with his mother at the wheel. His hands appear in front of him with his fingers stretched out, almost as if waving. His mother appears with sunglasses and a serious facial expression. Out of the frame of this screenshot, his DSLR camera sits on the dash. He performs a series of rehearsed moves that he choreographed for the scene.

16   SPECTACULAR LISTENING

for what section of a song is most popular. The chorus or something that can be really funny mimed out . . . I don't like making it so choreographed, because it takes away from the genuine feel of it." Finding ways to stage this kind of dramatic listening as both spontaneous and rehearsed, Motoki modeled these performances after other online performers, Ryan Higa, Kev Jumba, Brandon Rodgers, Nathan Zed, and the duo Ethan and Hilla. One of the first viral lip-syncing videos came in the form of two Chinese college students named Wei Wei and Huang Yixin, who posted a video to YouTube in 2005 that featured them wearing Rockets jerseys and lip syncing Backstreet Boys' "I Want It That Way." Motoki told me that digital platforms offered an important cultural scene for Asian American people: "I'm half Japanese. So it's cool for me to see these Asian American guys doing their thing online." He set these videos up using a DSLR camera on the dashboard, choreographing elaborate montages of musical clips, and strategizing about how to spread the clips online.

The prevalence of normal listening may be most apparent in instances in which these norms seem to be disrupted. Motoki's viral videos show how lip syncing can play with ideas about normal listening, in ways that evoke humor from transgression. His video actively challenges the idea that listening should involve (1) ear-based engagement and contemplation, (2) sound as a bounded object, and (3) meaningful listening as capable of being described. In his videos, Motoki presents listening as something that (1) causes involuntary responses throughout the body, (2) treats the body as a porous vehicle that sounds may pass through, and (3) uses the body to reveal how music makes one feel. The whole joke of his routine revolves around taboo modes of listening, which challenge expectations about serious and sophisticated listening.

Alongside with the rise of normal listening, a wide range of historical examples have challenged narrow ideas of how people listen to popular media. For example, Mark Katz gives the example of "shadow conducting" among phonograph listeners, who would animate sounds by pretending to conduct the orchestras in recordings—not unlike their air guitarist counterparts in the late twentieth century.[43] Tim Taylor describes the interactive player piano that allowed listeners to play with its "tempo levers, accenting apparatus, sustaining pedal lever, and usually, a softening button."[44] David Goodman writes that the radio "stood in clear moral contrast to the kind of deliberate, calm, rational, fully attentive and time-bounded listening that was always recommended by experts."[45] During World War II, lip syncing served as a humorous activity to entertain troops abroad, and these performances eventually integrated into local performance genres, such as drag performance and avant-garde theater.[46] Televised musical acts also played with simulation, as shows like *American Bandstand* and the *Smothers Brothers* put live musicians onstage to pantomime along with their sound recordings, and these practices evolved into elaborate music videos on MTV that synchronized images and sounds in novel ways.[47] Karaoke rose to popularity in the United States in the 1980s, allowing people to sync their voices with pre-recorded backing tracks.[48] Music video games formalized many of these activities into distinctive performance genres. Listening devices, such as the turntable or the smart phone, have become musical instruments.

All of these practices reveal listening as an interactive mode of engaging with musical sounds, in a direct challenge to ideas that align ideal listening with ear-based reception of musical works. However, many of these examples may not initially strike people as listening, but at the very least, perhaps most would agree that they involve ambiguous relationships between performers and recipients.

Contemporary digital platforms simply formalize trends that have been prevalent throughout the twentieth and twenty-first centuries. These interactive modes of media reception have been described by scholars as "participatory culture," "remix culture," and "configurable culture."[49] All of these terms acknowledge that media production does not go from producers to consumers in some linear way. Instead, consumers customize the media that they receive, creatively adapting popular media for new uses. These customizations include a wide range of online media activities—from memes to Photoshop to retweets. Digital platforms not only enable these forms of remixing but also shape it. As media scholar José van Dijck puts it, "the construction of platforms and social practices is mutually constitutive," in the sense that platforms engineer interactions in particular ways. Tracing the rise of social media in what has been called Web 2.0, José van Dijck describes an evolution of the World Wide Web in the early 1990s from "networked communication" to "platformed sociality."[50]

The body plays a critical role in these circulations. Many contemporary media techniques combine pre-recorded media with new bodily performances. These practices challenge narrow definitions of dance, listening, and instrumental musical performance, revealing how all remain

18 SPECTACULAR LISTENING

inextricably linked. Is a reaction video a dance, an act of listening, or a musical performance that treats a recording as a musical instrument? Deborah Kapchan writes: "listening acts enact."[51] Listening creates a relationship between popular media and the body. In contemporary digital cultures, the body is not simply something abstractly evoked or represented. A body presses, swipes, scrolls, taps, sees, hears, holds, and thinks—all in accordance with the particular capabilities of that body, the platform, and the many technologies in between. A body is implied in the circulation of all digital media, and a body puts that circulation in motion.

Spectacular Listening invites readers to understand how normal listening represents a narrow construct, primarily by offering numerous examples of ways to listen otherwise. Tobin Siebers writes: "[W]hen a disabled body moves into a social space, the lack of fit exposes the shape of the normative body for which the space was originally designed."[52] When we acknowledge the many types of bodies that people bring to musical listening experiences, then we begin to understand how normal listening serves only a narrow type of body and suits only narrow ideas of musical reception.

Scope and Methods

As an ethnomusicologist, I organize this book around four case studies, in order to emphasize the relationship among the body, popular media, and digital platforms. None of my case studies come from traditional fields of inquiry within the discipline, so I take methodological approaches from media studies, cultural studies, and various subfields within music studies, while combining them in a way that entwines with core ideas in ethnomusicological fieldwork. I adapt my methods to each case study, which involves different scales and scopes. I describe these in detail in each of my chapters. Across the chapters, three core values inform my methods: a recognition of the importance of low theory, attention to embodied practices, and a deliberate approach to interdisciplinary insights.

In terms of low theory, I explore areas of culture at the margins, which often get excluded from academic research and disciplinary boundaries. I take these areas of culture as sites of critical resistance and musical excellence. I model my approach to low theory after the work of Jack Halberstam. Drawing upon Stuart Hall, Halberstam theorizes "low theory" as "a mode

INTRODUCTION   19

of accessibility . . . assembled from eccentric texts and examples and that refuses to confirm the hierarchies of knowing that maintain the *high* in high theory."[53] Air guitar competitions, reaction videos, lip syncing, and podcasting tend to not be regarded as high art. I gather these seemingly eccentric practices together to make an argument about a broad shift in listening techniques. Attention to formal or high domains of culture can obscure the critical renegotiation of values that takes place in more nascent, underground spaces.[54]

Indeed, as I elaborate in my conclusion, the marginal status of many of these musical practices makes them particularly valuable for rethinking dominant values related to musical listening, since these performance genres have not been co-opted, formalized, historicized, or institutionalized as serious musical techniques. I choose to take them seriously, in order to show how serious activism does not require serious aesthetics. I build on the work of musicologists and ethnomusicologists who have turned critical attention to sites of play that others might dismiss as unserious or superficial.[55] As these scholars point out, musical activities deemed unserious are often designated as such because they come from marginalized groups.[56] Ethnomusicologists can be particularly equipped to explore marginal musical communities, asking questions such as: What parts of these activities count as part of a musical performance? How do these playful practices evoke broader values or invoke larger systems of belief? How does the performance structure of this activity reflect broader systemic structures of oppression?

I explore these practices through attending to the body, and in particular, bodily difference. Ethnomusicologists have not taken up social media in any extensive way, but our ability to analyze bodily performance has significant value for new media scholarship. Countless studies of new media either present a theoretical body (i.e., an abstracted, non-disabled body) or ignore the body altogether, focusing on technologies, media, and platforms. My approach here focuses on the point of contact among bodies, screens, and sounds. In so doing, I connect work on social media with the work on the body within ethnomusicology.[57] Attention to the body gives research on social media an additional dimension, by emphasizing the physical contexts of use in which bodies interact with a physical device and digital platform. I draw upon the work of scholars engaging with the body and disability in particular, while emphasizing how insights from ethnomusicology can deepen and expand these approaches.

Participant observation is a key aspect of this focus on the body. My four case studies involve a combination of interviews, fieldwork observations, historical research, and my own participation. I competitively air guitared, filmed my own reactions, learned to make lip-syncing videos, and consumed and worked with audio-media producers. Conventional ethnographic research in ethnomusicology involves fieldwork in a non-digital community, but anthropologist Tom Boellstorff makes the case that all ethnography is, in many ways, always virtual.[58] Ethnography involves assuming a role in a particular situation, whether in a physical location or a virtual community, and people can assume these roles online and offline.

Ethnography also involves attending to many aspects of experience, including those inside of the body (self-perceptions, thoughts, and beliefs), on the surface of the body (appearance and touch), and in social interactions among many bodies (hierarchies, relationships, and identities). These layers are important dimensions of a person's experience in any musical community. Kiri Miller's work has profoundly shaped my sense of the role of the body in these digital and physical worlds. She draws attention to the role of repetition and structuring practice, demonstrating how bodily knowledge enters digital contexts in what she calls "visceral ethnography."[59] Her work resonates with my own approach to learning to play air guitar or make lip-syncing videos, and her work also applies to the work of my interlocutors, who study the gestures of others in order to learn to enact them themselves. Miller theorizes the "playable body" as a key part of this dynamic: "The playable body is the body as playback device, capable of reenacting a repertoire that has been stored away in the archive of cumulative embodied experience."[60] Miller prioritizes the importance of the body as an archive of experiences that can be called upon to enact bodily knowledge during a performance. The act of spectacular listening involves restaging the experience of listening to share with others, in a way that involves translating visceral practices into staged performances of play.

Attention to the body also involves a recognition of the importance of performance. In the field of performance studies, Richard Schechner offers the classic definition of performance as "restored behavior." Thinking of these performances of listening as restored behavior calls upon us to also think about how these extreme examples reference mundane, everyday listening acts. Kyra Gaunt's concept of "somatic historiography" offers a useful way to consider how gestures can "re-present, re-member, and re-perform," particularly within the context of games and play.[61] I show how listening involves choreographies, both in the formal sense of gestural repertoires and in a more cultural sense of bodily techniques that people subconsciously inherit and reproduce. For example, a podcast conversation can be a staged representation of an everyday conversation. A reaction video can be a curated version of a visceral reaction to popular media. My case studies offer examples of these re-stagings of familiar contexts, in order emphasize various aspects about them to audiences. I situate these techniques at the junction of bodies, devices, and cultural contexts in physical and digital platforms.

Finally, I take an interdisciplinary approach to these topics, connecting the work on music disability studies with the work on disability in other adjacent disciplines. The field of music disability studies has proliferated over the past ten years with work that effectively emphasizes critical intersections between disability and topics such as virtuosity, musical ability, performance, aesthetics, and composition. George McKay's *Shakin All Over* provides an expansive engagement with popular music and disability, inviting scholars to rethink well-known topics and consider lesser-known ones.[62] The compiled works in *Sounding Off: Theorizing Disability in Music* and the *Oxford Handbook of Music and Disability Studies* offer extremely valuable insights into how disability connects to many fields of music studies, including music theory, historical musicology, and performance.[63] The work of Will Cheng influenced my ideas of musical narratives and an ethics of care within particular musical communities, as well as impacting my broader sense of music as disciplinary knowledge.[64]

My work offers fresh perspectives about listening in this growing body of work on music and disability. The most popular musical activity is listening, and yet listening can be incredibly hard to analyze, particularly in terms of the everyday experience of listeners.[65] The performance of listening offers a valuable frame through which to examine listening practices, given that these performance genres represent curated representations of typical acts. I am hopeful that this work can generate important attention to disabled listening communities, expanding the existing work in music disability studies. My approach has been influenced by a few excellent works in this area. For example, discussion of listening in Joseph Straus' *Extraordinary Measures* significantly shaped my conception of listening and disability, as has the work of Jessica Holmes and Nina Sun Eidseim.[66] My work contributes an ethnographic approach to these examples, which shows how people think about listening and share that with others.

22 SPECTACULAR LISTENING

My interdisciplinary approach also seeks to unite disability studies with some of the non-disability-focused work in the fields of performance studies, media studies, American studies, English, philosophy, and others. I model this approach after scholars who have helped push disability into conversations about media, technologies, communication, and culture. The work of Mara Mills, Katie Ellis, and Mike Kent has been particularly influential.[67] Mack Hagood, a scholar working across ethnomusicology and media studies, has offered a particularly useful approach to musical listening among disabled listeners.[68] Within the subfield of disability studies, many scholars offer critical insights about disability from a historical and cultural standpoint, including Lennard Davis, Tobin Siebers, Rosemarie Garland-Thomson, Ellen Samuels, Alison Kafer, and Eli Clare. I bring their discussions to my music case studies, while also showing how music can crystalize many of the ideas that they offer. My hope is that this work can create synergistic moments of awareness across disparate fields.

One final value runs throughout my work. As a scholar researching disability who doesn't share in the disabilities of those in my case studies, I approach my case studies with Michael Bakan's "ethnographic model of disability" in mind. In his book *Music and Autism*, Bakan acknowledges the limitations of his own perspectives and emphasizes the need for fieldwork to engage with participants as collaborators.[69] A spirit of mutual respect and collaboration has motivated my conversations with folks in this book, and I hope this book represents part of that dialogue and not some sort of conclusive statement. Many performers in this book got to know me and watched my project develop, as I shared ideas with them, presented them with my research findings, showed them drafts, and allowed them to get to know my motivations and preoccupations. I asked them to make themselves vulnerable in sharing their perspectives with me, so I also strive to do the same. For example, I begin Chapter 1 with a personal anecdote, which I hope demonstrates a mutual investment in the kinds of sharing I asked from others. As part of this mutuality, I also research my lifelong and daily-lived culture, in order to reflect deeply on a set of values that have been part of my own musical and cultural life.

With this methodological framework in mind, I approached my case studies with these overarching questions: How do people translate listening into a performance, and how does this differ across media and platforms? How liberating is spectacular listening as an alternative to normal listening? Does spectacular listening enable community, or does it heighten the privilege of individual consumers?

Outline of the Book

The following case studies offer a wide cross-section of spectacular listening, in order to reveal how listening techniques appear across digital and physical platforms. I focus on four different ways to frame my case studies: individuals (Chapter 1), community (Chapter 2), performance genres (Chapter 3), and practices (Chapter 4). Many of the themes in each chapter apply to the others. By focusing on different scales and scopes in these chapters, I hope to offer a cross-section of contemporary listening, which can reveal how seemingly trivial performances can represent a much more widespread shift in listening that occurs in different platforms and media.

In Chapter 1, I focus on the US Air Guitar Championships, an annual competition consisting of local, regional, and national air guitar competitions. The winner goes on to represent the United States in a Eurovision-style global air guitar competition in Oulu, Finland. These competitions feature hundreds of competitors and thousands of spectators. Competitors do not simply perform as themselves but construct elaborate personas that come to represent the powerful potential of listening to rock music. My research focuses on five competitors, all of whom experience a range of impairments—from anorexia to chronic pain to PTSD. I show how air guitar competitions enable them to objectify their listening experience (quite literally, through constructing an imaginary guitar), which ultimately allows them to expose and disclose impairments to a community. Air guitar competitions enable performers to masquerade and exaggerate impairments, fostering a feeling of intelligibility and mutual recognition between performers and audiences. I grapple with how these performances can be both liberating and stigmatizing.

In Chapter 2, I analyze a community of creators on lip-syncing apps, primarily focusing on a relationship among musical.ly, TikTok, and YouTube. Lip-syncing videos stage the act of music reception, as people flaunt their fluency in musical styles and idioms. I use *fluent circulation* as a construct for exploring these performances. *Fluent circulation* refers to the manipulation and circulation of media, demonstrating proficiency in a certain mode of reception with the intention of securing prestige and power. Lip-syncing videos showcase many overlapping and intersecting forms of fluencies and other "vocabularies": English, Russian, American Sign Language, dance genres, genre-specific gestures (like dabbing, tutting, fist pumping, or air guitar), affects, technical proficiency, and social-media conventions. All of these fluencies represent various types of knowledge that are made visible

24   SPECTACULAR LISTENING

and audible through performance. I demonstrate how these fluencies can transcend individual platforms, enabling a style of popular-media transmission that can create continuity for digital subcultures.

Chapter 3 explores popular music reaction videos as a performance genre. A core content on YouTube, these videos stage reactions to media as a performance of listening, using a response to media to generate a new form of content. In this chapter, I focus on creators who identify as disabled and non-disabled, in order to emphasize how they variously engage with disability in their reaction videos. I show how staging a reaction to popular music enables creators to react to and with disability. They perform how their bodies receive media, and I consider how these videos can offer a form of crip music criticism. I offer an overview of reactions as a type of media, followed by an examination of a particular series of chain reactions to a specific viral performance.

In Chapter 4, I examine podcasts as a practice, focusing on a collection of disabled podcasters who highlight music and art in their work. I examine how these hosts present listening as audible, emphasizing accessibility as a critical musical practice. These podcasts include *Disability Visibility*, *Power Not Pity*, and *Reid My Mind*. These podcasters present listening as their subject, while they model listening through their performances. I consider how listening in this audio-based format can actually invite a recognition of the entire body in the listening experience. I theorize these approaches as accessible listening, and I consider how podcasts can inform the way we consider other forms of sonic art, particularly popular music.

In my conclusion, I consider what happens when spectacular listening becomes standard. By drawing upon works in music studies and media studies, I consider what happens when and if spectacular listening becomes a much more prevalent and institutionalized mode of listening. I organize my conclusion into three themes: the sharing imperative, syncing out loud, and marginal practices. These categories help me generalize about trends that appear across my case studies and elsewhere, considering the ways that they empower and disempower listeners. I suggest that the need and desire to make one's listening legible to other people and our devices represent the potential widespread acceptance of new cultural ideas around listening, which entails questions about oppressive and disruptive possibilities.

An implicit theory of listening sits at the foundation of any discussion of music. In this book, I demonstrate how pervasive ideas about music often revolve around extremely narrow ideas about how we listen, imposing normative assumptions about bodies and music. I present a series of performers who creatively imagine ways that we might listen otherwise.

1

Use Your Illusion

Disability Masquerade in the US Air Guitar Championships

During the year of 2017, a massive blood clot developed in my upper arm. My right arm swelled to twice the size of my left, producing bulging veins and Hulk-like contours. Spending the spring in a succession of hospital and doctor visits, I struggled with a fear that I might die or spend my life swimming in an ocean of medical debt. After multiple ER visits, a visit to the ICU, surgical removal of a rib, and a slow recovery, I gradually began to emerge from this difficult place, carrying an enduring sense of fear (will it happen again?), fragility (what is safe for my body to do?), and melancholy (can anyone understand?).

During this period, I also found myself in the bizarre situation of preparing for my first air guitar competition at the Hard Rock Café in Boston. I suppose I could have postponed this performance until the following year (the next air guitar season), but I felt compelled to continue, because I had long anticipated my air guitar debut. Air guitar offered a nice counterweight to other heavy life circumstances. I had already conceptualized a stage persona—The Professair—a white-wigged, turtlenecked caricature of a stodgy professor. This persona felt like a rejection of the pretentious, privileged domains of academia. I needed something totally absurd in my life to offset so much seriousness. In the course of medical tests and procedures, I spent spare time combing through YouTube videos of metal guitarists covering classical music, in an attempt to find a good backing track for my air guitar routine. I found two videos from across the globe—a Japanese man playing Chopin's Nocturne No. 20 in C-sharp minor and a French woman playing the third movement of Beethoven's Piano Sonata No. 14 in C-sharp minor (Moonlight Sonata). I downloaded, edited, and spliced the best parts together. Then I stood in front of the mirror and over time learned how to make the air guitar visible, trying to synchronize various moves to the music. As my air guitar (routine) took shape, I found ways to work around

Spectacular Listening. Byrd McDaniel, Oxford University Press. © Oxford University Press 2024.
DOI: 10.1093/oso/9780197620458.003.0002

Figure 1.1 Professair at Hard Rock Café in Boston. Photo credit: Clara Schwager.

i. The Professair at the Hard Rock Café in Boston.

mobility limitations in my arm and neck, using finger tapping, holding the guitar neck almost vertically, and fingerpicking so as to avoid sharp alternating arm motions. I felt afraid that I would damage a vein by playing air guitar, so I practiced with reserve. When the time to compete finally arrived, I decided I would let go of inhibitions, releasing the caution that felt so prevalent in my everyday life. I took to the stage, delivering a magical pantomime with transcendent shredding. I felt the thrill as my fingers drilled each successive note on the air fretboard, perfectly in sync. People in the audience laughed. They seemed awe-struck. They applauded wildly. I felt seen by them, recognized as a member of this community through this vulnerable act of imagination.

The annual United States Air Guitar Championships give performers an opportunity to stage themselves as embodied interpreters of music recordings. By exaggerating the theatrics of real guitar playing, performers proudly display gestures often associated with embarrassing forms of fandom. Air guitar often connotes the private pantomimes of doting fans who simulate the gestures of their beloved guitar gods. By taking these taboo forms of listening to the stage, air guitarists draw power from humorous antics, turning these gestural interpretations into a distinctive artistic practice. The US Air Guitar Championships—part farce, part performance art—give listeners license to imaginatively interpret guitar solos for audiences across the country, inviting people to understand music reception as a creative act.

While these competitions may seem superficial on the surface, they offer sincere forms of self-expression for their participants. Their dedicated practitioners belong to a large community, which consists of local air guitar scenes and a national organization of air guitarists called US Air Guitar. This national organization belongs to an international consortium of air guitarists, housed under the umbrella of the Air Guitar World Championships. Contemporary air guitar competitions come from a long history of air guitar competitions in the United States and abroad. The media representations of these competitions rarely take them seriously, given the explicitly comedic approach competitors take to their routines, and air guitarists typically welcome any kind of media coverage that helps build the audience for their events.[1] But the sensationalist depictions of these competitions can often belie their serious dimensions. While the absurdity may draw many to air guitar, people often stick around because they find a community that celebrates non-normative bodies, unconventional lifestyles, and many forms of musical appreciation.

In this chapter, I focus on the serious side of air guitar, articulating the practice as an exercise in disclosure for those with disabilities, impairments, and non-normative bodies. Air guitar playing enables folks to translate something they feel—something others cannot see—into a demonstrable display, which can be vulnerable yet liberating. I describe the experiences of five competitors in the 2017 competition season, in order to demonstrate how playing air guitar enables them to grapple with social anxiety, broken bones, depression, post-traumatic stress disorder, chronic pain, bipolar disorder, and many other impairments. Air guitar playing enables them to represent aspects of their bodies to the public, disclosing parts of themselves that they might be otherwise forced to suppress.

I draw upon the concept of disability masquerade, a technique for disclosing disabilities to the public in order to receive accommodation. I argue air guitar playing enables an artistic form of this disability masquerade, helping competitors translate their daily experiences into performances that can generate validating forms of public recognition. Air guitar performances do not represent disability in ways that are always accurate, complete, or nuanced, but they are exercises in disclosure, crafted on terms constructed by these performers in order to confront the stigma of bodily difference. Air guitarists turn these differences into assets. Performers

28 SPECTACULAR LISTENING

treat their bodies as amplifiers for recorded sounds, transforming the taboos of private listening into a theatrical animation of popular music.

Methods

From 2014 to 2019, I conducted research on many dimensions of air guitar competitions. I attended events in Boston, New York City, Washington DC, Kansas City, and Nashville. I traveled to the international competition in Finland twice, including both the Dark Horse competitions and the World Championships. During these years, I frequently livestreamed competitions that I could not attend in person. On my second visit to Finland, I presented my research at the 20th Anniversary of the Air Guitar World Championships to approximately forty-five of the world's best air guitarists at Sauna World in Oulu, and I also attended a weekend-long air guitar retreat afterward. I conducted twenty-eight formal interviews with air guitarists during this time, in order to engage in more focused conversations about aspects of air guitar. I introduced the Air Guitar World Champion to my World Music course at Northeastern University in 2019. I competed in the local Boston competition at Hard Rock Café, which earned me the title of the third best air guitarist in Boston in 2017, and I returned two years later as a judge in this local competition. I also received the privilege of being asked to judge the 2019 US Air Guitar Championships in Nashville at the Exit/In, a rare opportunity and a true honor. I have become friends with many air guitarists over the years, resulting in countless conversations about air guitar.

During my research, I found myself constantly confronted with conversations about embodiment. I sweated in saunas while discussing gestures with air guitarists from around the world. I chatted with air guitarists backstage before competitions, as they nervously stretched and rehearsed their routines. I heard stories of injuries, impairments, and out-of-body experiences. Conversations always seemed to come back to the body. In some sense, air guitar competitions enable people to embrace music-related fantasy and play, and in another sense, competitions force competitors to confront the possibilities and limitations in representing these fantasies to others using their bodies. This tension between private fantasies and public spectacle forces people to think about many issues related to embodiment: mobility, movement, bodily representation, pain, injury, vulnerability, prejudice, power, and the public display of intimate states.

I decided to focus this chapter on performers with invisible impairments in the 2017 competition. I sent a Facebook post to the 406 members of the US Air Guitar group, asking people with impairments both physical and psychological to get in touch with me if they wanted to share their stories. I received an overwhelming number of responses, including these:

- "I struggle with mobility issues due to nerve damage suffered in a stroke in 2009."
- "What if it just helps me get through life in general?"
- "i've torn my meniscus and have also ruptured a disc in my back from playing air guitar"
- "My lyme disease may be coming back or maybe my knee is just still shitty. I'm also overweight, and working on that. Does that count?"
- "I've got rheumatoid arthritis, but onstage it disappears."
- "I specifically started doing this to overcome a mental obstacle, I figure it's appropriate to throw my story out to you. I'll email you when I get a break from my little ones."

After a few initial conversations, I chose five people to follow throughout the 2017 competition: Cindairella, Shreddy Boop, Giant Junk, Damaged, and Kara. All experience impairments that are relatively invisible or at least not entirely apparent to others who do not know about this aspect of their lives.

I bring these five stories together in order to craft a widely inclusive approach to disability. Disability can be temporary, fluid, and contextual. These competitors' conceptions of their own bodies as disabled/non-disabled vary and depend on their circumstances. I chose these five competitors in order to represent a broad spectrum of experiences. As Michael Bakan has argued, depicting disability as a discrete category can be advantageous for certain forms of activism, which acknowledge unique forms of discrimination that people with disabilities face, but these essentialist ideas can also separate people into non-disabled/disabled categories, creating a false binary that treats disability as self-evident and unchanging.[2] In this chapter, I work against this false binary, by bringing together folks who might fall on a spectrum of disability. All of these competitors experience stigmatized aspects of bodily difference, which largely fall outside of the social categories of race, gender, sexuality, and class. I call this disability, while hoping that such an inclusive definition does not foreclose other definitions or exceptions. In this spirit, I include my own experience of impairment in the introduction.

30   SPECTACULAR LISTENING

I experience the privileges of a non-disabled person in most aspects of my life, but I begin with that anecdote to acknowledge disability as fluid in my own experience. I hope such a disclosure mirrors the kinds of honesty I asked of my interlocutors.

Overview of Air Guitar

The contemporary US Air Guitar Championships come from an over fifty-year history of air guitar playing,[3] which first rose to prominence in the rock subcultures in the late 1970s, and early depictions of this viral fandom (in today's parlance) tended to align air guitar playing with pathology, an association that contemporary air guitarists actively work to reclaim as a non-derogatory source of pride. In the 1980s, air band competitions proliferated in malls and college campuses across the country, usually characterized in the style of this *Milwaukee Sentinel* article from 1982: "Many fans suffer from air guitar mania, an affliction—often called 'electric stomach'—that forces them to mimic favorite guitarists and singers for hours, on imaginary Stratocasters and invisible microphones."[4] These depictions of air guitar tended to traffic in ableist ideas of madness, and air guitar was viewed as symptomatic of a kind of uncontrollable automatic response to heavy metal music, which often incorporated ideas of madness as a part of the genre's aesthetic.[5] The associations between air guitar playing and madness were crystallized not only by news media but also in air guitar memorabilia, such as *The Complete Air Guitar Handbook* (1983), which offered this tongue-and-cheek history of the phenomenon:

> Air guitarists were arrested, jailed, and sometimes institutionalized. Whether their frenzied motion was a sort of seizure, or perhaps a rebellious ritual, or even total lunacy—whatever the cause, the air guitarists were, at least, disturbing the peace, so they were persecuted.[6]

Such pathologizing language makes light of issues of carcerality and forced institutionalization, which have long posed an existential threat to disabled people, but these pathologizing ideas of viral fandom are important to acknowledge, because many disabled air guitarists today have gravitated to air guitar playing primarily *because* of these connotations. They reclaim negative or stereotypical depictions of air guitar playing, by embracing non-normative minds, bodies, and modes of listening.[7]

Founded by Cedric Devitt and Kriston Rucker in 2003, the US Air Guitar Championships represent the largest and most organized air guitar competition structure in the history of the United States. In 2017, 281 competitors competed across the country in twenty-seven air guitar competitions, all hoping to advance from local to regional to the national competition. Competitions occurred all over the country—from Custer (SD) to Brooklyn (NY) to Conway (AR) to Philadelphia (PA) to Des Moines (IA). The semifinals and national competition averaged 1,900 viewers per live stream online. Before the national championship, performers competed in the Dark Horse competition in the hopes of getting a last-minute bid to compete in the national championships two nights later in the Black Cat in Washington DC, and nearly 35,000 viewers tuned in to watch the event on Periscope (a live streaming platform). The events received national press from *VICE News* and the *New York Times*, and Edward Snowden tweeted about the competition when he found out his lawyer would be a judge at the national championships. Alongside approximately 400 other attendees at the national championships, I sat in the Black Cat and watched fans live tweet, stream, and cheer, as they hung on every note of air guitarists' routines onstage.

At all levels, the competition features two rounds. In the first round, competitors perform a sixty-second routine to a backing track that they prepared for the competition. These backing tracks are not simply unedited rock songs but rather a mix of popular music, original compositions, and sound effects—all seamlessly integrated to create a narrative arc within the allotted time. Competitors use their bodies to emphasize timbre, dynamic shifts, transitions, riffs, solos, and sound effects. After the first round, the top competitors advance to the second round, where organizers give them a surprise song to which they must improvise an air guitar solo. They hear the sixty-second cut of the song onstage (some may recognize it, some may not), and each competitor—one by one—comes onstage to improvise an air guitar routine to the song, in the hopes of nailing all of the transitions and syncing their bodies with the track. The second round rewards air guitarists who have an extensive knowledge of rock solo history. Judges score each round based on three criteria: technical merit (does it look like they're playing guitar?), stage presence (is it entertaining?), and airness (does it transcend imitation of a real guitar and become an art form in and of itself?).

32   SPECTACULAR LISTENING

These competitions do not revolve around pretending to play a guitar, in the sense of attempting some fidelity to real guitar mechanics. Air guitar competitions exaggerate and distort guitar theatrics, enacting fantasies related to imaginative listening. In order to create one-minute routines for the first round of the competition, competitors use digital audio workstations and various music software to remix popular music, in order to craft solos that conform to a particular choreography onstage. The "edits," as air guitarists call them, help set the stage for their elaborate performances. In my previous work, I have analyzed the connections between these edits and the onstage routines, particularly for the ways that the choreography can represent a physical interpretation of the digital manipulations.[8]

Air guitar competitions represent one genre within a broader phenomenon of remixing popular music in the late twentieth and early twenty-first centuries. Before musical.ly or TikTok existed, air guitarists were using digital audio workstations to craft customized gestural representations of popular music snippets. These manipulations of popular music clips are part of a phenomenon that I call "syncing out loud," on which I elaborate in my conclusion. Indeed, the trend of syncing the body with popular music has been a major facet of popular music consumption in many genres, enabling people to synchronize gestures with increasingly mobile music in both digital and physical fields of practice. Digital music apps simply formalize some of the diffuse practices that existed long before Web 2.0.

In the US Air Guitar Championships, performers don elaborate costumes, embodying memorable stage personas. Some people choose comic or absurd personas, while others choose personas that are slight modifications of their daily identities. Some people invent a new persona every year, while others stick to one persona that slowly develops over time. Names of these personas fit particular conventions, referring to well-known guitarists or genres (Eddie Hans Flailin', Agnes Young, Shred Nugent, Operation Rock), war or violence (Rear Admiral Kickass, Kingslayer, Lieutenant Facemelter, 6-String General), body parts (Blurred Knuckles, Ricky Stink Fingers, Aireola), illegal substances or objects of power (White Flame, Dry Ice, Windhammer, Sir Lord Snake Bite), famous people or cultural archetypes (Mom Jeans Jeanie, Lumb-AIR-Jack, The Airtiste, Rocka Khan, El Airiachi, Captain Airhab), and alterations of a person's real name (Doug "Thunder" Stroock, Andrew "Flying" Finn, or Eric "Mean" Melin).

Personas also exist in a complicated relationship to a person's everyday embodiment. As Sydney Hutchinson points out, sometimes these air guitar avatars take on political valences, giving performers license to challenge cultural stereotypes.[9] The late air guitarist Andres SegoviAIR, for example, frequently performed in a chair, due to mobility issues related to the loss of his leg after complications with diabetes. His onstage persona codified a form of air guitar performance that he termed "chair guitar," which, in his specific iteration of it, emphasized virtuosity through technical proficiency of classical Spanish guitar. "I realized that, as a disabled performer with balance issues, I was not going to be able to compete with able-bodied folks on their terms—I had to figure out a way to compete on my own terms," he told me. Indeed, many other air guitarists have found ways to convert their everyday experiences of stigmatized bodily differences into assets in the air guitar realm. In 2017, the Canadian air guitar champion, The Phoenix, was featured in a *VICE* documentary, disclosing this process:

> I have a hyper-mobility disorder that causes my joints and my skin and in some cases my organs to not be properly formed and be very, very loose. And sometimes that's a pretty big disadvantage. Some days I can't really walk all that properly, or I have to use a cane. And when I'm up onstage doing air guitar, sometimes it's an advantage 'cause I'm really flexible, and my body moves in ways that, you know, other people's bodies can't.[10]

During her 2017 routine, she trudged onstage with a fake IV bag that caught fire as she dramatically kicked it away and began air guitaring—all while dressed like a fire-breathing zombie who had presumably come back from the dead to play air guitar. So while air guitar clearly plays with fantastical imagery of rock guitar lore, the personas onstage, as well as the performances of gestural listening, always come from a particular imagination, which is informed by a person's real life experiences and bodily possibilities.

Disclosure and Masquerade

Air guitar playing enables performers to translate their experiences of disability into abstract representations onstage. They do not necessarily use these performances to disclose a specific diagnosis, but these performances provide outlets for exploring how one might be perceived by others, using a persona as a proxy to exaggerate aspects of the body. Air guitar competitions

34 SPECTACULAR LISTENING

challenge the idea that private experiences should be kept that way. They facilitate forms of sharing that can treat disclosure as a source of power.

In everyday life, the stakes for revealing or concealing one's disability can be high. The need to hide disability comes with legitimate fears that expressing neurological or physical difference can result in the loss of a job, pervasive cultural stigma, and judgment from others. People may refuse to acknowledge disability in themselves, as a result of an internalized ableism that associates disability with weakness or inferiority. For these and many other reasons, people work hard to hide their disability, engaging in forms of passing that conceal aspects of the body that might diverge from the norm.[11] The difficulty disclosing disability can also lead many to suppress it.

In addition, people often respond to disability disclosures with doubt. They may view someone as exaggerating an impairment. They may see the request for accommodations as needy, selfish, or a burden on others. They may judge someone against a stereotype of what they imagine disability should look or sound like. To disclose disability means to be confronted with other people's ableist assumptions, which often manifest as disgust, discomfort, or doubt in the face of disability.

Disabled folks often engage in practices that involve translating disabilities to others, using a technique that disability theorists have called "disability masquerade." Building on the masquerade as a feminist concept,[12] Tobin Siebers describes how people might "engage in a little-discussed practice, structurally akin to passing but not identical to it, in which they disguise one kind of disability with another or display their disability by exaggerating it."[13] This could involve dramatizing a mobility impairment so that others recognize someone needs physical assistance in an airport, or over-describing a psychological problem in order to receive basic accommodations in a college course. Disability masquerade does not imply a vast conspiracy in which disabled folks exaggerate their impairments to manipulate others. Rather, disabled people must constantly contend with stereotypical ideas of how disability should manifest, so they often leverage normative expectations of disability to achieve some of kind assistance or accommodation. Disability masquerade simply acknowledges that the personal experience of impairments can be hard for others to understand, so a translation—a performance—often takes place that enables others to grasp the situation.

All of the air guitarists in this chapter struggle with questions about disclosure, both onstage and offstage. Their performances onstage enable them to disclose aspects of their lives to the general public with varying levels of abstraction and specificity. But in all cases they engage in a disability masquerade, selectively and strategically revealing aspects of themselves to the general public through their air guitar routines. These routines help them rehearse aspects of disclosure in their daily lives. I present each of their stories as complex vignettes here, in order to sketch the multi-faceted dimensions of air guitar within their lives.

Shreddy Boop

As the child of Greek immigrants growing up in the Washington DC area, Shreddy lived what she called a "sheltered life." A conservative home and parochial school limited her exposure to other kids, so she found herself bonding with her uncle, who came to live with the family and brought his record collection along. "He had the most amazing albums," she told me, as we talked via FaceTime in our respective living rooms. "He would let me look

Figure 1.2 Shreddy at Dark Horse. Photo credit: author.
i. Shreddy Boop shreds at the Dark Horse in Washington DC. She appears in traditional Greek clothing made to look like that of Jimi Hendrix at the Monterrey Pop Festival. Her hair swings across her face. The crowd watches her perform.

36 SPECTACULAR LISTENING

through his albums. Back then, I would look through all the artwork: Rolling Stones, the White Album, Billy Joel. It was cool to visually engage with the music, not just audibly. I grew up having visuals and art and having music videos too . . . I actually got to create my own heroes and discover my own heroes." Shreddy relished the chance to perform for her family, entertaining people with stories and performances, but social anxiety also severely limited her experiences outside of her comfortable spaces. She told me: "My anxiety is usually around new situations, new people, any situation where I may not have control."

As an adult in 2008, she combed through a local newspaper, where she saw an ad for an air guitar competition at the famous 9:30 Club in Washington DC. When she attended the event later that night, she watched performer after performer embody these fantastical personas and bring the music to life, and she began to reflect on air guitar as an art form: "I guess you're sharing with other people what that music makes you feel. You might listen to it when you're walking around, but, when you're on stage, you get to bring everybody on stage with you and show people how that song makes you feel or how that riff makes you feel. Great sense of freedom . . . But I noticed there were no women up there," she told me. "So, a year later I went ahead and signed up."

Signing up brought forth immediate fear of exposure. She felt "nothing but anxiety from the thought of it." I asked her to reflect on her feelings as she approached her first competition. "I knew I had to do it and fully immerse myself into this new situation, and that was the only way to see if I could get through it. I was a hot mess. Total anxiety around the entire thing." As much as she wanted her performance to bring forth a sudden transformation, she actually found it quite painful, once she finally got onstage: "I ended up being completely frozen onstage. My feet felt like lead weights. Getting in front of strangers is scary." In many ways, her initiation brought forth the worst of her symptoms—confronting her with a kind of pain she worked hard to avoid in daily life. But air guitar also gave her a sense of control and allowed her to channel the pain toward an absurd performance practice.

Eight years later, Shreddy was a mainstay in the Washington DC air guitar scene. Her social anxiety persisted, but she found ways to leave it backstage. "Every other year I get the frozen feeling, and every other year I feel comfortable and do really well." During the summer of 2016, she performed a routine to "Panama" by Van Halen, inspired by the theatricality of David Lee Roth and Eddie Van Halen. When her round one routine came to a close, she leaped offstage with a giant kick, landing in the area beyond the stage and shattering her heel bone. "The heel itself was fractured in a bunch of pieces," she told me. "When I started walking again, it was winter."

As we spoke throughout the 2017 season, she found herself coming to terms with anxiety in ways she never had before, while trying to grapple with a heel injury that severely limited her daily life (her commute, her work, and her social life). The anxiety, at first, seemed diffuse and somewhat uncontrollable to her, and she came to terms with how to objectify it. She learned to see it as a kind of bounded reality. Shreddy spoke of her previous experience of anxiety like this: "I hadn't separated myself from my anxiety. I hadn't figured out that this is a separate thing I can put aside." As she discovered ways to manage her anxiety, her heel impairment turned out to be somewhat more ambiguous than she at first thought. She frequently expressed frustration at the slow recovery, and, when I saw her a year after her initial injury, she had just seen a doctor, who was weighing surgery in light of complications with her recovery.

The dismissiveness with which people treat air guitar actually made Shreddy somewhat attracted to the practice as an absurd type of performance art, but it also made things challenging for her after her heel injury. In the case of "real" instrument playing, an injury resulting from a performance may be seen by people as true dedication to a legitimate craft, but a broken heel stemming from an air guitar competition could seem to many to be a ridiculous price to pay for such a pointless hobby. So she felt the need to hide air guitar as a pastime from many people in her life, including at her job, which revolves around dealing with people who expect a certain degree of seriousness. For many reasons, she could not disclose her air-guitar-related injuries to others.

Within the air guitar community, she could embrace these impairments. Many people mentioned her to me, when I told them of my interest in disability and air guitar, and they almost always recognized her foot-related impairment—not social anxiety. Her foot injury was indeed an event that made people take notice during the 2017 air guitar season, but I think sudden physical injuries, in general, are easier for others to empathize with than social anxiety, which tends to evoke more suspicion to those who cannot relate. People often recognize visible forms of pain and completely dismiss psychological ones—part of the fallacy that all disabilities are visible on the body. In Shreddy's case, her foot injury may have actually given her license to disclose her psychological struggles as well, because it brought about conversations with air guitarists about bodily struggles on- and offstage.

38 SPECTACULAR LISTENING

In 2017, I saw her perform at the Dark Horse competition in Washington DC at Nanny O'Briens, as part of the weekend-long air guitar festivities. She wore a Jimi Hendrix–style outfit, which consisted of traditional Greek clothing she converted into a 1960s counterculture aesthetic. Following her doctor's orders, she wore a boot all day and applied steroid cream right before her performance. Earlier in the year, we talked many times about her decision to perform a Jimi Hendrix song. ' "Voodoo Chile' makes you feel invincible," she told me, while describing listening to it on a bus and imaging a potential routine. "I feel that way. I feel so giant. I want to let go of this." In the context of our conversation, "this" referred to a lot of things—struggles with body image, social anxiety, heel injury, and, on top of all of that, simply having a bad day. When I saw her perform that night in DC, she seemed unguarded. She shredded up and down the imaginary fretboard, glaring at the audience, and delivering what could have been either a grimace or a smile. At the end, she knelt on the ground and lit her air guitar on fire, in the style of Hendrix at Monterey Pop Festival. She flickered her fingers above the flames to beckon them higher and higher, and, as the music came to a close, she threw herself onto the flames, disappearing into the smoking pile of air fire.

Damaged

Damaged's pain is invisible, but he wears it on his sleeve. After growing up in Arkansas, he served as a paramedic for eighteen years, and we spoke about his career: "I wasn't a paramedic who likes to work in small towns, where you go get grandma from the nursing home and take her to the hospital because her family hasn't seen her in three months. I was a trauma junkie." At the age of fourteen, he knew he wanted to help people in some of the worst moments in their lives, so he eventually became a firefighter. After receiving a litany of credentials (EMT, medic, flight medic, critical care medic, and FEMA certification), he worked in Little Rock (AR), Helena (AR), West Helena (AR), Mariana (AR), and New Orleans (LA)—work that included Hurricane Katrina and Hurricane Isaac. His work caused him to endure others' trauma, which in turn became his own.

As we spoke, he turned to look at the ceiling and began ticking off major life experiences: "I had a lot of things happen to me. I had a guy try to shoot me on scene. I've been stabbed. I had a guy who was shot in the back of my truck while I was working on him." He told me a story of a guy who came

Figure 1.3 Damaged at Dark Horse. Photo credit: author.

i. Damaged appears at the Dark Horse in Washington DC. He holds an air guitar onstage, as black face paint drips down his face. The word "Stronger" appears on his shirt. A crowd of onlookers gather around the stage.

up to him with a gun that he put to Damaged's chest and pulled the trigger six times. Fortunately, the gun didn't work, but, in that moment, he was convinced he was dead. "All these things you see, you're on call, as soon as it's over, you're on the next call. Your brain don't have time to process what you've seen and what you've done. Everyone has a box in their head where they take things and put them. My box got full. The last thing I put in there happened to be a hand grenade with a pulled pin. It broke me."

Four years ago, Damaged quit working and was officially diagnosed with Complex Post Traumatic Stress Disorder—a condition in which people get PTSD not from a single event but rather from a series of traumatic events. "I'm 100% disabled now. I go see a psychiatrist in Little Rock at Big Baptist. I have major depression disorder. Social and general anxiety." He cannot sleep at night and takes a cocktail of medications to manage his mood and temperament. "My bad days are awful. On a bad day, I will sit down in my chair in my living room and the TV won't come on and the kids won't be there to distract me. I will sit there for hours staring at a TV that's off and will stare at the stuff I've seen and done throughout my career."

40   SPECTACULAR LISTENING

Leaving home is difficult—he is averse to loud and surprising noises, will only sit at a restaurant if his back can face a wall, and hates crowds. He lives in a remote, mountainous area of Arkansas with his family. He doesn't like being suddenly approached by people and tends to worry that people will act panicky and violently in crowds. This causes a tension for Damaged. He's a friendly guy with a great sense of humor and clearly seems animated by interactions with others, but this is also the source of a lot of his pain and anxiety.

"So, given all of this, why would you ever want to enter an air guitar competition?," I asked him. I continued: "It seems like air guitar competitions would have all of the triggers that you try to avoid—loud noises, people intentionally trying to surprise one another, big crowds in small spaces." In order to understand his answer, it's important to understand his relationship to his CPTSD. Damaged wants others to recognize first responders as particularly vulnerable to some of the same problems that many people recognize veterans as having. Suicide rates, he told me, are especially high among first responders, and stigmatizing or suppressing PTSD and CPTSD makes life harder for first responders. I saw a green ribbon (Mental Health Awareness) tattooed on his arm, and he told me that his mantra is "stronger"—to be stronger each day than the day before. A desire for the visibility of PTSD and CPTSD presents somewhat of a paradox for him. He wants to raise awareness about his own experience and that of others, but doing so involves engaging other people, whom he finds hard to trust and be around.

His entry into air guitar occurred by accident. "I love music. I have a very eclectic taste in music. 90s metal. Bands like Metallica, Pantera, Soul Asylum. I also like the older country Hank Williams, Conway Twitty." He's also a musician who sometimes plays guitar at home. When he found himself a local festival in Newport, Arkansas, he heard there would be an air guitar competition, which he wanted to see but felt hesitant. He found a place where he could put his back against a wall to feel secure. Thunder Stroock, the national organizer for US Air Guitar, stood on the Newport stage and announced a $250 prize for the winner. After a lot of goading by his wife, Damaged reluctantly agreed to enter the competition. Backstage, he nervously told people about his story, giving them an explanation for his anxiety. He finally took the stage: "And the whole time I was doing it, I couldn't look out on the crowd. I was terrified the whole time." He claims he can hardly remember it. He did not win, but he felt like getting on stage was a huge victory. "For sixty seconds, I wasn't [the person] with my issues."

In the following weeks, organizers heard about his story and invited him to the regional competition in Chicago. Damaged did not want to participate in any more air guitar. "I talked to my therapist and she's ecstatic. She was like it's a huge step in the right direction." He laughed. "I really wanted to take a *smaller* step at that point. Like [playing air guitar for] six people in my front yard. Not a bar full of people." Damaged turned down the event in Chicago, but, after a little more convincing by organizers, he reluctantly agreed to go to a regional competition in Kansas City—a little closer to home. When he got there, he felt extremely welcomed by people in the community. "When I got to Kansas City, everybody in the group knew that this was how I was going to be. They gave me that space. And by the end of the night, I was talking to Harvey Wallbanger, the Lone Heartbreaker, Cindairella, Airiachi, Sonic Bitch."

After the event in Kansas City, Damaged got invited to his third air guitar event of the 2017 competition season—the Dark Horse in Washington DC. After thinking hard about going to DC, which involved weighing not only his disability but also kids and family, he decided he should go. He worried mainly about the physical spaces in the venues, the public transportation he would have to ride, and the general density of people around everywhere. His family and therapist supported the decision, thinking it would be a big step in the right direction. Having never competed in any US Air Guitar event before 2017, his commitment to the community rapidly escalated—from reluctance to compete in an event to participating in three events across the country. Throughout the trip, he posted on the Facebook event message board about struggles in DC, which is a bustling city that can trigger a lot of intense responses for someone who doesn't like crowds or sudden noises.

I first saw him play air guitar live at Nanny O'Briens. After speaking with me a bit before the competition, he moved to the front of the crowded bar, where he watched people compete and cheered them on. When his time came to compete, he stood up on the bar and began his performance by taking a huge leap to the stage. He played wildly, drawing attention to the word "Stronger" on his t-shirt. Eye-black paint streaks dripped down his face, as his wrists flashed with a studded bracelet and ring. The audience sound level noticeably increased when he took the stage, and I saw a handful of people on the right side of the stage air guitaring along with him, a sign of respect and enthusiasm for his performance. After his performance, the judges gave him modest scores, but he came over to me afterward feeling victorious.

Two nights later at the Black Cat, the 2017 US Air Guitar Championships came to a close with Mom Jeans Jeanie as the victor. The competition ended, as it always does, with everyone air guitaring to Lynyrd Skynyrd's "Freebird" onstage. I usually spend the nearly fourteen minutes of "Freebird" air guitaring, but occasionally I will take a step back and scan the crowd to reflect on the scene. As I sat in the back and stared at the stage, I noticed Damaged slumped over in the corner of the stage, such that his back faced the crowd. His hands were over his eyes. I cautiously approached him and put my hand on his back. "Are you alright?" He barely moved his head. "Just overwhelmed?," I asked. He nodded. In many ways, the "Freebird" moment represents the culmination of the entire air guitar season—the moment in which the competition has ended and people come together to collectively air guitar to what is perhaps the most beloved guitar solo of all time. In that moment, all the momentum of the air guitar season reaches its climax, and the solo can feel incredibly moving and powerful.

Damaged doesn't think air guitar will make his pain disappear, but he feels that air guitar allows him to stop fighting against the pain and suppressing it. He went from reluctantly joining an air guitar competition in a remote area of Arkansas to air guitaring the "Freedbird" solo on one of the most famous stages in the United States—an incredible arc of visibility and vulnerability. Air guitar can make people feel recognized as individuals—not for some virtuosic feat of guitar playing but for their willingness to subject themselves to the vulnerable act of air guitar playing. I think Damaged felt validated by being accepted as both different and the same as others. He describes how hard it can be to articulate his experience of his disability to others: "It's just hell. I can be honest with you about that. I have to fight through it everyday . . . Some [people] think it's something you can snap out of one day. They don't understand that the guy I was four years ago is gone. But I can be a better version of what I am now." Claiming his condition—talking about it in a casual and bold way—is his way of rejecting the idea that he should be ashamed of it.

I asked him about choosing his stage name. "When you're in our line of work, you just don't tell people you have a problem," he told me. "You don't come out and say you need to talk to somebody. You're looked at as weak or you can't handle the job. It affects everybody differently." He paused. "Some people can go on their entire lives and stuff things in that box. It never bothers them. Some are like me and the box gets full. And it cracked. And I'm forever going to be damaged. I'm damaged goods. So that's how I picked my stage name."

Cindairella

Air guitar for Cindairella is in many ways a family business. Her brother won the Air Guitar World Championships in 2013. She met her husband through air guitar, and her husband also competes. She incorporates US Air Guitar events into family road trips, traveling to competitions all over the United States. I met her in 2015 in Oulu, Finland, when she attended the Air Guitar World Championships and placed ninth in the world. We sat outside, before the competition, and she and her husband told me the story about how they met through US Air Guitar. If some are reluctant to share their air guitar hobby with outsiders, Cindairella is the opposite—fully embracing air guitar as central to her adult life.

On one of her family road trips, she found herself driving down to Austin, Texas, from Lawrence, Kansas. After dropping off her daughter at an event, she decided to go to the Austin 360 Bridge (Pennybacker Bridge) with a friend—a sightseeing destination that involves a steep hike followed by a scenic overlook. While hiking, she slipped on some rocks and broke her fifth

Figure 1.4 Cindairella in Lawrence. Photo credit: Whitney Young. Form attached.

i. Cindairella appears with a tank top that bears her name in glittering letters. Her outstretched arms sketch an air guitar slightly larger than a "there guitar." A purple light shines around her, as she makes a serious face in her routine on the stage in Lawrence, Kansas, in 2019.

44 SPECTACULAR LISTENING

metatarsal (little bone in her foot). "I heard or felt it crack," she told me, unable to separate the sound from the sensation. She eventually decided to go to the emergency room. She immediately began to realize that she might not be able to compete in an upcoming air guitar competition. "I'm in the emergency care room, and I'm trying not to get emotional, because if I think about air guitar too much I'll start crying." As she tried to deal with this pain in the following months, she began to experience intensified pain from a herniated disc in her back as well. "That's chronic," she told me. "That's going to follow me the rest of my days: chiropractor and physical therapy. I think it's just a thing that happened over time and that's where I am for the rest of my life." Her foot provided the most acute pain—sharp pain followed by tenderness and occasional twinges—and her back provided a more subtle ache that ebbs and flows.

Cindairella found ways to channel two sources of pain in her performances, by developing an invincible persona. I asked her about the development of Cindairella, and she emphasized personality traits she wanted to cultivate through this character:

MCDANIEL: How did you develop Cindairella?

CINDAIRELLA: Cindairella is the epitome of the powerful women I wish I could be in life everyday but haven't gotten there yet. I think I developed that character out of that. Some people say she comes off as sexy. But I'm not aiming for sexy. I'm aiming for powerful. And sometimes people read that as a sexy trait, and, if that happens, fine. But when I pick songs, I don't want to come off as "sexy, shake your ass." I want to come off as "powerful, this is who I am, deal with it" . . . I could've come up with any kind of character. Why did I come up with her? I curated her so she comes off as a strong, powerful type of woman who can do what she wants and doesn't take anyone's shit and, if necessary, she would defend and kick someone's ass. In real life, I hate confrontation. I can't even watch shows where it happens. It's super uncomfortable . . . As I have gotten older, I've wanted more out of myself that way, so I created this character. I feel like there's some feedback. Since I notice [those traits] in Cindairella, it's come out in my real life too.

MCDANIEL: I can imagine there's some spillover that way—that creating Cindairella in a certain way nurtures a side of you. Has she evolved over time?

CINDAIRELLA: I think so. This year I'm doing less of the black eye makeup. Before, when I created her, the makeup was my own mask, so, when I put it on, I could be her . . . . Like the Batman mask. It doesn't just cover up who I am but makes me feel like I'm in that costume, in that body. This year I've gotten away from the makeup. I can now become Cindairella really easy. I don't need a mask anymore.

MCDANIEL: So you're closer to being her?

CINDAIRELLA: Yeah.

MCDANIEL: You compare her to a superhero, and their powers usually come at the expense of some fatal flaw that they have to wrestle with. Does Cindairella have a weakness?

CINDAIRELLA: The way I developed her . . . She was very similar to me in that, because she's so powerful and doesn't give a shit how you think and feel, she's standoffish. Feelings are separate from her. In real life, I have a similar weakness of building walls. It stems from lower self-confidence. I feel like I'm better now than I ever have been. Still there's that element of fear of putting yourself out there.

When Cindairella confronted her bodily pain in her foot and back, her first thoughts grappled with how physical pain and mobility limitations might undermine her persona's power. She described to me her feelings in the emergency room in Austin, making references to Andres SegoviAIR's style: "My first initial thought is: I can't do air guitar with a broken foot. I can do chair guitar, but that's not my thing. Cindairella is not a chair guitarist. She likes to kick for god's sake."

As a result of internalized ableism as well as fear of disability stigma, Cindairella worried that a physical impairment might undermine some of the feminist power of Cindairella.[14] Physical mobility aids in the competition can often entail a gendered double standard. A few women air guitarists expressed concerns that mobility aids, as well as other signs of a physical impairment, may signal weakness to judges and others, while many men expressed that signs of physical impairments could confirm their strength (e.g., as battle scars).[15] Cindairella grappled with the ways her own bodily impairments could impact her persona onstage, whose invincibility might be premised on a kind of non-disabled superheroism.

However, in the subsequent years of the competition, she challenged the idea that Cindairella should be all powerful, while further integrating her

46   SPECTACULAR LISTENING

daily life with her persona. After her broken foot in 2016, she got her doctor to write her a prescription for a knee scooter. "I went to Toys-Rus for LED lights to put on the scooter. I went to Michael's to get stuff to bedazzle the boot with pinks and silvers." As she worked on her adaptation of Poison's "Talk Dirty to Me," she "tried [her] damnest" to work the scooter into the routine. "I did the routine most of it sitting down and sometimes got up on my knee and leaned on the handlebars."

The following year she grappled with multiple dimensions of pain, although she ditched the knee scooter. Her foot ached, often made worse by the weather and changes in humidity and barometric pressure. Her back occasionally flared up. But she found ways to make these issues part of her performances.

During her 2017 routine, Cindairella was on top of her game, winning the Kansas City regional competition and looking poised to place high in the national competition. She no longer used the knee scooter. Her routine presented back pain as a humorous consequence of a bad hangover. She entered the stage, with a bent back and her hand pressed against her head. Her feet moved slowly. She looked sickly, nauseous, and achy. Peeking through sunglasses, she contorted her face to express exhaustion and anguish. Her aches and pains evoked pain from aging, overexertion, and a bad hangover. She plodded to center stage. Suddenly, as the music began, she emerged with a sudden burst of energy and precise coordination. She channeled the pain into something powerful and potent. She kicked high above her head and danced around stage. For air guitarists in the audience, this narrative had two layers of meaning—1) her recovery from a hangover leading to rocking out at a party and 2) her persistence in dealing with her physical injuries leading to an extremely impressive air guitar routine.

I found myself in awe of her second-round routine and shocked that she didn't win the national championships. During the second round, competitors had to improvise a routine to "Take the Power Back" by Rage Against the Machine. Cindairella was most likely too far behind after the first round to make up the deficit in scores with Mom Jeans Jeanie, but her routine presented an incredible combination of big moves and subtle gestures. At one point, she managed to hit a series of power chords, and, in between one power chord and the next, she lifted the guitar and snorted a line of (air) cocaine along the neck of the guitar, after which she flipped the guitar back into her arms and continued strumming—never missing a beat. This circled back to her first-round routine, signaling a recovery from hangover into full-blown party mode. Her snorting fake cocaine mirrored the kinds of adrenaline marshalled by air guitar competitions, where music becomes a controlled substance for the display of intense feelings. For her, air guitar competitions did not necessarily allow her to avoid pain so much as they allowed her to experience pain without feeling guilty for it—like she should be taking it easy on her body and taking better care of it. Pain and fatigue can sometimes bring about a sense of shame and guilt for not taking better care of ourselves. Cindairella embraces the freedom in throwing caution to the wind.

Figure 1.5 Kara Portrait. Photo credit: Lenny Gotter.
i. Kara appears on a beach in one of her air guitar costumes. She appears dressed up as Furiosa from Mad Max with face paint, colorful hair, and hands on her hips, as long chains hang from her neck down to her sides.

Kara

For many air guitarists, playing air guitar represents a unique experience with their own bodies—one that calls on them to acknowledge how their body feels and how it looks to others in performance. This kinesthetic knowledge comes slowly but provides a foundation for a good air guitar career. Learning about the body is something that Kara has been doing long before air guitar. Her knowledge of the body emerges from both work and hobbies. She's a massage therapist in Portland, Oregon, and she enjoys karaoke, belly dancing, hula hooping, pole dancing, and burlesque performance. When she first discovered air guitar competitions, she had a reaction that many fellow air guitarists share: "Who the fuck does this kind of thing?" Seven years later, Kara is a regular competitor in air guitar competitions, and she also organizes them, coming up with elaborate pre-shows and half-time shows. She likes the stage and loves the side of air guitar that can be entertaining for others. "Any kind of performing, you focus on people in the audience," she told me. "Yeah you look at [music] like playdough, like clay. You have to create a little story. It has to be something that will translate into something to somebody else."

Air guitar came into Kara's life at an opportune time. At the age of thirty-two, she experienced sudden and chronic pain that stemmed from an injury thirty years earlier. When she was two years old, she got into a car accident with her grandmother. Her body flew in the air, and her grandmother grabbed her leg to prevent her from flying out of the window. She recovered from the car accident, but, three decades later, the injury was triggered during a massage. Something initiated deep searing pains in her legs—sciatica from the car accident that manifested all of the sudden. "It was so bad. Luckily we had a walker in my house . . . because I couldn't walk." She spent a lot of time working through the pain. "I went to therapists, acupuncturists, massage therapists, chiropractors—different ones doing different exercises. It got to the point where my back would go out quarterly, and I couldn't function."

Kara gave up a lot of her beloved hobbies. "At that point, I had to stop belly dancing. That's a lot of hip movement, and you move your hips like an infinity symbol. So that was over for me." As she was struggling to come to terms with her new limitations, she found air guitar. "I was like: this is actually really fun, and I can do something creative." Kara embraced air guitar, which helped her work through some of the pain. "Air guitar helped me get motivated to get better." At the same time, it also brought forth many other forms of pain. She blew out both of her knees. She torqued multiple ribs. She even made friends with a chiropractor who acts as a sort of on-call specialist for air guitar events. "She loves it. She's actually come to competitions. She's fascinated by it. She's got a picture of me on her wall."

Because of her kinesthetic knowledge, she recognizes the ways air guitar is similar to other embodied exercises, activities, and sports. She told me that stage routines can condense a lot of motion into a single performance, which can be extremely dangerous: "So it's like a race. It's that energy where you go from static to this combustible movement for sixty seconds, you're bound to injure yourself and you're bound not to feel it when it happens." When developing her routines, Kara views choreography as a kind of science:

> I look at music as an equation. I'll be like: "Oh I can do this here, and I can do that there." So I listen to a lot of music that I would never listen to. I listen to it differently. And bellydancing has helped me listen to music differently. That's given me more a musicality in a different way. You hear people that will have the idea: you've just gotta rock, if you love it . . . Ok that's fine for you're if you're in your bedroom. But, I think that's selfish. You have to think that these people bought a ticket to see you onstage. You have to make them laugh. Blow their minds.

Her emphasis on controlling and manipulating music also gets her into trouble, since she finds that over-choreographing a routine can ruin some of the spontaneity and energy in the moment. Having too much bodily control can make a routine seem too mechanical.

Kara views bodily and psychological pain as one in the same—one always producing the other. When I reached out to air guitarists for my research on disability, Kara responded:

> I have dealt with a chronic low back injury that has been so significant in my life that I have at times had to use a walker. I have blown out my rib a few times in competition mode and planned an air guitar competition with the death of my mom looming, she passed a few days after the show.

I was curious how her story of her mom's death relates to my request for narratives about disability. I asked Kara about this. For her, air guitar involved grappling with both bodily and psychological pain together. She explained her mom's death to me in this way:

> Planning a competition is different than just showing up and competing. It was a great distraction actually. My mom had cancer, and the previous

50 SPECTACULAR LISTENING

year [my husband's] mom was dying. So, [my partner and I] had *that* experience. And my mom actually had cancer for over a year, and last April her doctor was like: "You've got a month." She had lung cancer. She was one of those types of people who is suicidal until she finds out she is going to die and then she wants to live. She was like: "No I'm going to live. I'm going to beat this." So that April I had a weird relationship with my mom, so I had to start going there. That sucked—going to my mom's place and dealing with what was going on there. So she decided to get worse the week of the competition. I decided the show has to go on. My mom was going to die on my birthday, but she didn't die on my birthday. I told my mom I was going to do the show and not see her that day. I was going to do the show. And while putting my makeup on (I have this girl who does my hair), I just blanked. I couldn't put my makeup on. I didn't know how to get ready. She took over and did my makeup and put my hair on. I had a moment. It was interesting. *(long pause)* When you're going through a situation like that you're kind of looking outside of yourself. I'm still processing it . . . There's no reason for air guitar. It's the silliest thing in the world, but it's so fun. It gets people out of their heads and out of their lives for a moment.

Air guitarists often explain air guitar with some version of the saying: "It's a stupid joke that people take extremely seriously." Kara's story reveals the way air guitar can be hilarious *and* significant as a force in people's lives— a source of pain but also a way of coming to terms with significant life experiences. After her mom's death, Kara began to experience additional physical symptoms. "And here's another part of my story," she told me. "I've got some serious intestinal issues going on right now—IBS, colitis. So I'm working through my intestinal issues. It started after my mom was going into the last of her life. That's when it started and continued to get worse. If I have any kind of stress, then that adds an element to what's going on."

In 2017, Kara debated whether to take a self-care vacation or fly to Washington DC to play air guitar. Both could contribute to her happiness in different ways. Air guitar won out. Kara's routine revolved around anesthesia, all encapsulated by her performing as a tooth. "Actually, as a meta-tooth," she corrected me. Always tweaking her stage name, she went by Kara PAIRriodonté—a play on previous stage names. In her routine, she was dressed in a t-shirt with an image of a molar, and her performance began with powerful licks from AC/DC's "Beating Around the Bush." She thrashed around stage with muscular arms and animated facial gestures. In mid-performance, her routine was suddenly interrupted by a clip of Steve Martin from Little Shop of Horrors. She lip synced along with his line from the film: "Open up, here I come!" Then Pink Floyd's "Comfortably Numb" kicked in, and her performance entered a kind of anesthetized dream state in slow motion. She wanted to include sounds of dental drilling but felt like it would "be painful to all the dental phobics out there."

Giant Junk

"I've got something to prove, because people think I'm fucked up because of this whole stigma thing. I'm sure people have problems and want to use air guitar to work through them. I'm not afraid to say what's wrong with me and why it's better." Giant Junk and I spoke on the phone, as he was trying to hunt down a raccoon that had somehow made it into the attic of his home. "I suffer from a slew of mental illnesses, mainly bipolar. I'm also ADD. This is surprising to people because I'm so well built, but I'm also anorexic. I have had to learn over time to turn those things into advantages." Giant Junk spent much of his professional life post-college coding algorithms for a major healthcare company, and he spent much of his private life performing in a metal band in Nashville. He spends a lot of his time thinking about ways to make his skills and passions serve his desire to help people. Over the course of our conversations in 2017, he was considering some major life changes—whether or not to go back into the tech and/or healthcare industries, whether he wants to unplug from technology and go off the grid, and how he can get his dog Robocop to Mount Rushmore. He explained the crossroads to me:

> I'm 39 years old. I've got no kids, no wife. What do I want to do with my life? It's kind of like you dive into a big algorithmic problem and have a general direction of where you're going and have a sense of the outcome you want, but, in the process of developing the algorithm conceptually and code to execute it, you're going to encounter things you didn't expect that you're going to have overcome but also new insights that will change what you decide to do.

I replied and asked him if he's trying to perfect the algorithm or accept its imperfections, and I realized that I wasn't fully grasping what he was saying.

He said it's not the algorithm itself that he's trying to change but rather the methods used to make the algorithm—that's what he's working on.

As part of his love for music, Giant Junk loves air guitar, and he even has "air guitar" tattooed on his body. "I've always wanted to put on a spectacle," he said. But he also feels critical of US Air Guitar for a handful of reasons. He sees air guitar as an opportunity for people to let go of their inhibitions and have fun, and he hates seeing the competitive side of air guitar rise to the surface. "I've always struggled to put routines together. I never enjoyed that. The thought of practice—I just don't get it. It doesn't resonate with me." He joked: "I've got my last place streak going."

He doesn't aspire to win competitions and thinks that competitiveness within air guitar undermines the spirit of the event—the inclusivity that people purport to celebrate in the US Air Guitar community. As a former division-one athlete and musician, Giant Junk was drawn to air guitar precisely because it does not require training your body and practicing for performance. For him, the notion that it should become a competitive arena, in which judges deliver critical comments and harsh scores, completely goes against the air guitar ideals of spontaneity and passion.

His vision for an inclusive, spontaneous, and weird air guitar community also cuts against the top-down management style of US Air Guitar—perhaps his biggest grievance with the group. Although air guitar competitions take place all over the country, the ones in dense urban coastal areas tend to be much easier to sustain, since they draw on a consistent population of competitors and fans. Events in the South are much harder to run, and national organizers tend to place the onus of advertising and organizing on individual organizers in the South, who must do a lot of free labor in service of the national organization. "Nashville is the hardest scene to promote something ever," Giant Junk told me. The city has tons of competition, in terms of music and entertainment, and it doesn't have the luxury of dense urban foot traffic, as does New York City or Washington DC. Giant Junk saw organizing as an opportunity to use his unique qualities as assets: "I can use the engaging personality and shit that comes with my diseases to be more successful. And finally to be different from everyone else. I'm not thinking about the problem in the same way."

In the course of promoting and organizing competitions, Giant Junk ran ads on Facebook and promoted on the radio, giving away free tickets. He put flyers up all over the city. He raised money for Notes for Notes, a charitable organization that opens music studios in Boys and Girls Clubs. He brought Notes for Notes rappers and performers to shows to open for air guitar competitions, and he featured them in his radio advertisements for air guitar. He recruited judges and worked hard to ensure that they would treat competitors in positive and non-discriminatory ways. He told them: "If I hear anyone evaluated based on their gender, their religion, the way they look, I'll throw you out. No one will be mistreated at my event." Even though the judging scale is from four to six, he told judges that no one should receive something in the fours. Low scores are unnecessarily critical toward people doing something extremely vulnerable. And Giant Junk should know—he's received plenty of fours. In this instance, Giant Junk's skills played a big role the event's success.

His insistence that air guitar should be a judgment-free occasion for self-expression came to a head in Arkansas years later. He competed in Newport—the same event where Damaged made his debut. The event in Newport turned out to be a conservative event, which sometimes happens when a community hosts an air guitar event for the first time. I've seen air guitar events where people strip off their clothes onstage, and I've seen air guitar events where cursing was disallowed. "Air guitar is really weird," Giant Junk told me, and, for the most part, he is right. Occasionally, it surfaces in a festival or local arts event that kind of neutralizes much of this weirdness, but the question for many air guitarists is: should air guitarists bring the weirdness to the event or accept the conservative values that the local community would prefer? Giant Junk embraces the weirdness.

When Giant Junk showed up to compete, he came onstage in a thong— in the style of Olympic swimmers. The judges—three local radio DJs—were hostile to his costume. At the beginning of the competition, he was the only person signed up, and he helped convince others to compete, so, in some ways, his weirdness served to promote the event. However, he felt nothing but animosity from the judges, and they eventually kicked him offstage for his costume. After his routine, they made snide comments about him not wearing boots and gave him low scores. As he was walking away, one judge shouted criticisms about his body. For someone with anorexia and a victim of bullying and felony assault as a kid, this kind of criticism was triggering. He felt really shaken up by it after the event. The whole affair rubbed him the wrong way and underscored the exact problems with organizing and competitiveness that undermine how fun US Air Guitar should be. In many ways, being vulnerable onstage proved to be a painful experience and reinforced the division he felt between the community and him.

54 SPECTACULAR LISTENING

Giant Junk is not alone in mixed feelings about the competition. For Giant Junk, who has familiarity with both being onstage and organizing, the pain he felt onstage was a consequence of bad organization and leadership. I witnessed a somewhat veiled exchange between people in the air guitar Facebook group after this event, where people came out in support of both Giant Junk and the organizers. Giant Junk unplugged from the Facebook group long ago. In this exchange on social media, a lot of people in the community did not seem to realize how this situation affected Giant Junk, and I did not feel like it was my place to tell them—I remained neutral in the situation. But I do think representing the story here serves to underscore the ways judges' comments have undesirable effects on competitors that could be prevented. I also think people would be more sympathetic to Giant Junk's situation, if they knew the details. But Giant Junk doesn't seem to want the onus of having to explain his perspective to everyone—he seems like he'd rather just let it go. The last time we spoke, he told me: "At this point with air guitar, it's more of an itch I want to scratch once a year."

Conclusion

Air guitar competitions can function like a roast. Roasts—in the sense of roasting a king or a celebrity—can expose someone to ridicule but in a way that shores up the person's power. It shows their tolerance for insults, reinforcing their invincibility. At the same time, a roast can allow someone to tap into an empowering vulnerability, allowing them to let go of all pretenses and embrace a side of themselves that they might be tempted to suppress. Sometimes these roasts can be validating, bringing about a heightened sense of self-acceptance, and sometimes they can take an unpredictable turn, where criticisms go too far or strike a nerve.

When they take to the stage, air guitarists masquerade as fantastical personas, while representing real dimensions of themselves to audiences. Learning to play air guitar heightens one's awareness of how others might perceive your body. When you learn to play air guitar, you must develop a sense of the air guitar as an object, considering its imagined weight, length, and contours. You learn to move with it. You learn to convincingly show others the physical dimensions of the object, so that they believe it exists.

The air guitarists whose stories comprise this chapter often spoke about their impairments in similar ways. Damaged refers to his struggles as a box in his head. Shreddy Boop talk about her anxiety as a part of her that she can reflect on objectively. Kara says, "When you're going through a situation . . . you're kind of looking [at yourself] outside of yourself." The tendency to see impairments as these imagined physical objects reflects the process of air guitar playing, which requires physically manifesting an invisible object for others to see. Perhaps we could think of many musical practices that involve translating everyday experiences into musical performances, but air guitar competitions revolve around the humorous tension between something being imaginary yet obviously present. "Air guitar is the greatest thing you've never seen," air guitarists frequently say. The comedy and poignancy of this practice come from the fact that something invisible can exert such a powerful physical force over someone.

Two years after the 2017 competition season ended, I received a formal invitation to judge the US Air Guitar Championships, alongside four others: Ben Wizner (of the ACLU and Edward Snowden's lawyer), Tony Tapatio (air guitarist who proposed to his fiancée during this particular air guitar competition), Jeanne Basone (former professional wrestler known as Hollywood), and Jay Knowles (well-known Nashville songwriter). I accepted, dropped all prior engagements, and flew down to Nashville for a weekend, which served as reunion of sorts with the folks mentioned here. I saw Cindairella and Giant Junk, the latter of whose itch to air guitar brought him back into the fold with an enthusiastic vigor. I bumped into Shreddy Boop, who told me she's actually started disclosing her air guitar career to the general public. She even publicly shared her story recently with a news outlet, using interviews to proudly align her air guitar presence with her real world one.

And I saw Kara. In the time since Kara's periodontist-inspired routine, she kept feeling recurring symptoms that she attributed to IBS, the pain from which felt most acute in moments of stress. After going to the doctor to check up on this situation, she found out that she had Stage 4 colon cancer. When she told me on the phone, she spoke with a kind of resigned sense that the end of her life would come soon, as she tried to process what that might mean for her spirituality, creatively, practically, and relationally with her partner. In the time after we spoke, she populated a blog with the many stages of her process. She described her chemotherapy and her new colostomy bag, which she named Klaus. Humor has always helped her offset the heaviness of difficult life situations.

Being confronted with death only made her cling more tightly to her air guitar dreams. She posted frequently about air guitar, conceptualizing a

56   SPECTACULAR LISTENING

routine that might be possible in her changing body. When I appeared in Nashville to judge the national competition, she showed up to compete. Many air guitarists had chipped in to help her pay to fly to Nashville, a huge task logistically for her and her partner. She barely had the energy to travel, essentially spending the entire weekend in Nashville resting up for and recovering from her brief minutes onstage. Most of her routine was conceived in her mind, since she couldn't physically practice, but she decided not to hold anything back in that moment at the *Exit/In*. When she finally competed, she performed a routine to Lizzo's "Boys," calling on the way Lizzo played air guitar in the original music video for the track. She did so well that she made it to the second round, though she placed fourth overall at the end of the night. During the end of an improvised routine in the second round to "25 or 6 to 4" by Chicago, she abandoned the air guitar altogether, instead playing the air trumpet along with the track. She spun around such that her back faced the audience, moving her hands around to the backside of her body to play what she has since called the "butt trumpet." While this spontaneous move appeared funny at the time, it enabled her to turn the site of her cancer into an instrumental part of her creative practice.

For many air guitarists, their routines onstage enable many forms of disclosure related to a wide range of identities and experiences, and this form of sharing can produce memorable moments of community for participants in these physically co-present spaces. As they develop skills and avatars for these public performances, air guitarists find ways to leverage disability as a masquerade, exaggerating aspects of the listening experience to others in strategic performances. They deploy humor, virtuosity, and stagecraft, in order to make bodily arguments about how they want to be perceived.

Air guitar competitions make listening loud. They offer an outlet for individuals who feel comfortable on a stage or want to become that way. However, they can also privilege forms of listening that are theatrical and over-the-top, at the expense of more subtle and quieter forms of listening. Not everyone can translate the felt power of music into such apparent representations onstage. In my conclusion, I consider what happens when these forms of sharing feel imperative for listeners, leading people to believe that the truest forms of fandom always manifest as elaborately orchestrated and emotional performances.

In the next chapter, I focus on the contours of entirely online subculture, which revolves around these theatrical representations of popular music. This online community enables performers to create performances quite similar to their air guitarist counterparts, as they pantomime to popular music through theatrical displays of listening. In ways that complement the personal dimensions of syncing practices in this chapter, the following chapter explores how a community can persist online, when participants lack a clearly defined geography, membership, and even sense of distinct musical events. Online networks can exacerbate a sense of vulnerability, complicating questions of sharing, belonging, and inclusion. And they can also vastly expand the reach of spectacular performances of listening.

2

Fluent Circulation

Lip Syncing from Musical.ly to TikTok to YouTube

In the region today called Silicon Valley but a hundred years before the region acquired that name, laws circulated that made disability an actionable offense in public. These "ugly laws," as they came to be known, appeared after the Civil War.[1] According to disability scholar Susan Schwiek, San Francisco may have been the first to pass these laws, which then became replicated across the country in almost identical language. This version from Chicago exemplifies this formula:

> Any person who is diseased, maimed, mutilated, or in any way deformed, so as to be an unsightly or disgusting object, or an improper person to be allowed in or on the streets, highways, thoroughfares, or public places in this city, shall not therein or thereon expose himself to public view, under the penalty of a fine of $1. (Chicago City Code 1881)

Similar laws swept the country—from Portland to Chicago to Denver to Reno to Columbus to the entire state of Pennsylvania. As each of these places sought to become a great American city, their leaders excluded those whose bodies did not match their aesthetic ideals, those whose disenfranchisement and social alienation would bear testament to their limits of inclusion. Such is the idea taken up by disabled poet Lateef McLeod in "I'm Too Pretty for Some Ugly Laws," in which he writes: "I am not suppose to be here / In this body, / here / speaking to you. / My mere presence / of erratic moving limbs / and drooling smile / used to be scrubbed / off the public pavement . . . Whatever you do, / my roots are rigid / like a hundred year old tree. I will stay right here."[2]

* * *

According to reporting based on leaked moderation-policy documents obtained by the German *Netzpolitik*, *The Intercept*, and others in 2019,

Spectacular Listening. Byrd McDaniel, Oxford University Press. © Oxford University Press 2024.
DOI: 10.1093/oso/9780197620458.003.0003

FLUENT CIRCULATION   59

TikTok actively suppressed videos of disabled people, keeping the videos of disabled users from being recommended in the "For You" feed on this digital application—henceforth "app." A key part of the way videos spread on the platform, the "For You" section feeds users an endless stream of new content, boosted by a secret algorithm that promotes new videos based on user criteria. This alleged process of suppression—carried out by human moderators instructed to label videos as "Risk 4" in order to inhibit their spread on the platform—singled out users with "facial disfigurement," "autism," "Down Syndrome," "abnormal body shape," "chubby," "obvious beer belly," "obese," "too thin," "ugly facial looks," "fangs," "lack of front teeth," "senior people with too many wrinkles," "eye disorders," and "crooked mouth disease."[3] According to this reporting, spokespeople from TikTok argued that such policies were meant to inhibit bullying on the platform by protecting these vulnerable users.

Disability often gets scrubbed from public view. Throughout United States history, disabled people have been suppressed in many ways—political disenfranchisement, media inaccessibility, an exclusionary built environment, forced institutionalization, wage exploitation, and outright eugenics. Alongside these forms of exploitation, aesthetics have been a key part of such projects, as people have worked to segregate disabled bodies from shared spaces. These policies often come with the suggestion that they benefit disabled people, since they prevent vulnerable people from harassment, but much like gender- and race-based forms of segregation, these forms of segregated "protection" never entail equitable treatment with those of privileged identity categories. Segregation simply becomes a way to treat a group as a subordinate class of people or worse.

However, despite these persistent forms of discrimination, disabled folks find one another, creating communities that challenge these systems of oppression. Let me describe one example. In the year 2017, I am sitting alone in my living room consumed by a particular app on my smartphone. *I open muscal.ly and watch.* A bald middle-aged person in a leotard runs as fast as possible in an empty gymnasium and does an elegant front flip, while "Middle of the Night" by the Vamps plays. *Swipe up.* A trans youth in a backward baseball cap takes up most of the screen, as Bastille's "Pompeii" plays in the background. The person's hands shake as they slowly come together, and their lips are steady. Caption: "I have cerebral palsy, and I refuse to be anything but proud . . . " *Swipe up.* A person in a gray t-shirt and black nail polish performs to the same clip. Their steady hands pop in crisp motions, as the person signs and lip syncs to the lyrics "and the walls kept tumbling down in the city that we love . . ." *Swipe up*. A young person with acne and faint facial hair earnestly lip syncs to "At My Best" by Machine Gun Kelly. The faint outline of a wheelchair headrest appears behind the person, and they pull the phone near and far from his face. They point to the screen and give a soft glance at the camera. These videos contain hashtags such as: #disabled, #lgbt, #ALS, #Deaf, #Bored, and #CarCrash.

This example represents a community of disabled users on the app musical.ly. The musical.ly app revolves around circulating lip-syncing videos, in which users animate popular music clips with their own bodies through gestural performances. They circulate these videos with captions and hashtags, and their videos then become part of a vast landscape of videos far beyond the physical site of their creation.

I am merely one of 215 million users on this app,[4] which existed from 2014 to 2017 until ByteDance bought and transformed the app into TikTok. During this time, I learned to navigate the app to find disability communities, just as the app learned my own preferences to curate content for me. I began to feel like part of a community, but the word "community" feels not quite apt, since the app did not clearly delimit this community into a formal group. Within many digital cultures and apps in particular, defining a community can be particularly difficult. Communities can often be porous, ill defined, and constantly in flux. But I at least came to feel a sense of belonging, connected to a particular subculture on the app.

Many online subcultures have porous boundaries with constant interactions from new and old users. These subcultures travel across platforms, and participants remix old media to form new media. These communities may consist of people who may know very little about the offline realities of one another's lives, and at the same time, the participants may know a lot about one particular dimension of one another's lives, particularly in subcultures that revolve around a hobby or identity.

I offer the concept of *fluent circulation* in order to describe how community members come to recognize one another in these fluid and diverse online spaces. Fluent circulation may be defined as culturally coded forms of transmission that signal competency in a particular community, providing a means by which people can sustain connections with one another.

The term "fluent" helps describe a shared language within a community. Fluency refers not only to language, in the sense of words and hashtags, but

I use the term to refer to technical knowledge, gestural vocabularies, and a style for circulating media. Fluency is a subconscious demonstration of a kind of technical and bodily knowledge.

I emphasize "circulation" as a method that people use to express this fluency. In more conventional musical performances, we might describe a guitarist as playing with a particular genre, aesthetic, or style. I am suggesting that people circulate media with a particular style in lip-syncing performances. People make use of multiple platforms, languages, technical proficiencies, musical idioms, hashtags, memes, gestures, and editing techniques—all in a way to circulate media in a style that signals their belonging to a particular community. They create a shared sensibility around sharing media.

In this chapter, I articulate the struggles and triumphs of this small disability community on musical.ly, placing it within the backdrop of a broader media landscape that often suppresses and individualizes disability. I theorize fluent circulation in order to show how these users create and maintain this community. The musical.ly app was hardly a utopia, but the struggle for solidarity within the app exemplifies strategies that online disabled communities have undertaken to challenge erasure, posing important lessons for future struggles in digital cultures. My attention to controversial issues, as well as forms of connection across physical divides, traces the contours of this in-app community, in ways that show a creative defiance that often pushes against the idea that disability should be individual and invisible.

Methods

Ethnomusicology has only begun to take digital cultures seriously, so analysis of a particularly niche area within digital cultures—a musical app—required a creative assemblage of methods. I sought to understand musical.ly on three fronts. First on a theoretical level, I researched the history of lip syncing, as well as cultural norms of listening that render lip syncing so taboo or embarrassing. Through historical work on karaoke and other forms of embodied performance with pre-recorded media, I came to understand a vast history of practices that informed the development of musical.ly, as well as the many subsequent ones influenced by musical.ly after its end. I realized the importance of documenting musical.ly, since musical apps rarely receive the same levels of scholarly attention as bigger streaming and participatory platforms

62   SPECTACULAR LISTENING

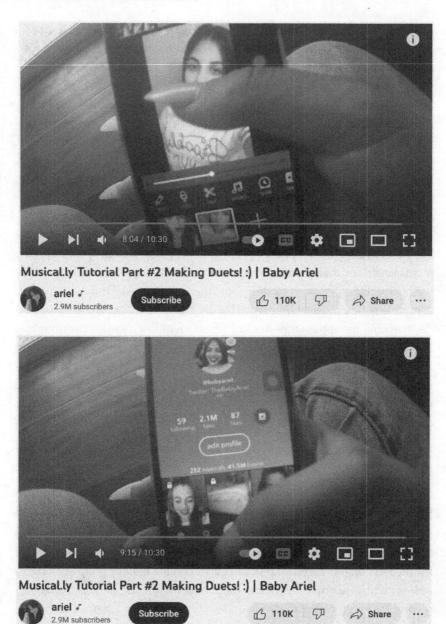

Figure 2.1   Ariel Rebecca Martin. "Musical.ly Tutorial Part #2 Making Duets!:) | Baby Ariel." Screenshot by the author on July 17, 2022.

A screenshot appears from a YouTube tutorial, in which a famous performer named Baby Ariel demonstrates how to navigate the app to create duets. Her thumb hovers over a cell phone, as she edits her video. In the screenshots to the right, she presents two alternative views of this process, which involve filming a video and curating a channel.

FLUENT CIRCULATION   63

Figure 2.1 Continued

(though TikTok has dramatically changed that). The app's users skew younger with more women and significant numbers of LGBTQ+ members, which also likely explains a dearth of research on the platform. The fact that the app was bought and sold during my research made me feel like this work should be especially pressing, since recollections from musical.ly users will soon fade as time goes on.

Second, I sought to understand musical.ly through participant-observation on the platform. I dedicated a specific period of time to observations. During the winter of 2017, I spent an hour per day (five days per week) for four weeks formally observing performances and interactions on musical.ly, while taking fieldnotes on my observations. This fieldwork involved scanning through videos on various feeds, directed searches for types of videos, and detailed dissections of a single video. But I also learned just as much through more casual use of the app outside of this formal period of observation, while waiting in line somewhere, riding in the car, or spending time in my apartment. I would follow trends, support performers whose videos I admired, and talk about the app with friends. I also sought out experts in various fields when a controversial topic arose on musical.ly, and I feature these people in particular in what follows.

64 SPECTACULAR LISTENING

Third, I learned about musical.ly as a performer. I created my own lip-syncing videos, following the numerous tutorials I watched on YouTube. I learned to significantly improve my lip-syncing abilities, while honing skills in some of the technical aspects of musical.ly transitions (as they're called using emic terminology). I also participated in lip-syncing events outside of the app, in order to understand how to contextualize the specific affordances of musical.ly.[5] For example, I judged an in-person lip-syncing competition with Brown University's president Christina Paxson, performance-studies scholar VK Preston, and professor emeritus of engineering Barrett Hazeltine. This experience helped me reflect on lip syncing on an app, as compared to lip syncing in a live in-person context.

Defining musical.ly

This chapter situates musical.ly within a broader context—what José van Dijck calls an "ecosystem of connective media."[6] While I center musical.ly, I consider both YouTube and TikTok as important elements within this ecosystem over time. On musical.ly, users could like and share videos. Feeling these options to be somewhat limited, many users would frequently record, download, and combine videos in large compilations, which they would then upload to YouTube as a sort of archive. YouTube also provided a critical site for tutorials, where users trade knowledge about how to use the app. So YouTube proves to be an essential component of my research on musical.ly, as well as the work in the next chapter on reaction videos.

TikTok looms in the history of musical.ly, given the way TikTok transformed many of its affordances into an even-more-popular and widespread platform. With over 500 million users, TikTok has become more than five times the size of musical.ly in 2016, catalyzing all kinds of new disability subcultures as well as widespread controversies about disability censorship. As this newly ascendent digital platform takes center stage, musical.ly offers an important case study, as a precursor to our current digital domains. And musical.ly's demise ultimately raises questions about the longevity of these performance genres and the political implications of these forms of content over time.

The history of musical.ly itself began in 2014, when Alex Zhu and Luyu Yang created the app in Shanghai. The two were trying to create an educational social-media app, but the app did not succeed in the ways they had hoped. So they used remaining funds to create a lip-syncing app, which allowed users to create short fifteen- to twenty-second videos to accompany popular sound clips. The app launched in August 2014. On the app, users could combine multiple shots, use filters and effects, change the speed of the recordings, and "re-muse" (or reuse) sounds by other users. Users called one another "musers." Users could upload unofficial found clips for people to use, but musical.ly also supplied official sounds, through multiple partnerships that include 7digital and Apple Music. The platform hosted specific lip-sync challenges, such as #EverythingsADissTrack (parody a diss track) or #LiteralSongLyrics (post a funny literal interpretation of metaphorical lyrics). Musicians would frequently promote songs on musical.ly, and many amateur musical.ly performers accrued enough popularity to parlay musical.ly power into musical careers.

By the end of 2017, the app fully transformed to host a range of content—sports, gaming, visual arts, makeup tutorials, DIY, and so on—in ways that capitalized on the downfall of Vine (another video-hosting app). On musical.ly, people could like other musical.lys (represented through "heart" icons). They could follow a user, as well as comment on a video. They could populate a profile with links to a YouTube channel, as well as complete their bio with a thumbnail and description. Users could block one another, as well as cultivate a "Best Fan Forever" list of companions on the app. In-app purchases enabled people to buy gifts for one another. They could navigate to various in-app spaces, finding videos based on song, popular trends, or a leaderboard with particular challenges, and people could also choose to scroll through one of two curated feeds called "Following" (people one follows) and "Featured" (people featured on the app). In distinction to my other case studies in this book, the musical.ly performers tended to be young, especially in the initial stages of the app, and I imagine younger born-digital users tend to be early adopters of new platforms. Over time, more adults began to join the app, and I focus on adult users in the content that follows. On musical.ly in 2017, an estimated 70 percent of users were women, and 49 percent of users participate on the app in the United States.[7]

Lip syncing on musical.ly may seem sui generis, but lip syncing emerges from a much more expansive history, in which people sought creative ways to use technologies to sync the body with pre-recorded media.[8] I elaborate on this phenomenon in my conclusion, in what I call "syncing out loud." Within a more recent and specific historical framework, lip syncing emerged

66 SPECTACULAR LISTENING

as a particularly prominent cultural practice online, made possible by the affordances of video-sharing sites.

In the early 2000s, popular memes and viral videos often featured lip syncing as a prominent trope. In one particularly notable example in 2004, Gary Brolsma uploaded a video of him moving his mouth to the words of "Dragostea din tei" by O-Zone (a pop group from Moldova) to a flash-animation site called Newgrounds. The low-quality video features Brolsma sitting at a desk in front of a computer, throwing his arms in the air, and making goofy faces as each line of the song plays in the background. In 2006, someone uploaded a mirror of this video to YouTube and titled it "Numa Numa." The video went viral, and Brolsma became an overnight celebrity. People now celebrate the video's anniversary every year. In the years that followed, people began posting amateur music videos featuring large groups lip syncing in public and office spaces. For example, in 2006, Jakob Lodwick, founder of Vimeo (a YouTube rival), directed "Dubbing: Endless Dream" followed by another video "Lip Dub: Flagpole Sitta by Harvey Danger."

The most famous lip-syncing video of the current century comes from a disabled performer named Keenan Cahill. In the late aughts, Cahill posted a series of lip-syncing videos, including "Teenage Dream" by Katy Perry. In the video, he delivers a passionate singalong with the Katy Perry track, complete with dramatic facial expressions, dancing, and an overly-sentimental-yet-purposeful passion. On September 2, 2010, Katy Perry discovered Cahill's video and tweeted at him: "I heart you." Soon thereafter, the video skyrocketed in popularity, receiving 3 million views within a week. Cahill ended up collaborating with Pauly D, 50 Cent, LMFAO, and David Guetta, appearing on commercials for Smart Water and the Chelsea Lately show.

The fame that brought Cahill into the spotlight also tended to dwell on his Mucopolysaccharidosis condition, and many news stories sought to paint Cahill in a patronizingly inspirational light. An alternative narrative would be to place Cahill as an artistic innovator within the history of lip syncing, as well as someone engaged in a disability masquerade in the style I theorize in Chapter 1. Given the ways disabled folks must often manipulate the affordances of various technologies to accommodate different bodily needs, the rise of a disabled star in the history of lip syncing is perhaps not all that surprising.

Ultimately, musical.ly took some of the diffuse and random forms of lip syncing in digital cultures and organized them in an app. The app made lip syncing easier, visually stimulating, and formally organized around

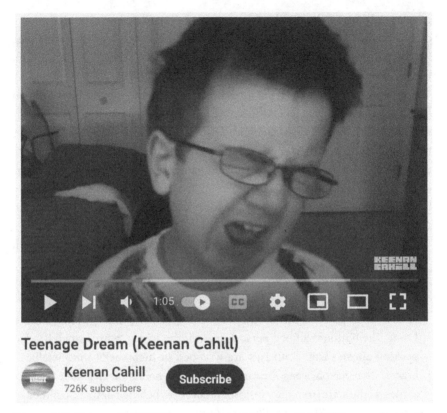

Figure 2.2 Keenan Cahill. "Teenage Dream (Keenan Cahill)." Screenshot by the author on July 17, 2022.

In this YouTube screenshot, Keenan Cahill sings "Teenage Dream" by Katy Perry, in one of the first major viral videos on YouTube. He appears with glasses and an open mouth, as he belts out the tune in his bedroom. In the video to the right, Cahill looks directly at the camera and delivers the lyrics with gusto.

particular trends. As a result, many users flocked to musical.ly in order to delight in the possibilities of creating these mini-music videos to circulate on and beyond the app.

Defining the Disability Community on musical.ly

In contrast to some digital and physical music scenes where membership may be formally organized, the app does not enable people to gather in such a formal way. I sought ways to trace the boundaries of communities of disabled

68 SPECTACULAR LISTENING

users, but I ultimately felt like the community could be constituted in many different ways. In other words, users can use the app in ways that create particular parameters, which create in-groups and out-groups. In this section, I offer a few ways that community forms on the app.

Disabled users on musical.ly form communities through follows and fan lists, as well as likes that teach the algorithm to favor a particular type of content for a user, but perhaps the most obvious way to form community comes from hashtagging, which enables users to organize content around a particular theme. Hashtags enable users to expand the reach of their videos, by linking their content to other content with a similar label. The #disability hashtag is the most widely used disability-related hashtag (as opposed to #crip, for example).

In one instance, I searched for the #disability hashtag. Confronted with approximately 1,000 video results, I documented what I saw as I swiped through a series of videos:

"I can't change," spits out of my phone speakers—the hook from "Same Love." The bottom half of a person's legs fill the screen, with a small head peeking above them. Both legs are wrapped in high socks and metallic braces. The person leans forward, putting her hands on her knees, and smiles, as the glare from the sun obscures her eyes behind her thick-rimmed glasses. *Swipe up.* "Don't act like you forgot. I call the shots shot shots. Like blah blah blah." A blue-haired white woman rests on the floor, simulating a talking mouth with her right hand just as Rihanna says "bitch, better have my money." She crinkles her eyebrows and twists her head, as her eyes dart around inside a pink hoodie that obscures her whole lower body. *Swipe up.* A young Latina girl with a New York accent talks about how disabling her Twitter account "killed [her] vibe." *Swipe up.* An empty wheelchair appears in the frame, in a black-and-white filter. "First rule, never let them change you. Rule two, do you to fullest. And never be ashamed too." The screen flashes to show a white girl lying on her side, and I can only see one arm and her torso. She raps along with Lupe Fiasco, nailing the lines and flexing her arm. When the lyrics say, "You just good at what they can't do," the screen flashes to an empty wheelchair.

Disability-related content on the app does not always carry the hashtag of disability, so these examples represent videos in which users wanted to explicitly acknowledge disability as a subject of their performances.

FLUENT CIRCULATION   69

These posts accumulate into an archive of disability performances, enabling other disabled folks to find this type of content through searching for the hashtag. Of course, these videos often occasion inspiration-driven comments that traffic in ableist tropes, but these tags can also call upon other disabled users, who would often react to these ableist comments through a wave of supportive replies. So the hashtag both makes one visible to stigma, while also calling upon allies to participate in a chain of circulation.

As this example may reveal, disability communities on the app often intersect with other marginalized identities. As of December 2017, nearly 80,000 videos were tagged with #queer. The hashtag #queer would often couple with a range of other hashtags, such as #lgbt or #nonbinary, as well as emojis such as a rainbow or unicorn. The vast array of #queer-labeled videos often encompassed much more than sexuality and gender, and they often referred to a wide range of differences from some of the normative heterosexual, cisgender, non-disabled user-generated content.

Scholars of disability have forged similar connections between queerness and disability, leading them to theorize "neuroqueerness" as a way of acknowledging how neurodivergence intersects with gender, sexuality, and queerness more generally.[9] Many disabled users would use either #disabled or #queer to register non-normative affect on the app. In the words of José Muñoz, "minoritarian affect is always, no matter what its register, partly illegible in relations to the normative affect performed by normative citizen subjects."[10] Indeed, many videos seemed to aim for ambiguity as a kind of commentary on the more normative affects or straightforward hashtags elsewhere, and the hashtag of #queer often accompanied these kinds of videos.

Hashtags can also invite other complicated overlaps, through accidents that aggregate content in mutually reinforcing ways. The hashtag #depression offers a telling case. Let me give two videos as examples, along with my reactions as I reflected on these videos.

> *Video One*: The chorus of "When a Man Loves a Woman" comes through, as I see a white middle-aged man with backward cap and a gold chain lip syncing passionately to Percy Sledge. He holds back a smile. Hashtags: #Depression #PTSDAnxiety #FeatureMe #Disabled #MyLife #AlwaysBeYourself.
>
> *My Reaction*: The man must watch tutorials, following the belief circulated in many of them that #FeatureMe hashtag will make one featured on the app. But his lack of transitions (special effects) makes me think he

70　SPECTACULAR LISTENING

won't be featured. His quite specific disclosure of #PTSDAnxiety makes clear he means #depression in a clinical sense (rather than metaphorical) sense. And his lip syncing to this Percy Sledge clip makes me think he doesn't use the app often, since it's not a trending song.

Video Two: The lower half of a face appears in a mound of blankets in a dark bedroom. In the black-and-white video, I can faintly see lips moving to the lines: "You hate me. Don't you? It's ok. Don't worry, because I hate me too." Hashtags: #depression #depressed #sad. The person's shoulders shake, as if crying, and sounds of sobbing spurt from the recording.

My Reaction: This recording is also a popular meme among angsty folks on this app, featuring an unknown child-like voice uttering those lines over "Sad Song" by We the Kings. The line between #depression as mood and #depression as diagnosis is blurry here, particularly given the use of #sad. Either way, the presence of so many obscuring elements—darkness, blankets—makes me think of this person as feeling vulnerable. The person's crying is likely fake, because of the way it perfectly syncs with the pre-recorded audio. But maybe it's manufactured crying that manifests some true desire for compassion?

I offer these reactions not to criticize or evaluate these performers but rather to demonstrate how the use of the app constantly involves ambiguity about context, given the endless scroll of videos.

These videos—two of the many archived with the #depression hashtag—bring up a few contentious issues within the disability community. First, many instances of the #depression hashtag reveal how people frequently reference disability through figurative language, often in ways that completely disregard those with clinical diagnoses or actual disabilities. The common use of disability terminology to describe art, for example, as "schizophrenic," "bipolar," "lame," or "crazy" perfectly encapsulates the ableist dimensions of this trend, which leverage disability stigma to give a rhetorical flourish to descriptions of aesthetics.

Second and alternatively, these hashtags can also allow people to name something that they feel, which could very well accumulate into a medical diagnosis. Many disabled people reject medical diagnoses as a need to legitimize a person's bodily experience. Without knowing these two performers or their relationship to each other, I could at least imagine that someone who first feels symptoms of depression might explore the hashtag, finding videos of people (like the man in the first video) who claims the term with a more clinical sense. Sometimes a mood can indeed be something that approaches a more long-term psychological condition.

And, finally, these hashtags can also categorize musical clips according to a mood evoked by the music (rather than genre, which rarely functions as a hashtag). So a hashtag can provide an archive of a wide range of disability-associated themes—both ableist and affirmatively disablist. And it is because these archives are so open-ended that they facilitate both connections among folks with different orientations to disability, as well as interlopers who might partake in the language of disability but ultimately be at odds with disability communities.

The reasons that disabled users on musical.ly might disclose or conceal disability can perhaps be made evident by musical.ly's biggest disabled star, Kaylee Halko. Trained in dance styles ranging from jazz, lyrical, and hip hop, Halko became a star on musical.ly, accumulating three million followers with a dozen fan pages.[11] As a child with progeria, Halko appeared on ABC's "20/20" at the age of eight. Her father spoke to a local news station about the social stigma she faced, resulting in bullying and death threats, causing her to transfer schools. However, she found a following on musical.ly, leading to some profiles in online publications as a rising star. Many of the fans commenting on her videos on musical.ly seemed to offer genuine appreciation of her dances and humor on the app, and these fans would often operate with a mob-like intensity to shut down anyone harassing her. And yet her visibility on the app also resulted in news coverage that tended to fixate on her rare condition, describing her physical body in medical-curiosity-like language and even speculating about her likely death at a young age. In ways that echo the coverage of Keenan Cahill a decade earlier, the coverage of Halko tended to reproduce harmful ableist tropes for a non-musical.ly audience. Popularity on the app can be hard to control, inviting both wanted and unwanted attention.

Disabled communities on the app—networks of followers who frequently consume one anothers' content—also craft a sense of community in more covert ways, primarily through performing with a particular set of conventions that avoid disability labels. For example, disabled users on the app would frequently substitute their own bodies for avatar alternatives. I could not find an instance of people explicitly acknowledging this aesthetic choice, but

72 SPECTACULAR LISTENING

many disabled performers who I followed would substitute their bodies for their pets or bitmoji-style avatars.[12] Sometimes jokes accompanied these decisions. Other times they operated as a kind of performance art. For example, I followed a user named Alberto, a published author and online provocateur. A man with cerebral palsy and scoliosis since childhood, he communicates with an augmentative alternative communication device, and he frequently featured videos of himself lip syncing on the app, albeit not moving his lips in these videos in order to simulate how he actual speaks (with an AAC device). But just as often he would make comedic videos with an animated avatar that he called his "mini me," who would serve as a kind of stunt-double in his videos.

A willingness to tweak the affordances of the app—to use them in ways that they're not initially intended—can seem to some as going against the ethos of the app, but disabled folks often must contend with technologies built for non-disabled bodies. These adaptations are creative reinterpretations of these affordances, born out of exclusions in their design. For example, three disabled users appeared in my circles on musical.ly: an Arab American man named with Duchenne muscular dystrophy, a white man with Autism, and Black man with a tumor that covers his right eye. The three decided to share an account on the app, under the username @inspirationaldudes. While I initially almost swiped past their posts as a result of the "inspirational" framing that signaled problematic yet prevalent disability content, I came to understand the username as ironic. These three collaborators would leverage humor, technical effects, and various animations, sharing an account in what might be considered a form of rotational programming. For example, in one video the Arab American man appears lip syncing to a song from *asdfmovie* (a flash-animation comedy series). As his wheelchair scoots forward in a few short bursts, we see a picturesque background of blue skies and green grass, with him gleefully singing: "It's a lovely day to walk down the road, and, if I ever stop singing, I will explode." The screen cuts to someone who shouts at him, and he stops to see where the sound came from. Suddenly, a look of shock takes over his face, as he realizes that he has indeed stopped singing. He suddenly explodes, eviscerating his entire body in a flash of imaginary fire (in ways that echo Shreddy in Chapter 1). The video ends with a plume of smoke. Through this kind of slapstick humor and other more serious videos, these three collaborate to produce multiple videos each day, achieving a level of consistency that would be hard for a single performer to do all alone. They turned their feed into a TV channel of sorts. They even reached out to other disabled folks on the platform in what they called #FeatureFridays, in order to craft a disabled channel through using a single account. In January of 2018, @inspirationaldudes had over 13.5 thousand fans.

While researching musical.ly and discovering these creative transformations of its affordances, I frequently wondered what an accessible musical.ly might look like, where built-in features could enable even greater participation without placing the burden of inventive adaptations on individual users. A more accessible app might include auto-captioning, visual or sign-language representations of sounds, alt text, and video-recording functionality for those without normative hands. I thought of how audio description could enhance the app for some users.

And yet I also saw users thrive on this strange musical app, in ways that provided evidence for its inclusivity of people marginalized in more conventional musical practices. In their theorization of "dismediation," Jonathan Sterne and Mara Mills describe impairment as a given in all media technologies, and these impairments "scale to disabilities unevenly within particular media systems."[13] As all of my case studies in *Spectacular Listening* reveal, different performers find accessibility in different places, but the presence of some forms of inclusion should not preclude the work toward design that can be even more inclusive.[14] Sterne and Mills argue that all design is imperfect, requiring constant improvement that works toward greater inclusion.

The work of these users on the app reveals how disabled folks often catalyze these changes. When I consider contemporary music media apps today, I think of TikTok accounts that largely function as large media channels centered around particular identities, and I think of the earlier work of @inspirationaldudes. I also think of the rise of virtual influencers and the prevalence of AI-generated voices on TikTok and Instagram, and I think of the folks on musical.ly who experimented with similar aesthetics. Of course, musical.ly is not the single origin of these practices, and cultural change mostly occurs through mass movements rather than individual creatives. But the presence of disability among innovators has often been erased in media histories, whether in the history of captioning, text messaging, or electronics.[15] So acknowledging these artistic precedents serves to emphasize that impairments often provide the impetus for improving technology toward greater accessibility, a charge led by disabled folks in ways that benefit everyone.

Musicking on musical.ly

When scrolling through the app, lip-syncing performances may seem seamless, featuring a fluid synchronization of sounds and bodies, but shooting a musical.ly video requires a lot of skill. Let me take you through one of my performances.

I open the app and select the "Pick Music" tab. I find Kesha's "Learn to Let Go." I know the song well, but I start to memorize the specific eleven-second clip, playing it over and over again as I train my lips to exaggerate the words. As I prepare to record my video, I hit the little magic-wand icon, which filters out blemishes on my skin. I survey my apartment, looking for an uncluttered backdrop with good lighting. I settle on an area next to a window. I select "Fast" in the time filters (following the style guidelines of famous musical.ly star Baby Ariel's YouTube tutorials). This enables me to record my video in slow motion and then speed the final video back up to regular speed, making it much easier to record. I hit the record button once, just to hear the song. I hear Kesha sing at two-thirds of the original tempo. I move my lips in slow motion to the track—a dry run. As I'm holding the button, I move my phone to various angles with respect to my face, in order to punctuate Kesha's words—"LIVE and LEARN and NEV-er FOR-get IT." I use one hand to manipulate my phone angles, while my other hand interacts with the camera through dramatic gestures. Through watching tutorials, I learned that you should always move your hands and the phone in concert, in order to enhance the dramatic appearance of the gestures. When Kesha sings "forget it," I move the phone close to my face and point to my head, indicating "forget." I shake the phone, as if the intensity of my words has somehow made the camera quiver. When Kesha screams "Woooooah," I move the phone in a big arc around my body, as I keep my eyes locked on my phone camera. Then I pull the phone back in, and, as I hear "learn to let it go" in slow motion, I pretend to slap my phone such that it flies through the air.

Each of these moves involves a lot of trial and error—record, view, delete, repeat. Once I have the whole sequence in my head, I practice doing it all in one take. I perform this routine twenty to thirty times, each bad take marred by extremely small issues—a missed word, I drag/rush in my lip-syncing speed, a bad camera angle, bad lighting, the camera capturing something I don't want in the background, and so on. When I finally have a recording

I'm pleased with, I watch the video, and I see that, in real time, it looks like I'm magically dancing and singing into my phone with fluid motions and precise synchronization. I apply some subtle visual filters that change the saturation and contrast on the video. Then I post the video.

Similar to millions of other musical.ly users, I learned this process primarily through tutorials on YouTube, which explain the various techniques required to craft these videos, and one of the most prolific instructors is a woman named Eliza. In order to craft tutorials online, she told me that she first became an astute observer on the app, recognizing various trends and dissecting the physical techniques required to perform them on her own. While TikTok dances may come to mind, these musical.ly tricks—sometimes called transitions—were much more elaborate than a dance in front of a still camera, involving props, camera movements during performances, and optical illusions. For example, in the middle of 2017, people would perform while holding their phone, and in the middle of the performance, they would let go of their phone, which would then just hover in mid-air. I discovered that people were accomplishing this effect via a combination of dental floss (invisible on the screen), a physical technique using spoons and phone cases, and digital editing. Eliza learned how to do these tricks on her own, mirroring the embodied knowledge she observed in others.

She also learned how to teach these techniques, crafting a YouTube channel with various tutorials. These tutorials would often feature a picture-in-picture depiction of the techniques, as she would walk users through the act of filming a particular effect. She would also give the technique a name, atomizing complex embodied repertoire into specific items for instruction (as a dancer might break down a dance into steps).

When I spoke with her, I asked her about her history performing, assuming she must have a good deal of experience with music, and she described her musical background in this way:

> Not at all. Not one tiny bit. I was painfully shy as a kid. Yeah. Not the best with people. I had Tourette's Syndrome, which caused a lot of bullying as a kid. Kids are mean in general, and when you have Tourette's, it's a disaster. I was viciously bullied throughout school. I had very very few friends, and I experienced bullying all the way up through college honestly. So no I was not outgoing.

She explained that these feelings coupled with a lack of musical skill.

> I have shown no musical talent. I've taken piano, clarinet, cello, a bunch of instruments and never shown any talent in any of them. But I do have good rhythm, which is very important. I think to be good at musical.ly you have to be predisposed to have really good timing. That's one of the most important things.

So her desire to participate in musical.ly, as well as to formally disseminate knowledge to help others participate, comes from both an awareness of disability stigma, as well as a desire to express a latent musical desire that might not have found an outlet in more conventional musical practices. She even went on to speak of muscal.ly as connected to a complete change in her career—from pursuing a science-oriented career path to embracing a career in film and media.

Figure 2.3 Eliza Caws "GLITCHY MUSICAL.LY TUTORIAL // Tips and tricks [Eliza Caws]." Screenshot by the author on July 17, 2022.

Eliza appears with a black shirt in a bedroom, as she films a tutorial for musical.ly. One hand holds a phone that is directed toward her body, and the other hand appears open with her fingers stretched out, in order to create a gestural effect in the recording. She demonstrates how to move the phone relative to her hands to create a sense of motion.

The success of musical.ly largely depends on the labor of folks like Eliza, who help generate participation on the app through these tutorials. Here's an example of the language of one tutorial. In a video called "MUSICAL.LY TRANSITION TUTORIAL//NO EDITING REQUIRED!," she describes a set of moves:

> The first transition we're going to do, I'm going to call this one the "cartwheel," because it looks like the phone is rotating this way. The way that you do this one is: you have the phone straight ahead of you. All you're going to do is rotate it all the way upside down and let go of the record button. Then you reset the phone. You bring it as far as you can. I know your arm doesn't really bend that way. But you go as far as you can. Press the record button when you're ready. And then bring it back up to center.

She proceeds to demonstrate a series of gestures that correspond with musical shifts, helping users cultivate the embodied knowledge and technical skills required to produce content on the app.

These musical.ly tutorials can attract millions of viewers, and each of these teachers has cultivated their own followers on the app and on YouTube. Their instructions are not simply teaching some official set of moves on the app, but rather each presents a kind of conscious translation of embodied knowledge for their viewers.[16]

In her work on musical.ly, Jill Rettberg describes how visual social media increasingly makes use of gestural languages to communicate, using the body to represent imagery in the lyrics, and she locates the app within a broader history of pictograms in online communication.[17] These gestural languages emerge through iterative reproductions, where people perform over and over to the same song in order to develop conventions.

The work of Eliza and others demonstrates how people play a key role in the development of these languages, serving as important influencers within this economy of gestures. Indeed, as I developed proficiency on the app, I learned to make my moves more crisp and visually expressive. These techniques did not simply require a conscious understanding of the app's affordances, but I also had to learn a set of gestures from watching others that eventually became intuitive. I came to understand how to combine these gestures with trending songs and the appropriate affect, in order to participate in a fluent circulation of these videos on the platform.

78 SPECTACULAR LISTENING

ASL In-Groups

As a result of the emphasis on gesture as a way of enhancing videos, sign language became a site of much conflict on musical.ly. Many hearing people readily made use of sign language on the app, enhancing their videos with an additional linguistic element, but these performances often reproduced a caricatured misrepresentation of actual American Sign Language and other sign languages, which has an enduring and harmful legacy.

d/Deaf performers have robust musical traditions. The term "d/Deaf" encompasses a wide range people, some of whom belong to the d/Deaf ASL-fluent community and others who may be hard of hearing and use hearing aids or cochlear implants. Artists with a wide range of hearing and listening abilities have created musical practices despite significant forms of discrimination throughout history. Including a denial of many human rights (related to property, children, driving, and employment), d/Deaf people have been victims of audism, a form of ableism that refers specifically to the privileging of normative hearing.[18] This prejudice manifested in suppressing d/Deaf language in the late nineteenth century, through forced instruction in lip reading called oralism. Oralism aimed to assimilate d/Deaf people into hearing cultures, yet the effect was to suppress rich cultural practices that d/Deaf folks already had in place. And yet despite an attempt to suppress d/Deaf culture in the midst of a hearing-centered society, d/Deaf innovators produced many musical traditions, ranging from d/Deaf poetry to percussion signing to d/Deaf hip hop to d/Deaf musical theatre.[19] d/Deaf musicians have made many contributions to hearing-centric music circles as well. So musical.ly manifests both an embrace of possibilities for gestural engagement with popular music that might sit outside of the category of dance, while also forcing a lot of d/Deaf users to witness hearing people misrepresenting their language in ways that call to mind the very forms of epistemic violence they have long faced.

Amy Cohen Efron, who identifies as a teacher and d/Deaf activist, caught my attention during my research, as a result of blog posts criticizing the tendency for hearing people to profit from ASL-inspired lip-syncing videos. Amy was born d/Deaf in a hearing family, and she attended Gallaudet University, where she obtained three degrees and found a footing in activism. As a member of the 1988 d/Deaf President Now Movement at Gallaudet University, Amy helped fight to shift Gallaudet's leadership to employ d/Deaf leaders, rather than have oversight of d/Deaf education by hearing folks, and she saw the ways that social media changed d/Deaf activism in the years that followed. After the suppression of sign language (leading to many underground language communities), d/Deaf schools re-introduced sign language in the 1960s and 1970s, and in the 1980s, a few companies released VHS tapes, which helped both hearing and d/Deaf people learn ASL. She told me: "These videotapes were not always accessible to the community because its costs were too high. Usually a one-hour VHS tape costs over 50 dollars, and no one is able to afford that. Until YouTube comes along."

YouTube had a profound impact on the d/Deaf community, and it spawned many similar video-hosting sites specifically geared toward d/Deaf people, including d/Deaf-oriented sites like DeafVideo.TV and other newly video-enabled social-media sites like Facebook, Snapchat, and Instagram. However, the popularity of signing on these video sites also brought about instances in which hearing folks sought to capitalize on their fluency in sign language. Efron explained this process:

> YouTube becomes monetized and that was when sign language interpreters or sign language students decided to create "cool" videos in ASL to translate songs. They never asked the Deaf community or a Deaf person who uses ASL for feedback. They just simply take the money and run. You can clearly see the numbers of views of hearing people using sign language, compared to Deaf people sharing their art. That is cultural appropriation, especially if there is no collaboration between sign language students who are hearing with the Deaf community . . . Yes, it is a hearing privilege to be able to hear the music, and use English as a dominant language, and "adding" signs for the "visual"/"movement" impact . . . it downgrades our cherished language that has been suppressed for a very long time.

Such a perspective reveals how increased visibility on these platforms has brought about increased appropriation of the language.

Examples abound of these kinds of cultural appropriation. In 2014, a controversy erupted around a video uploaded by a woman and a man. They posted a video on YouTube that featured them lip syncing to "You're the One I Want" from Grease. The woman, a hearing ASL interpreter, taught her fiancé how to do some signs, and the two posted a video featuring them syncing their lips and bodies to the music. After their video went viral, the

80   SPECTACULAR LISTENING

two appeared on TV, and Los Angeles councilwoman Nury Martinez gave them an award for promoting ASL awareness. The popularity of the video stirred a backlash among ASL speakers, which was further exacerbated by the media attention the two received. The two even launched a Kickstarter campaign to make more of these videos and continued to profit from them. This controversy was hardly an outlier. In another example, a young hearing girl received criticism from the d/Deaf community for posting "Dirty Signs with Kristin," a video that featured her signing curse words in sign language. She accrued thousands of subscribers on YouTube, sold a book on Amazon (*Super Smutty Sign Language*), merchandised her brand, and appeared on Comedy Central.

In ways consistent with these high-profile examples, these forms of culturally appropriated signing on musical.ly appeared especially prevalent. Users not only crafted ASL signing videos, but they or others would assemble compilations of these videos, in order to upload them to YouTube to profit off of this content. Such videos often appeared as gestures of inclusion, but hearing folks reaped the profits. In one exemplary video, I see a white guy with a University of Alabama t-shirt, who lip syncs and signs in American Sign Language to Justin Bieber's "Stuck in the Moment"—a throwback. His lips and hands move together, each syncing a different language to the music. I wonder: Is this guy a hearing person? *I swipe left to profile.* I read: "Not deaf just love ASL."

And yet musical.ly also offered an opportunity for some incredible d/Deaf art that challenged these highly visible ableist alternatives on YouTube. Shaheem Sanchez, a professional dancer who is d/Deaf and whose brother won *So You Think You Can Dance*, posted videos under @ASL_Incorporated. His profile read: "Bridging the gap between the hearing & deaf community." His videos blended breakdancing with ASL, fluidly blending the two in elaborate interpretations of contemporary songs. In distinction to some dancers on the app who made use of the special effects to simulate slow-motion dancing or generate popping-and-locking movements, Shaheem demonstrates his ability to do these techniques without special effects. In interviews, Shaheem described using a Subpac to feel the beat (a device that looks like a backpack and makes an audible beat into a physical vibration), and he also posted videos on Instagram and YouTube. His videos speak multiple discourses at once—they succeed as lip-syncing videos for hearing viewers/listeners and use sign language to embed meanings into these performances that only ASL-fluent speakers could appreciate. As a form of

Figure 2.4 Shaheem Sanchez. "Pills & Automobiles—Chris Brown (in Sign Language)." Screenshot by the author on July 17, 2022.

Shaheem performs "Pills & Automobiles" on YouTube, documenting his dance performances across platforms that incorporate ASL with hip hop. He appears in a striped shirt with his two hands blurry in motion. He lip syncs along with some of the words.

signifyin', Shaheem's videos draw on a range of signs that cite and incite in varying ways for different audiences.[20]

Thus the play with languages—from lip syncing to ASL—can invite multiculturalism and cultural appropriation, and ultimately these videos complicate the idea of a single musical voice. In her work titled *Multivocality*, Katherine Meizel explores how musical performers use multiple voices, offering a case study on d/Deaf singers in a way that yields "an inclusive view of *musical voice* that encompasses multiple embodied modes of meaning-making."[21] Meizel pushes against the idea of "a singular, static vocality for every individual," instead suggesting a much more encompassing idea of voice that includes bodies, sounds, and identity. Building on the work of music-cognition scholar David Huron, she considers celebrity impersonation as a "special kind of kinesthetic listening" that enables someone to engage with another's body through performance, and this "kinesthetic listening" could certainly describe lip syncing as well.

Meizel's concept of multiple voices informs my theorization of fluent circulation, which includes the voice and expands to add additional vocabularies. Fluent circulation encompasses multivocal musical performances and brings these into dialogue with the many quasi-musical and extra-musical techniques (e.g., editing, hashtags, memes, and sharing) that impact how one's voice might translate across a platform and beyond. Fluent circulation considers a creative identity across technical and social domains, acknowledging them as musical in various ways.

Conclusion

What holds a community together? In the previous chapter, I present the personal stories of performers who work to stage representations of themselves, and in this chapter, I consider how a community of performers maintains a collective language, particularly in the ever-changing landscape of music apps. Sometimes these users organize a community around affordances created by app designers, in the forms of lists or hashtags, and sometimes users adapt affordances for creative new uses, such as sharing accounts to create a channel or introducing glitches as a performance aesthetic. These online communities can be porous, leaving opportunity for interlopers and appropriation, but these communities can also be inviting because they arise in such an improvisational manner.

Fluent circulation puts a name to a strategy for performance that helps communities congeal around a particular set of values. The term incorporates language, gestures, editing, and modes of circulation. Fluent circulation involves common languages, gestural vocabularies, and circulatory styles. The term points to the fact that communities can recognize community members, in ways that transcend a platform or formal organizational structure. Fluent circulation blends performance and listening, enabling people to draw attention to reception as a creative possibility for a new performance.

On musical.ly, fluent circulation takes many forms within disability subcultures. We can notice strategic alliances, where disability and queerness meet. We can observe the potential and pitfalls of being recognized as disabled, as users archive their disabled performances explicitly, or as they embrace obfuscation. We can become aware of the ways popular gestures carry a politics, rooted in deeper systems of embodied knowledge, and we see creators work to incorporate two subcultures, such as d/Deaf music and hip hop. We can also witness the curatorial aspects of these performances, as YouTube creators compile similar performances to generate thematic compilations that emphasize disability and other identities.

In the three years following the acquisition of musical.ly by Bytedance, these communities of disabled users on musical.ly appear fragmented and widely dispersed on TikTok. In a recent Kaylee Halko video on TikTok, she seems bored with the app, claiming she doesn't know what to make videos about anymore. Eliza no longer creates tutorials about these apps. One of the @inspirationaldudes passed away. Shaheem appears to have moved into a career in acting, appearing recently in the *Sound of Metal* (2019). Perhaps the most famous musical.ly star—a young performer on the app—is now a musician who has begun disclosing struggles with mental illness, despite an early career producing non-disability-related content on the app.

And yet despite the demise of musical.ly, TikTok has inherited many of these cultural practices, creating a context for many disability subcultures to thrive. Much of content on musical.ly has been moved to TikTok. I begin this chapter with anecdote that casts TikTok in a critical light, in order to emphasize the challenges that disabled creators face in gaining visibility on the app. These challenges endure, but TikTok has enabled many disability subcultures to flourish as well, giving opportunity for communities of Autistic creators, d/Deaf creators, and creators with a wide range of impairments and disabilities. TikTok is the site of much ableist content online, as well as some of the most important anti-ableist content.

The communities on musical.ly represent critical subcultures that paved the way for TikTok activism, and musical.ly also serves as a reminder that TikTok will not last forever. The stories of disabled users on musical.ly, in their brief and temporary flourishing on the app, can demonstrate some strategies for collective agency in a community in flux. These many fluencies can transcend platform and build an accumulated knowledge that can mobilize in new contexts. The appeal of musical.ly, much like many of the other practices in this book, can be a receptiveness to those on the margins, and these marginal musical practices can challenge ideas at the core of more traditional musical practices.

84   SPECTACULAR LISTENING

While researching musical.ly, I noticed a trend on YouTube, in which creators would react to musical.lys, while filming themselves viewing musical.ly videos for the first time. I came to recognize the importance of reactions, as a way of enabling people to record their feelings about a particular piece of media. For disabled users in particular, the act of filming oneself as a consumer of media felt like an important cultural practice, given the context I present in my Introduction about the tendency to ignore disabled consumers in popular media.

Let me provide a contemporary example from TikTok, which encapsulates how these reactions take place. On YouTube, I find a channel called Wheels Not Heels by a disabled creator named Gem, and I see a particular video that bears the title: "Reacting to Disability Awareness TikTok Videos." In the video, she praises TikTok for helping to familiarize disability, and she proceeds to react to disability TikToks, as she goes through a series of them. In one video, she reacts to TikTok creator Maria Muscle. Maria's TikTok video appears superimposed on Gem's screen, in order for me to see Gem react to Maria's content. I watch the TikTok video play and watch along with Gem:

> Maria wheels through a parking lot, while Audrey Mika's "Y U Gotta Be Like That" plays in the background. Maria makes it from the back of the parking lot to the front near the store, finally reaching the disabled parking spot. A car has parked in the spot, preventing her from using it. Right on cue, Maria shrugs while lip syncing the line of the song: "Why you gotta be like that?"

Watching this TikTok video, Gem shakes her head in approval and then says: "I mean it speaks for itself . . . Raising awareness in quite a funny and entertaining way gets the point across."

This example may feel relatively unremarkable, and indeed the TikTok video does not aim for a kind of sensationalist virality. But the video nonetheless exemplifies an important cultural practice, where disabled creators film themselves as spectators in their consumption of the art of other disabled creators. In this video, Maria curates an everyday life experience for TikTok, in a way that frames a daily annoyance, and the reaction on Gem's YouTube channel exemplifies a form of validation. In the early days of musical.ly, these reactions appeared in many diffuse ways on YouTube. They have now become commonplace. The ability to react (an affordance that emerged out of a duet feature) is now part of the artistry of TikTok.

In the chapter that follows, I examine reactions as a particularly notable practice online and on YouTube in particular. In distinction to the previous two chapters on music communities, the following chapter dwells on a performance genre, which enables creators to leverage reactions to disclose powerful feelings about disability in popular media.

3

Tactical Reactions

Toward a Crip Music Criticism

In "The Only Music Critic Who Matters (if You're Under 25),"[1] music journalist Joe Coscarelli describes Anthony Fantano as an "influential evangelist" for the "notoriously insular and endangered art form—the record review." Riding a "wave of reaction and review videos" in order to build an "independent one-man empire . . . from his suburban Connecticut home," Fantano caters to his nearly 2.3 million subscribers on YouTube by filming meme-laden, theatrical reactions to popular music, which consist of bodily gestures, charged facial expressions, and imaginative language. Coscarelli presents Fantano as the "most popular music critic left standing," after the demise of the music magazine industry and the increasing corporate oversight of *Pitchfork* and *Rolling Stone*. Since his channel (The Needle Drop) launched in 2009, Fantano's success has included a generation of devoted fans, the development of an additional YouTube channel, a partnership with Amazon's livestreaming platform Twitch, a bevy of Patreon subscribers, and a whole range of young imitators across platforms for whom a record review means a reaction video. Fantano has popularized a formula for reviews that treats them, above all else, as performances. In the piece, Coscarelli quotes renowned rock critic Robert Christgau, who says of Fantano's work, "I don't 'watch' reviews. I read writing," claiming he doesn't "know his work well enough to dis it." Fantano's reactions exemplify an emergent form of music criticism that supplants reflective writing with riveting reactions.

Reaction videos certainly represent a digital update to the written record review, offering a new way to package timeless debates about music aesthetics for a younger generation that favors video over text. But they also impose a more subtle and significant shift in music reception. They dramatically reimagine listening, idealizing a mode of reception that favors affective bodily responses in the act of consumption. Downplaying subtlety,

Spectacular Listening. Byrd McDaniel, Oxford University Press. © Oxford University Press 2024.
DOI: 10.1093/oso/9780197620458.003.0004

Figure 3.1 Anthony Fantano. "Danny Brown—XXX ALBUM REVIEW." Screenshot by the author on July 17, 2022.

Anthony appears with black glasses and a black t-shirt against a yellow background. The album cover for Danny Brown's "XXX" appears in the top left corner. Anthony's one hand appears in the screen and is made blurry by being in motion.

ambivalence, private reflection, and extended contemplation, they emphasize a thrilling collision between the body and popular music, which may be performed in front of a camera for others to witness. As I argue in the introduction to *Spectacular Listening*, digital cultures have increasingly transformed private music reception into a public spectacle, enabling people to convert personal consumption into prestige, profit, and power. Reaction videos on YouTube epitomize this process, where word-based arguments about music are subordinated to histrionic portrayals of how music feels in the moment of listening. The body becomes a source and site of experiential knowledge about music.

For many who appreciate written reviews, reaction videos may appear to offer a superficial gloss of popular music, downplaying careful reflection in favor of instantaneous judgment, but they can also enable a form of activism that lurks beneath their clickbait veneer. In the media landscape dominated by high-profile creators like Anthony Fantano, a collection of disabled YouTube creators has leveraged reaction videos to emphasize

88   SPECTACULAR LISTENING

disability as a significant factor in music reception. They take advantage of the emphasis on the body in these reaction videos, foregrounding listening as something influenced by a wide range of disabilities, impairments, and bodily differences. The popular music tradition of written album reviews so often ignores techniques of listening, in favor of reflections on the music itself and its cultural context. Reaction videos provide a format for centering techniques of listening, since they take the act of listening as their explicit subject matter.

On YouTube, disabled creators showcase diverse sensory perceptions, various mobilities, assistive devices as props, and a range of neurodivergent ways of appreciating music. They use the reaction video genre to assert disability as an affirmatively claimed source of musical knowledge. Further, this coterie of disabled creators reveals the ableism implicit in idealized conceptions of listening that prioritize the ears, the mind, and neurotypical contemplation. They reveal how discussions of listening that fail to acknowledge bodily abilities simply reproduce an implicit ableism, by assuming all listeners share the same normative framework for music reception. By staging reactions that assert bodily difference, these creators undermine some of the foundational white, male, and non-disabled critical perspectives that dominated a previous era of popular music criticism,[2] celebrating how bodily diversity can provide new ways to access popular music.

In this chapter, I present my ethnographic work on YouTube in order to demonstrate how disabled creators leverage reaction videos to promote a crip music criticism. I organize this work into three sections that get increasingly more granular. The first section focuses on the broader context of reaction videos on the platform, while the second section concentrates on disabled creators who make reaction videos. Finally, the third section spotlights disabled creators who staged a series of chain reactions in response to a particular viral video from *America's Got Talent*. I ultimately challenge the idea that reaction videos are shallow, superficial content that fails to critically engage the depths of popular music. Instead, I demonstrate how disabled creators have turned these videos into reflections upon listening itself, challenging more dominant frameworks of reception that have long diminished, discounted, or discarded disabled perspectives. In so doing, these creators animate a history of crip criticism that is often pushed to the margins in the history of popular music.

Methods

I use the term "disability" as a catchall term, in order to describe people for whom bodily differences result in significant forms of exclusion, stigma, and/or segregation, while recognizing the fluid, contextual, and cultural aspects of these experiences.[3] The social model of disability acknowledges that disability can often be produced by assumptions built into our physical and digital environments.[4] For example, a concert venue with stairs-only access renders those in wheelchairs as disabled, while one with an elevator does not. The social model implicates society for these exclusions, rather than treating disability as a personal problem to be overcome through medical intervention. The stigma that disability always produces a deficient and/or incomplete life leads many to reject self-identifying as disabled. Some people regularly experience impairments but refuse to think of themselves as disabled. Some people prefer to embrace their bodily differences as making them neurodivergent or cyborgian. And still others work to affirmatively claim disability as a way of being in the world, arguing that a proud embrace of disability identity works to destigmatize and broaden understandings of disability as simply part of life.

Many embrace the word "crip" to acknowledge an explicitly activist orientation to disability, transforming an ableist slur into a source of pride.[5] In this chapter, I strategically deploy the terms "disability" and "disabled" to acknowledge people who experience systemic oppression as a result of bodily differences. I suggest that their performances belong to a crip music criticism, because I also want to acknowledge the pleasure and possibilities of non-normative embodiments. These creators transform differences that can be a source of oppression into an affirmatively claimed social identity, which acknowledges forms of difference that often rest outside of the categories of race, gender, sexuality, and class (though are inextricably tied to them). My use of the term "crip music criticism" also stems from an awareness that these creators may or may not be disabled in the particular moment of creating a reaction video, but they experience the world in non-normative ways, which leads them to produce content online that proudly asserts these experienced differences as a core aspect of their identities.

As a mostly non-disabled white man at the time of writing this (see: Chapter 1), I recognize that these creators trust that my writing will convey their perspectives with fidelity and proper context, and I acknowledge that my own privileges enable many forms of access that made this research possible, both digitally and physically. I also know that the following examples of ableism, racism, sexism, and other forms of oppression impact readers differently, in ways I remain insulated from and thus cannot fully understand. I hope that these examples can document oppression, while simultaneously emphasizing the critical interventions staged by the listeners in this work, who are people with complex lives and contradictions (like all of us).

My research examines reaction videos in three ways: from the vantage point as a viewer of reaction videos, from the vantage point of creators, and through embodied performances. Reaction videos are hardly a typical topic for ethnomusicologists, so I creatively combined methods in this field with anthropology, media studies, and music studies in general. I ultimately spent two years between June 2018 and June 2020 following ten YouTube channels, in order to take fieldnotes on their content, comments, and various controversies. Analyzing large-scale platforms, whose algorithms remain obscure to researchers,[6] I balanced my observations as a viewer of these channels with first-person accounts from creators, in order to understand their qualitative experiences on the platform. I reached out to forty creators who represent a variety of identities, subscriber numbers, and musical content. Nine agreed to speak with me through phone conversations, Skype, and e-mails. Our conversations revolved around questions of labor, performance, identity, and channel-building strategy. Given the stigma of disability, I decided to give many of these creators pseudonyms, as well as modify the titles of YouTube videos, to make them less discoverable.

After speaking with these creators, I sought ways to situate their perspectives within a broader context of YouTube content creation, so in the spring of 2020, I attended PAX East as a part of a grant from the American Folklife Center. This annual conference revolves around technology, gaming, and online content creators. The conference helped me see two sides of content creation—the folks on panels with expert knowledge about how to succeed on the platform and the aspirational amateurs who eagerly attended these panels in the hopes of turning their hobbies into profitable career paths.

Finally, I have experimented with making my own reaction videos, including filming, editing, and circulation. I brainstormed something I could consume that would not necessarily be hindered by my own disciplinary background, so I decided to react to a variety of pre-packaged foods in short five-minute videos. I would open/unbox a pre-packaged food item (e.g., a new seltzer flavor or box of cookies) and then react to it in short, succinct clips. In so doing, I gained perspective on reactions as a bodily practice, which requires translating an affective experience into something demonstrative for others, and I also gained awareness of the technical skills required for editing, the equipment and space required for high-quality videos, and the kinds of extra-reactive activities required for wide circulation (e.g., the essential skill of crafting a good thumbnail). Such an approach helped me understand the skills required to produce reaction videos.

The Broad Context of Reactions

Reaction videos are a particular performance genre on YouTube with a set of conventions, which often consists of the following series of events. An ad or two plays. Then a creator introduces the channel, sometimes accompanied by theme music in a title sequence. Then the creator gives a little background on an upcoming reaction, including anticipatory ideas about the artist/song. At this point, a superimposed video appears on the screen,[7] which features a music video or a static image of an album cover (for sound recordings without an audiovisual component). The creator then proceeds to play the media, while filming reactions in real time for viewers to witness. These reactions may include wild gestures, potent facial expressions, and vocal exclamations. Some creators pause throughout to break up bodily reactions with verbal commentary; others play it straight through. When the video ends, the creator may summarize their reaction in a few words, followed by requests for their viewers to subscribe to their channel and find them on Instagram, Twitter, Snapchat, and TikTok. Describing reaction videos so clinically here does a disservice to the attention-grabbing affect of these videos, which often circulate far beyond YouTube with provocative thumbnails and sensational titles.

Reaction videos represent an extremely profitable and popular genre on YouTube, so much so that the two brothers behind Fine Brothers Entertainment attempted to license and trademark the term "React," an ultimately unsuccessful effort that led them instead to form an entire react-related empire across YouTube, Facebook, Snapchat, and Instagram.[8] Many people make money from reactions. Once creators meet certain watch-time and subscriber requirements, they may monetize their channel, which (pending YouTube's approval) means gaining advertising revenue through

92 SPECTACULAR LISTENING

display, overlay, and video ads. Creators may also generate revenue through channel memberships (subscribers paying for special perks), merchandising (selling t-shirts), Super Chat (fans paying for priority in chat streams), and YouTube Premium memberships (creators get a cut of subscription fees).

Many popular music-reaction videos exist in a grey area with respect to copyright violations, and as a result of copyright issues, many creators heavily edit and/or pause the media in a reaction video to avoid detection by YouTube. In other cases, however, reactions can actually generate more attention for the original media (thus appeasing the companies who own the original content). Reaction videos do not need to be individually monetized to benefit a creator, since they can be used as clickbait to bring potential subscribers to a channel, who can then be lured into viewing monetized content. Reactions are rarely the only type of content creators produce on YouTube. Rather, they serve as just one relatively reliable form of attention-grabbing content. According to *Forbes*, the highest-earning YouTube content creators made $22 million (Ryan ToysReview), $21.5 million (Jake Paul), and $20 million (Dude Perfect), during the single-year period between June 1, 2017, and June 1, 2018, but Stokel-Walker (2019) writes that "96% of those who upload to YouTube don't make enough money from adverts alone to break through the US poverty line."[9] So while reaction videos enable some to capitalize on their consumption, the majority of creators who hope to make money on the platform fail to achieve this level of wealth. Even high-profile creators recognize what they perceive to be increasingly finicky algorithmic tweaks from YouTube, leading them to invest in other revenue sources (e.g., other social media platforms, live tours, podcasts, their own apps, and even educational series for other creators).

One creator represents the high-profile creator class. A member of a synth-pop band, this creator has nearly one million subscribers and told me that reaction videos represent extremely easy-to-create evergreen content for his channel (i.e., content that doesn't require timeliness for its impact). He told me:

> The reaction video is a beautiful thing. You can sit down, shoot it, edit it in like an hour. It's all based on opinion. I think that's what the people come for. It's not the crazy production. Other content can take weeks. The reaction video brings in just as much revenue but takes an hour to make . . . It's an endless cycle of "I'm going to talk about this because you talked about this . . . " which ultimately always trickles back to you.

Although he downplays the skill and labor involved in these videos, his ability to craft a video so efficiently stems from years of practice, and he recognizes reactions as a good way to generate attention on the platform, even as a promotional tool for his band's musical performances.

Reaction videos may seem like a distinctive performance genre in a landscape of diverse content on YouTube, but they are one of many performance genres on the platform that feature people documenting their own consumption in the hopes that their emotional reactions will generate attention. They exist as part of a broader landscape of digital media that incentivizes users to share their media habits as an ostensibly empowering practice, which I call the "sharing imperative" and discuss in my conclusion to this book.

From technology reviews to food tutorials to travel vlogging, numerous YouTube genres depict people consuming something for others' entertainment. Ever since YouTube appeared in 2005,[10] many viral videos have appeared on the platform that feature people reacting to products, media, and bizarre situations: the kid who shouts in ecstasy upon receiving a "Nintendo sixty-fooooourrrrr!!!," teens pranking their siblings into watching "Scary Maze Game," or the pornographic "2 Girls 1 Cup." Stemming from a much longer history of reality TV, video blogging, and *Candid Camera*–style TV shows, these viral videos have spawned their own genres on YouTube, such as the unboxing genre in which people unwrap a product to capture their reaction in the initial moment of consumption (the format of choice for the highest-earning content creator in 2018, Ryan ToysReview).

The recommended video function helped propel these trends on the platform. Motored by an artificial intelligence system called Google Brain, YouTube's recommended video algorithm uses user data to recommend an endless stream of videos in order to sustain viewer attention and thus display more ads. According to Chris Stokel-Walker,[11] this recommended video function has increased watch time among users twenty-fold between 2006 and 2009, since 70 percent of the time users spend on YouTube is spent watching recommended videos. While the algorithm remains mysterious, creators began to suspect that reacting to popular videos could be a good way to gain new subscribers, since their reactions would pop up as recommended videos right after the original media played. Since popular music is an extremely popular form of content (twenty-eight of the top thirty most-watched videos on YouTube are music videos),[12] many creators started reacting to popular music videos in the hopes of drawing attention to their own channels. Popular music reaction videos therefore represent a particularly explicit and influential version of the kinds of performances of consumption that appear across the platform, but they exist as part of a broader landscape in which creators constantly upload videos of their own consumption in order to gain power as intermediaries in these chains of circulation.

Reaction videos enable viewers to experience music through the body of someone else, which can actually enhance latent or subtle feelings in the viewer. Part of the appeal of watching these emotional reactions stems from the fact that they feature everyday people rather than paid professionals. These creators can become micro-celebrities of sorts, generating their own memes, followers, and fandoms.[13] The skilled performers who create these videos become avatars for those who watch them, as they find ways to transform internal feelings into demonstrative displays. Reactions can express a wide range of affects, not simply positive feelings like pleasure, joy, or surprise. As Melissa Click describes in *Anti-Fandom*, media industries have actively promoted interactivity as a way to "motivate audiences' affective engagements with media texts," and even affect that appears undesirable—disgust, fear, and hatred—can bond people together through "powerful alliances and antagonisms."[14] Presenting a range of feelings, creators of reaction videos bond their viewers to them through creating mutual feelings toward the music in question. These reactions can also extend the life of new music, by allowing viewers to constantly re-experience a new piece of music *as new* by watching creators listen for the first time.

While reaction videos may seem entirely spontaneous, they must be understood as work.[15] Their framing as reactions may imply something involuntary about the bodily gestures that comprise them, but they represent laborious, carefully curated, and precisely edited performances. Much like some might imagine reality TV as an enhanced version of reality, reaction videos are an enhanced representation of listening. Creators learn all kinds of skills, including search-engine optimization, genre conventions, staging, thumbnail creation, audiovisual editing, and bodily techniques that enable them to translate internal feelings into overt expressions. In her book on musicians and digital communication platforms, Nancy Baym defines "relational labor": "the ongoing, interactive, affective, material, and cognitive work of communicating with people over time to create structures that can support continued work." Her theory offers a way of thinking about the work in a performance, as well as the work that exists in between and around these onstage on-camera performances.[16] In my article, "Popular

Music Reaction Videos," I describe how creators develop these skills.[17] As with musical performances, creators render themselves vulnerable by staging their bodies for others' consumption, even as they consume music in the process. Sometimes these supposed first-time reactions are extremely rehearsed, re-filmed over and over until creators get it right. Many creators will take down an unsuccessful video, revise, and resubmit the video to YouTube in order to improve the chances of wide circulation. As a unique type of musical performance, reaction videos can serve to merely entertain, feeding the algorithm to generate profit for creators, but importantly, they can also be persuasive, modeling an approach to music that can influence how subscribers hear it.

Interlude

While reactions may seem superficial or surface level, some reactions can offer important cultural interventions in racist, sexist, or ableist discourses. During her 2016 *Formation* tour, Beyoncé played a fan's reaction video to *Lemonade* on the big screen, so fans at her live concert could watch someone reacting to her music. The video featured a YouTuber named Evelyn from the Internets. Evelyn's reaction stitches together an imaginative and poignant pastiche of evocations that Beyoncé's music calls to mind: "She gave you Nina Simone, Nefertiti, Venus de Milo. She called on Trayvon Martin, Mike Brown, and Eric Garner's mother to give us the present, ok. And then she surrounded us with visuals of the Black future . . . " Evelyn makes content on YouTube that combines travel vlogs, beauty tutorials, first-generation stories, and Black pop-cultural commentary. Of course, after she found out Beyoncé played her reaction video in concert, she filmed another reaction video, in which she reacts to finding out Beyoncé used her reaction in this way. In her reaction to Beyoncé playing her reaction, she runs down the street, shouting in joyfulness.[18]

Evelyn does not disclose having a disability on her channel, yet much of her channel's content revolves around psychological struggles. Indeed, Evelyn's initial popularity on YouTube, which allowed Beyoncé to find her channel, was fueled in part by a viral video called "Call in Black." The video describes the psychological toll that police violence takes on Black people, and it imagines a world where such trauma could be acknowledged and accommodated in the workplace as a kind of sick or personal day. She acknowledges that a

96   SPECTACULAR LISTENING

panic attack inspired one of her videos, and she drops links to content in the
video description, such as "A Meditation for Overpoliced Black Girls."[19]

The Tactical Reactions of Disabled Creators

YouTube is a critical site for disability activism. Digital cultures often create
disability through design built around normative bodies.[20] In her expansive
work on accessibility online, Elizabeth Ellcessor writes that 54 percent of
people with disabilities use the Internet, while 81 percent of non-disabled
folks do. Disabled users of these platforms often face the challenge of
platforms that fail to follow web content-accessibility guidelines, and many
rely on all kinds of modifications to software and hardware—text-to-speech,
speech-to-text, voice-recognition, on-screen keyboards, captions, and so on.
And yet YouTube has given rise to disabled influencers and creators, who
find creative ways to acknowledge disability as a widely shared experience.
Estimates suggest that 26 percent of adults in the United States have a disability,[21] and disabled creators reach millions of subscribers.

For those with disabilities seeking community or others with shared
experiences, digital cultures—and YouTube vlogging in particular—can be
a valuable place to feel a sense of belonging. You can find a single person
on the other side of the globe who shares in your struggles and joys. Some
disabled creators push explicitly political agendas—from opposition to the
hyperpolicing of Black disabled folks in the era of Black Lives Matter to the
#CripTheVote initiative, which pushes political candidates toward disability
justice. But much of the work of disability activism on YouTube turns the personal experiences of disability into a politics of recognition, through which
an acknowledgment of bodily difference can expose a pernicious ableism in
society.

Even for those who might appreciate the personal-as-political activism of
YouTube vlogging, reaction videos may seem to be a relatively empty performance genre or worse. Such videos sometimes do reproduce some of the oppressive paradigms in popular music consumption, promoting racist, sexist,
and ableist cultural scripts of consuming in the Other.[22] But their widespread
popularity has led disabled creators to harness their conventions for political ends, producing productive frictions and useful connections with larger
non-disabled YouTube communities. The fact that they do not seem political

at all belies their radical potential. Indeed, they can help viewers understand subtle ableist listening norms that many take to be natural, universal, and obvious. These disabled creators purposefully accentuate listening in disabled bodies, exposing—for non-disabled and disabled folks alike—how listening can be informed and affirmed by disability identity.

One creator, who I will call Jacob, for example, purposefully accentuates his blindness on his two YouTube channels, showing how reaction videos privilege visual dimensions of music videos. His vlogging covers a wide range of content: bodybuilding, his progress learning the banjo, stories related to his Leber Hereditary Optic Neuropathy, and popular music reactions. A white southerner, Jacob creates videos that tend to have high audio quality yet fuzzy visual quality (experienced creators on YouTube will tell you audio quality tends to be more important than visual quality on YouTube).

As I scroll through his channels, I click one video and watch a reaction to Eminem's "Stan"—a song with a title that became synonymous with unconventional fandom. He sits with a laptop in front of him, and after a little preamble, he hits play on the track. Although the music video plays on his laptop, his head faces forward directly toward the camera. The track begins with a slow crescendo of Dido's hook, which competes with menacing sounds of thunder, lightning, rain, and rushing water. Jacob mentions he can hear a storm. When the beat and bass line finally drop, Jacob nods rhythmically. Dido's voice now sounds prominent in the mix, as she sings: "My tea's gone cold I'm wondering why / I got out of bed at all / The morning rain clouds up my window / And I can't see at all." He abruptly pauses the video. He forces a laugh that feels painfully drawn out, perhaps even planned. "It's funny," he repeats a few times in the midst of forced laughter, evoking both senses of the word—humorous and suspect. I begin to feel uneasy as he draws out this bout of forced laughter. "You know," he says, "I *can't* see at all." He lets that linger for a moment. Such an instance catches me off guard, as I realize the reaction video provided a pretext for his intervention. Rather than create a sense of empathy and sameness between himself and viewers, he immediately makes me aware of my sightedness, as he draws attention to how blindness informs his listening to the music video.

The discomfort Jacob evokes directly acknowledges the audiovisual assumptions of the reaction-video genre, which often assume normative vision for both creators and subscribers. For creators who announce their disabilities, the emotional labor required to educate others can certainly

98 SPECTACULAR LISTENING

take a toll, yet many dedicate themselves to actively confronting those who perpetuate stereotypes, whether out of a necessity for survival or a desire for activism. Jacob's approach employs what Johnson and McRuer, riffing on Sara Ahmed, call "crip killjoy."[23] Jacob's performance undercuts an understanding of reactions as feel-good content or politically neutral. His video takes viewers by surprise, pausing what appears to be a typical reaction video to emphasize the sensory assumptions implicit in these YouTube conventions. These techniques are somewhat similar to the creators in Chapter 2, who may label content with disability-related hashtags but also avoid hashtags to intervene in content that people do not imagine to be disability related.

While these reactions may feel spontaneous or improvised, they often come from a situated place, where creators work to maximize the impact of their videos while considering how such videos transform disability into fodder for others' consumption. For example, a creator, who I will call Michael, is a white British YouTuber with approximately 5,500 subscribers as of July 10, 2020. His channel features videos about his life, Autism, and various reactions to media. His reactions foreground the experience of Autism, including videos with titles along the lines of "Is Hamilton the Musical Autism-Friendly?" or "Autistic Man Reacts to Autism TikToks."[24] I reached out to him to ask about his decision to foreground Autism as a subject in his videos, as well as in his video titles and thumbnails. He told me:

> I feel that just the side of me that's intensified on YouTube is the Autism bit. I feel I'm more Autistic online, which is a weird one. Because I'm always posting these videos of me being stressed or moaning about stuff I'm stressed about. And saying how much it affects me. That's what people have in mind: that that's me constantly. Whereas in real life, I don't like to make a big fuss of being Autistic. I just like to get on with it. I internalize it all . . . I think, fair enough, most people do know someone on the spectrum. But there are a lot of people who don't. When you get these things in the media, neurotypicals don't really have as much . . . As much as they say they know about Autism, you still don't know what it's like to be Autistic . . . [YouTube videos] are different from writing an essay and all that stuff, because I'm very much in control of how I want it to come across . . . I am always honest. But it means I can edit it down to be the most effective way of delivering it that it can be . . . You can gauge more from a

video. People can gauge my tone. When I say I'm angry, they can actually see I'm angry. That's what I like.

Michael points out that videos offer a more potent approach to conveying how one feels, and he admits to playing up his Autism as a particular political strategy for educating folks on the platform—in a way that evokes the disability masquerade in Chapter 1.

Indeed, this agenda came into clear focus with the viral video "Autistic Guy's Reaction to Netflix's 'Atypical.'" Netflix's *Atypical* came under criticism for its stereotypical representations of Autism (e.g., white male savants), as well as its casting that featured non-Autistic actors playing Autistic characters. I asked Michael to describe his process of shooting it. Although this reaction targets a television show rather than a music video, I want to include his thoughts, because it encapsulates the political potential of reactivity. He told me:

I had seen the trailer on the day before. Ooops! There's a little insight actually. That wasn't my first time watching it. I actually don't [watch for the first time] in any reaction videos. If I did that, I can't speak and watch at the same time. So I have to watch it first to be able to react to it. So it's a little bit of a show. But it's still the honest opinion is what I hope for. I saw [the show's trailer] on Twitter . . . Everyone on Twitter wanted something to happen. At first it was boycott it . . . I wanted to see if I could make an impact on it. I thought, if I react to it, I know reaction videos do well on YouTube. Maybe it will get seen beyond my audience and maybe it will get seen by the show's producers. And yeah. And I decided to film it that way because that was kind of the format of the reaction videos . . . I must admit with that title, I was being slightly tactical, because I did want the video to be seen by a lot of people, so I followed the conventions of the reaction videos. How did people react to it? That was the first video that got seen by a lot of people. This was my first one to blow up on YouTube. Yeah, this was my first one to go viral on YouTube. I was gaining 50 subs a day. There was just a lot. A lot of people were like: "Wow, I didn't realize Autistic people could be like this . . . " People always say this to me. And I don't know whether to take this as a compliment or not. People will say: "If I didn't know, I wouldn't say you're Autistic." I'm like: "Well, I am!" *Exasperatedly laughs.* I don't know if they're trying to say, "oh you seem normal." I don't want to seem normal.

100 SPECTACULAR LISTENING

> I'm not normal. But like alright. Whatever . . . I was educating a lot of people
> with a video on that scale.

By dramatizing this conflict, Michael seeks to change public perceptions through what he calls "tactical" approaches, explicitly framing Autism as something that gives him authority. While his video ostensibly features a spontaneous reaction, his reflections here reveal the strategic agenda that undergirds this in-the-moment performance, scripting an affective approach to this media that his viewers might similarly adopt. Given the way definitions and depictions of Autism largely revolve around white boys and men, Michael being a white man no doubt enhances his ability to be taken seriously on YouTube. As activist Lydia X. Z. Brown has argued, women and racial minorities with Autism are often met disproportionately with doubt, criminalization, and denial of resources.[25] Michael's privileged status in these other aspects of his identity helps him claim authority, while mitigating the risks of exposure others might face.

While some disabled creators embrace the political power of critique and confrontation, others champion joyfulness as a direct challenge to the idea that disability should lead to some tragic, joyless life. Reaction videos offer a way for disabled creators to demonstrate how disability influences music reception in ways that make it pleasurable. For example, one creator who I will call Margaret makes content with her husband who I will call Jim. Their channel has followed their lives from Canada to South Korea to Japan to Canada (again) and generated 1.4 million subscribers along the way (as of June 29, 2020). Their content spans multiple platforms, including YouTube, Instagram, and their own website. Margaret is forthcoming about her life with Ehlers-Danlos Syndrome, describing mobility issues, chronic pain, a suicide attempt, and depression. But her serious videos about impairments also inform a euphoric embrace of pop music that appears throughout the channel. Dwelling primarily on K-Pop (from 2NE1 to Super Junior), she highlights the particularities of listening in her body. In one video, she talks about dancing to the oft-maligned artist she calls "Shitty George Michael," claiming he epitomizes music that "makes you feel really great [and] makes you want to dance, even if you're just elbow dancing because you can't support your weight." In another video, she describes channeling chronic pain into pleasurable experiences of "dancing at a live show and watching an amazing DJ." In yet another video, she models how to dance while wearing various mobility aids and offers fashion advice for wearing knee braces and using a cane. These videos exist alongside countless other videos that feature her promoting beloved K-Pop tracks, demonstrating K-Pop dances, and reviewing new K-Pop releases with her husband—many of which never mention EDS.

Disability is often in flux, producing different possibilities in a given moment, and in disability-focused videos and others, Margaret presents listening to music as a bodily affair that involves using what's possible given the props, muscles, and movements available to her. In contrast to Jacob and Michael, Jim and Margaret do not frame these videos as reactions, and their disability-related content seems to target the disability community in particular, celebrating ways of enjoying music and life in general as a disabled person. But their channel represents important work that performances of listening can do within a community. Shocking takedowns that confront ableism can promote awareness among large audiences of non-disabled viewers, but nuanced portrayals can help cultivate self-love within smaller, more insular listening communities online.

A communal politics of care can also emerge unexpectedly out of the relationship between creators and subscribers. I spoke with another woman, who I will refer to as Lindsay. A white Canadian creator with 1.1 million subscribers, she almost exclusively posts reaction videos. While her most recent fifteen videos averaged an impressive 535,000 views (as of mid-July 2019), the first videos on her channel hardly averaged 1,000 views. She then recorded a reaction to Lil Pump in 2017, which suddenly garnered 30,000 views. She proceeded to experiment with reactions to SoundCloud rappers and found that strategy to be the ticket to success. She told me she dropped out of business school to make videos full time: "It turned everything around. We moved out of our basement into a high-rise apartment. And we worked strictly on our YouTube channel." She developed merchandise for her channel, as well as a cross-platform branding strategy. By focusing on artists such as Juice Wrld, XXXtentacion, Mac Miller, and Lil Peep, she found herself grappling with the untimely deaths of many of these musicians on her channel, and she received many private messages from fans:

Every day, I get hundreds of DMs. I make an effort every single day to take care of all of them. One of the biggest tragedies of my channel was the passing of [XXXtentacion] last year [in 2018]. It was one of the most abrupt and horrifying and heartbreaking experiences. Once it happened, I think I got hundreds of messages from kids saying: "I can't go on. I'm heartbroken.

102   SPECTACULAR LISTENING

I'm suicidal." I felt like a real mom to a lot of these kids . . . I took on a role like I'm going to respond to all of these DMs and make sure all of these people feel loved. They don't need to make a horrifying decision . . . I was heartbroken myself. It was also a beautiful therapy for me and helped me cope with passing myself. The more I did that, the more I felt so connected with the people who watched me . . . But I don't know—How much I owe them? People on Instagram come to me and send me a heartfelt message. Sometimes I'll even answer emails. Instagram is the perfect place because I can see the person, their face, their profile. I can feel like I'm talking to them themselves. Now Instagram is adding some beautiful features to their operation. You can Facetime people now. You can call them. Send them voice notes. That's without phone numbers involved . . . People are very vulnerable and moldable. I want them to get the right message and make sure they're treated properly. I didn't grow up with a lot of this. Coming to a point where we get to see what YouTube does to people. I want to make sure everyone is thought about.

Lindsay came to realize the death of many of these rappers—often due to overdoses—had catalyzed both a grieving process in her subscribers, as well as self-awareness about their own psychological struggles. So her reactions took on all kinds of extra meanings, as mourning rituals, celebrations of life, and even acknowledgments that music can awaken difficult things within us. She and other creators in this chapter told me that they frequently deal with suicidal fans and folks with various mental-health crises, problems exacerbated by a lack of universal healthcare and widespread social stigma. Lindsay was one of the few who felt personally accountable to those who watch her reactions. One creator I spoke with had a fan die by suicide after a failed attempt to track him down in person. Recognizing how desperate and lonely some fans can be, Lindsay sought to manage these reactions as diligently and carefully as possible, recognizing that her reactions could reverberate powerfully among subscribers.

Reaction videos center the body, and in so doing, they create a context where bodily differences matter in the act of listening. Some creators may explicitly frame their disability in order to accentuate differences with non-disabled audiences, who might have internalized ableist assumptions. Other creators may seek to find common ground, showing disability as an inherent part of life and speaking on behalf of people with similar embodiments. And yet others may simply create content that opens up possibilities for their viewers to disclose disabilities in a safe community. In all instances, reaction videos become a particularly fruitful forum for disability activism, primarily because these videos center listening as their subject. They make space for everyday listeners—nonprofessionals—to consider listening in their own bodies, attending to aspects of the body that might not conform to the norm.

Interlude

I'm sitting at my computer, watching a video called something like "Disabled Man Reacts to Kanye," which reveals an Arab American man who wears round glasses and a white t-shirt. As he listens to the music, he looks down and away from the camera. The lyrics from "Yikes" appear as captioned text at the bottom of the screen, showing me what he hears in real time. Kanye says the lines: "That's why I fuck with Ye . . . That's my third person. That's my bipolar shit. That's my superpower. Ain't no disability. I'm a superhero . . . " After flinching a few times, the man finally pauses the music and searches for something to say. He gets choked up and apologizes. After clearing his throat, he launches into this explanation:

> That was some strong, strong stuff from Ye right there . . . Hearing Kanye describing his bipolar illness as a superpower. I completely understand what he means . . . It can be really hard accepting that you're a normal person, when you don't have an episode of mania but that's what you have to do. Hearing him telling me he's going to go off meds and all that kind of stuff. It's so . . . It feels like he's so close to accepting what's happening to him and then he ignores it.

He takes his glasses off to wipe tears from his face. While he struggles to find words, his body language—tears, hoarse voice, and anguished face—communicate a connection with the music that non-bipolar folks cannot know. His performance is not a review but rather a vulnerable act of demonstrating to viewers how the music brings out latent feelings he tries to suppress. At a time when Kanye has been heavily criticized for his white-supremacist and antisemitic remarks, this man brings a form of empathy to the music that he wishes to share with the nearly 500 others who watched this video.

104   SPECTACULAR LISTENING

Mobilizing Chain Reactions

While the broad genre of reaction videos can be a diverse terrain for addressing many ways of listening to music, these videos can also revolve around a particular piece of media, engaging in a kind of tug-of-war about how to interpret a specific musical performance. When a high-profile new music video, live musical performance, or music recording comes out, a cascade of reaction videos usually follows. These reactions may target the original media, or they may play out as a series of chain reactions—reactions to reactions to reactions. These chain reactions operate as a kind of dialogue between users. They not only involve language, but also emphasize affect as a critical aspect of exchange and negotiation between differing perspectives.

One notable example reveals how chain reactions can intervene in digital discourse: reactions to a viral video of Kodi Lee from *America's Got Talent*. These reactions offer an important addition to the examples in this chapter thus far, because they demonstrate a communal response to a single performance. This example represents a mobilization of affective reactions from disabled creators that work to re-script some of the patronizingly ableist receptions of Lee's original performance.

I first learned of a YouTube video from a student in a course called Music and Disability Justice. About half of the students in the class identified as disabled, so much of the work of the class revolved around navigating discussions between non-disabled and disabled people's perspectives. After one student's repeated suggestions, I pulled it up on YouTube, made it full screen, hit play, and watched it for first time with my class. Here is how I would describe my reaction as I stood in front of my class and watched the video on the projector:

> Two people walk out onto the *America's Got Talent* stage. A white woman leads an Asian American man to the center of the stage, as he grips a cane in his right hand. The judges welcome the two, and the man leans forward to say hello. His eyes wander in circles, and he never looks directly at the judges. When they ask him his name, the 22-year-old man responds: "I'm Kodi. I'm Kodi Lee." Upon uttering his surname, his voice drops dramatically in pitch. The woman beside him announces: "I'm mom. I'm Tina Lee." Kodi's jaw moves constantly. His whole body rocks back and forth. His mom chimes in to tell the judges he's "blind and Autistic." She explains that music saved him from a world of norms to which he could never conform. She leads him around to the piano. His Chuck Taylors touch the pedals. After a

TACTICAL REACTIONS   105

Figure 3.2 America's Got Talent. "America's Got Talent 2019 WINNER KODI LEE Auditions And Performances | Got Talent Global." Screenshot by the author on July 17, 2022.

Kodi appears at a piano onstage at America's Got Talent. He wears a blue hoodie with a white vest, and a microphone appears in front of his face, as he leans forward to sing.

dramatic pause, he begins, singing the first lines of Leon Russell's "Song for You": "I've been so many places in my life and time / I've sung a lot of songs / I've made some bad rhymes." Kodi's voice is magnificent. Precise. Rich in tone. Deftly moving between melisma and melody. When Kodi's falsetto gives way to the lines "when my life is over," I feel goosebumps, which then are immediately eclipsed by a sense of self-consciousness. *I should model a more detached demeanor for students who may be watching me*, I think to myself. When the final lines come in about "singing this song to you," I breathe a sigh of appreciation, and I see the audience thunderously applaud Kodi. Then Kodi turns to his audience and applauds for them. And then my class claps for the YouTube video.

In a previous class, we had painstakingly addressed how these slick media narratives often play up disability as a tragic deficit that may be heroically overcome, all for the purposes of inspiring non-disabled audiences. Will Cheng's "Staging Overcoming" proved essential for analyzing how reality competitions traffic in disability narratives that often play up their

106   SPECTACULAR LISTENING

emotional impact as human-interest stories, eschewing mention of the structural barriers that disabled people face in favor of depictions that render disability as an isolated personal struggle.[26] And yet despite Cheng's cautionary warning, we felt susceptible to the awe-inspiring affect that the clip encouraged us to feel.

While his performance brought about predictable forms of inspirational narratives of overcoming, many disabled creators called attention to the ways blind and Autistic listeners might understand Kodi's accomplishments differently. In order to understand these disabled creators' interventions, we first need to go back to the judges' reactions, which generated an ableist chain reaction online. Howie Mandel speaks first, calling his performance a "great inspiration." Julianne Hough, whose tears overflowed during the performance, says, "I heard you, and I felt you. And that was beautiful." Simon Cowell follows, "I don't know what it's like to live in Kodi's world . . . but your voice is absolutely fantastic," awkwardly switching his address from Kodi's mom to Kodi. Then Gabrielle Union hits the golden buzzer following her address to Kodi's mom. Confetti falls. Kodi's multiracial family storms the stage with Terry Crews, who announces that he is going to the live show in Hollywood. The whole scene is nothing short of a spectacular reaction to Kodi's abilities.

Such a scene scripted subsequent ableist reactions all over social media, enabling non-disabled creators to consume this piece of gut-wrenching media as a form of profitable clickbait. I find one of the top search results revealing a creator who I will refer to as Jack, a video of a long-haired white muscular man in a sleeveless shirt. Jack proceeds through a litany of cringe-worthy statements about the degree of Kodi's disability, suggesting that his musical skills come from some natural biological compensation for his deficiency in other areas, and he repeatedly calling his performance "crazy" and "insane" without any sense of irony at how these terms have been weaponized against people like Kodi. The guy concludes the video by suggesting that Kodi's performance gives "normal" folks "no excuse," echoing Howie's reaction by calling the performance "inspirational." Throughout the video, the man appears overcome with joy at seeing Kodi succeed, while occasionally fighting back tears. I mention these pain-inducing ableist terms here, just to emphasize how commonplace these ableist ideas about disability can be.

Many on YouTube filmed similar reactions, which work to transform Kodi's labor into a consumable product that creators can digest in front of audiences—an act that works to present these creators as benevolent people by showcasing their empathy. Yet these reactions disempower disabled folks in so many ways: accepting disability only when it produces exceptional art, imagining disability as a magical force that unleashes amazing abilities while downplaying the hard work to cultivate such abilities, and ultimately reducing people to their impairments. These reactions reveal patronizing orientations to disability, which center non-disabled creators' humanity primarily through dehumanizing the people whose art they consume.

In the wake of these initial reactions, disabled creators on YouTube reacted to these reactions. I click on one video of a white middle-aged blind man who I will call Daryl. He wears a blue shirt and gestures wildly in the air, speaking with a deliberate fervor. One eye looks at the camera, as he tells viewers that these reactions have "really been bothering" him. He appears agitated, exuding discomfort as he shifts in his chair. "None of this is to take away from the mastery and the beauty and the amazing story that Kodi represents. But I want to be really clear that I am so tired of people saying that he is succeeding in spite of his disability . . . " He seems to collect his patience to launch into an explanation:

> He is not succeeding in spite of his disability. He is succeeding because of it. His disability has given him the gifts that he has today. He wouldn't have those gifts without his blindness and without his Autism. And without his family that recognized those gifts in him . . . [The man sits back in his chair, reflecting on his own situation] Just like I am the man that I am today—I wouldn't change my disability for anything—because of the opportunities and the blessing and the knowledge and the insight (no pun intended) and all the other things my blindness has given to me.

In this video with nearly 400 views, he explains the labor and support required for Kodi to succeed, challenging the idea that disability proved to be an obstacle. He acknowledges disability as part of what Joseph Straus calls his "creative identity."[27] Indeed, Kodi's website credits Kodi's listening abilities for his talent, promoting his "audio photographic memory" that enables him to accurately recall music after a single time listening to it. In listening to Daryl's listening to Kodi, viewers come to understand how Kodi's success stems from harnessing his inherent abilities and also laboring to convert his listening abilities into these virtuosic performances.

I click on another video. In this video featuring an Autistic creator, I see a white gender-non-conforming person. I skip ahead in the video to

108 SPECTACULAR LISTENING

a scene with a superimposed video of Kodi on the person's screen. As Kodi performers, the creator—who I will call Sam—appears nonplussed, as they take drags from a cigarette. Their video has over 2,600 views. Breaking with their stoic appearance, I see the person nod knowingly when Kodi's mom says it's hard for him to conform to the normative expectations in his world. Sam continues taking drags from a cigarette, appearing somewhat withholding or skeptical. When the standing ovation finally occurs, they elaborate:

> Are people standing up and clapping and cheering because this individual and human being did some amazing music and sounds good? So if it's a neurotypical person . . . would people be standing up and cheering as much as they are? Or are they simply cheering and emotional and wowed because they view this person as . . . um . . . you know disabled and otherwise unable to do such things? . . . The first time I watched it, I did have tears because I was so excited for him because of the passion that he has . . . Like I don't think I have that confidence. He oozes confidence.

Disclosing being moved to tears in the initial viewing, Sam reveals that this second viewing reflects a growing skepticism about what Kodi's performance means for Autistic folks. Many of the reactions to Kodi's initial performance fixated on his stimming before his performance, attributing it to discomfort in the limelight, but this Autistic creator interprets this as a sign of confidence. Sam's affect in this reaction appears to script a less emotional interpretation of his performance, instead privileging a more restrained appreciation of his virtuosity as a pianist and singer. While Kodi's performance offered a pretext for many non-Autistic viewers to emphasize their emotions (and thus empathy), Sam's restraint encourages people to take Kodi more seriously— and perhaps to take the slick packaging more skeptically.

A subsequent video plays called "Autistic Woman Reacts to Kodi Lee Reactions," which features a young Autistic woman named Stephanie. Her reaction to Lee feels more clinical and precise. Speaking with a measured tone, she gives a play-by-play of Kodi's performance, carefully dissecting some of the reactions that plagued Kodi's reception online. She says:

> The way he talks *is* different. Now whether it's because he likes the way it feels to talk like that . . . Sometimes for me I say things or do things in a certain way. "Voices," it just is. If I had the ability to, I would indulge in it. It's the way he's finding it the easiest to get the words out.

As with Sam, she hears Kodi's vocal delivery as evidence of confidence and self-assuredness. She then addresses some of the circulations of the original *America's Got Talent* clip, versions of which claimed something like "Kodi Lee Defeats Autism and Blindness." The woman calls this a "stupid title," since "Autism and blindness aren't things to be defeated." She then directly confronts her non-Autistic viewers, encouraging them to take their amazement and make it conform to a broader disability acceptance:

> Let people be amazed. Let people wonder if maybe the next time they see someone just casually, when they're out and about who doesn't communicate in the way they're used to, maybe they're seeing them in a way that they're not. Maybe they can start to challenge their perception of people. Just like Kodi Lee, so so so many people might not be able to communicate in the way you're used to but are still human beings with talents and abilities and good things and have good lives and are happy and aren't just suffering and don't need you to go "poor them they must have no life."

This woman offers a tactical response (to use Michael's phrase) to re-script affective responses to Kodi. In a subtle way, she acknowledges amazement as a strong impulse among listeners, yet pushes for amazement to be simply a broader condition of musical appreciation, rather than a uniquely applied affect to disability in particular.

Such an emphasis resonates with Rosemarie Garland-Thomson's *Staring: How We Look*. Rather than criticize "the gaze" or staring as inherently exploitative, she suggests staring represents a widely shared human impulse to know something that seems distinctive. By "being conscious in the presence of something that compels our intense attention," we can embrace "a 'newness' that can be transformative," so long as we remain attentive to the desires of the staree.[28] As with staring, listening can compel our attention in a way that may be transformative. In her video with nearly 8,000 viewers, Stephanie's reaction to others' reactions pushes for amazement as a transformative receptivity to others, something equally applied to everyone.

While the top Kodi Lee reactions have generated hundreds of thousands of views on YouTube, the videos from disabled creators reacting to Kodi Lee total around 20,000 views, which may seem to be hardly enough to sway public opinion on a massive scale. But these ongoing interventions appear repeatedly across the platform in response to many musical performances, comprising small pieces that make up a persistent and concerted effort

Figure 3.3 Stephanie Bethany. "An Autistic's Thoughts on Kodi Lee (AGT Golden Buzzer)." Screenshot by the author on July 17, 2022.

Stephanie appears in red shirt with black glasses in what appears to be a home office. She reacts to reactions to Kodi Lee.

among YouTubers to insert disability identity into spaces that otherwise exclude it. Kodi Lee reaction videos by non-disabled creators often render disability as something that may be consumed, not as something inherently part of the community of listeners that engage with Kodi's performance. These disabled creators implicitly acknowledge the significance of disability as part of one's identity as a listener, representing subscribers who might share in these experiences.

Commenters on these videos chime in with statements such as: "As an Autistic myself, I can understand what's being asked here" and "I'm a person with autism[;] I know how that feels." Reaction videos can also challenge an unacknowledged ableism that informs many viewers' responses to Kodi. As a form of clickbait, these reactions from disabled creators can lure people into channels and broader communities that present more responsible representations of disability. Disabled creators on YouTube have millions of followers, and reaction videos represent a form of sensationalist content that can bring non-disabled folks into contact with more explicit forms of disability activism.

Conclusion

Reaction videos may feel like an odd place to find disability advocacy, yet attention to the more official and/or formal domains of culture—books, think pieces, public talks, activism-oriented concerts, and even music itself—can sometimes obscure some of the work that occurs within the less prestigious domains of popular culture. Though their performances require artistic labor, these creators are not widely revered as artists or even underground subversive musicians. Most are not millionaires or distinguished speakers. They are amateur listeners who want to draw attention to disability as part of their listening experience. They circulate these videos within a vast landscape of reaction videos on YouTube, which feature every possible problematic and productively counter-hegemonic approach to popular music imaginable. But their work serves to publicly acknowledge that popular music does not represent a one-size-fits-all format for all consumers. Creators' videos translate listening into a new performance, engaging in a form of spectacular listening that validates diverse forms of listening. Creators become listeners-by-proxy.

Thinking of those who have long advocated for greater awareness of feminist, LGBTQ+, Black, and/or people-of-color approaches to music criticism,[29] I would ask: how can we acknowledge the history of disabled music criticism too? The white male rock critic has long dominated musical discourse in the popular sphere, but while these perspectives represent the most privileged and prioritized voices in music criticism, they exist alongside numerous others, who often go unacknowledged and underappreciated. Ann Powers has been a prominent advocate for celebrating a history of women writers who challenge this paradigm, promoting what Daphne Brooks calls, borrowing from Zap Mama, an "ancestry in progress." This work advocates for more diverse contemporary perspectives, while publicly acknowledging women and people of color of the past for their critical contributions.

Much like the prominence of white men critics does not signal the absence of alternative perspectives, the absence of prominent disabled critics does not mean that all popular music critics embody an entirely normative, nondisabled perspective. But written popular music criticism in major outlets rarely mentions disability as it pertains to the critic. As I argue throughout this book, many people experience stigmatized bodily differences that they do not think of as disability, concealing this from others or simply ignoring an impairment as irrelevant to their identity. This dearth of disabled critics

112 SPECTACULAR LISTENING

has been compounded by barriers to accessibility for music criticism, as well as misconceptions of disability as a personal—rather than structural—issue.

In order for a crip music criticism tradition to emerge alongside and entwined with race, gender, and class, the general non-disabled public needs to be convinced that disability represents a widely shared social identity—and that bodily difference affects how one listens to music. These reaction videos, as a somewhat new music critical tradition, offer a way of effectively centering bodies as the material site of media reception. Perhaps these listeners could simply describe their experiences in writing, but reaction videos represent a more accessible format for many people. They also resist some of the elisions that writing can make possible, primarily because they stage the act of listening rather than describe it. They honor a broader tradition of media reception in which sensory differences, mobility impairments, psychological struggles, neurodiversity, and embodied difference can all be valuable for appreciating various dimensions of music. In so doing, they help recover crip perspectives in the much broader history of popular music criticism.

In the next chapter, I consider a group of podcasters who explicitly frame their work around disability activism. Their work resonates with this chapter in various respects, particularly questions about ancestry and listening through others. While reaction videos are a domain of culture that may not always be intelligible as activism, the following chapter highlights podcasters who very much embody an activist role, in order to emphasize intersections between disability, listening, and sound.

4

Accessible Listening

Podcasts as Audible Models

Podcasts resemble popular music recordings in many respects. Both may be streamed or downloaded, usually circulating with other visual or textual materials. Both popular music and podcasts may combine sonic media recorded at various times, woven together into a new performance. They both may involve compositional structures, which may make use of vocal performances, timbre, rhythm, tempo, momentum, motifs, and contours of pitch. They may take on subjects through direct narrative or artistic abstraction. Both art forms yield celebrities and controversies. Their creators hone their craft, through rehearsals, technical knowledge, and skilled performances. Both may involve planning and improvisation, which can generate immersive experiences. If we take John Blacking's classically broad definition of music as "humanly organized sound,"[1] we may find that podcasts meet the criterion.

Thinking of podcasts as musical enables us to apply musical questions to the art of podcasting. In *Listen*, Peter Szendy asks: "Can one *make a listening listened to*?" He points out that we may understand music history differently, if we consider the way translation and arrangement (e.g., arranging symphony works for piano) as a form of listening: "My hypothesis here is that the history of arrangement—due to the fact that an arranger is a listener who signs and writes [their] listening—does indeed open up possibility of a history of listening *in music*."[2] In other words, composition can involve the act of translating listening into a performance, in order for others to hear how one interprets music and responds *in music*. I argue that we can use this question to examine podcasting as a sonic art that revolves around listening.

In their many varieties, podcasts often present listening as an audible subject and a practice. Podcasts take many forms—from surveys of new music to serial investigative journalism to conversational banter. They may feature a journalist reacting to new information. They may invite listeners to explore a particular piece of media along with the hosts. They may facilitate a

Spectacular Listening. Byrd McDaniel, Oxford University Press. © Oxford University Press 2024.
DOI: 10.1093/oso/9780197620458.003.0005

114 SPECTACULAR LISTENING

conversation that involves give and take between various guests, modeling ways people might exchange perspectives.

In this chapter, I explore three podcasts as sound-based performances of listening. The three podcasts are Power Not Pity, Disability Visibility, and Reid My Mind.[3] In these podcasts, the hosts present listening as a subject. Hosts model listening, and hosts ultimately create objects that may be listened to. In these various layers, podcast hosts offer various versions of accessible listening.

I consider accessible listening as one particularly inclusive subset of the spectacular listening case studies in this book. Spectacular listening involves the translation of private reception into a public display of skilled interpretation. As my case studies reveal, these acts of translation may be theatrical, over-the-top, and ostentatious. Alternatively, spectacular listening may involve more subtle acts of translation that nonetheless still turn private reception into a public exploration of listening itself, as exemplified by the podcasts in this chapter. I define accessible listening as a technique that seeks universal inclusion of listeners by attending to a wide range of bodily and sensory capabilities involved in the act of grasping meaning from sound media.

In these podcasts, the hosts promote disability activism, using podcasting as a means to emphasize perspectives marginalized in both mainstream media and overwhelmingly white disability-studies subcultures. All examples in this chapter feature people of color engaged in conversations about disability. I highlight the explicit politics of these podcasts, while also drawing attention to their craft. As their guests offer a wide variety of perspectives, these podcasters demonstrate modes of listening for their audiences, modeling what listening to and with disability might sound like. I separate their ideas into three themes: listening as exchange, listening technologies, and listening through others. In my conclusion, I consider how accessible listening always involves all three components—an intersection of bodies, technologies, and communities.

What Is a Podcast?

A podcast can be defined as a digital audio file that listeners stream or download, usually existing in a serial format with installments released over a period of time. In *Podcasting: The Audio Media Revolution*, Martin Spinelli and Lance Dann offer eleven elements that characterize podcasts: (1) listening on headphones, (2) consumption in public due to mobility of listeners, (3) listener ability to rewind or do "back scanning," (4) discovery of new content in more selective ways, (5) niche global subcultures and audiences, (6) social-media integration, (7) fewer gatekeepers for content, (8) free or oriented around a free model, (9) evergreen and available in perpetuity, (10) can be modified by creators even after release of content, and (11) no timing or scheduling constraints as with some previous forms of radio.[4] They describe podcasting as an "audio media revolution," recognizing the ways that many call our current moment the Golden Age of Podcasting in a way that echoes the Golden Age of Radio in the previous century.

While podcasts may seem novel in the history of audio media, they stem from a long line of audio-media predecessors. Radio radically altered listening norms, by making listening more mobile and customizable.[5] The many new forms of music and narrative audio that found their way onto the radio often evoked feelings of intimacy, anxiety, and intrigue,[6] quite similar to the characteristics some might attribute to contemporary podcasts. In *Sound Streams*, Andrew Bottomly describes how the internet catalyzed transformations in radio practices, and he suggests thinking of podcasts as radio rather than some distinct break with the past.[7] Indeed, the contemporary podcast landscape, including major podcasting companies and platforms, stems from many developments in the 1990s with downloadable audio shows and the rise of MP3 players that came thereafter in the 2000s. Many radio shows—like *This American Life* and *All Songs Considered*—began to offer podcast versions of their shows and now exist primarily as podcasts, but ambiguity between radio shows and podcasts remain. When I worked briefly at the NPR headquarters, I witnessed the transformation of radio content into streaming apps and podcasts, as journalists navigated how audio stories might fit these new networks, and I watched how radio formats gradually transformed into these alternative forms of downloadable streaming media.

I refer to podcasts and radio as distinct entities in this piece, as a result of the ways my interlocutors refer to them. In other words, even if technologically and theoretically podcasts can be considered as radio, I use "podcast" and "radio" in what follows simply as a convenient way to distinguish between the two. I agree with Bottomly's assertion as a theoretical argument, but as an ethnographer, I also hope to characterize how people refer to these media in everyday language. I do, however, ultimately take up another of Bottomly's suggestions that we think of podcasts as a practice, one that consists of multiple media. Podcasts are one of many audio practices, and popular music is a constellation of audio practices too. So in this chapter, I describe how people experience podcasting as unique, while acknowledging that these practices should connect to the extremely long and diverse history of many audio practice predecessors and contemporaries.

What Is the Point of Listening?

In my previous work, I have described podcasts as persuasive demonstrations of listening.[8] While many podcast hosts actively promote these conversations as an opportunity to hear the perspective of the interviewee, I argue that they also feature the hosts themselves performing the act of listening. The podcast host—the central perspective that provides continuity across episodes—becomes a kind of avatar for podcast listeners, offering a particular point of view. Alan Beck calls this a "point of listening."[9] I suggest that podcasts do much more than let their audiences listen in to a conversation. They enable listeners to experience a conversation from the vantage point of the host, whose listening techniques implicitly persuade audiences to adopt similar forms of listening. The host guides the conversation, models particular emotional responses, and frames the audience's understanding of the interviewee. The host makes their point of listening audible, through recording the act of listening as a creative practice.

Despite the many ways podcasts can target niche audiences and affinity groups, podcasts are hardly an all-inclusive artistic practice, and the model listeners who host podcasts can affirm ableist or anti-ableist stances in subtle but pervasive ways. Disabled podcasters, as part of a much longer history of disabled innovators, have been pioneers in making podcasting more accessible. As part of the 2019 Werk It! festival for women in podcasting, the podcast host of Power Not Pity, Bri M., gave a talk about accessibility in podcasting. Bri's advocacy includes arguing for practical steps, such as full transcripts for all episodes and image description for all digital content, and Bri also argues for an increasing awareness about disability issues among all podcasters, which can make disability a priority in podcast development. Speaking to a room full of people who produce podcasts, Bri addressed the need for accessible workspaces that include accommodations, benefits, and health care, while avoiding industry hiring practices that disproportionally exclude disabled people of color. Power

Not Pity models many of these measures, through extensive transcripts and multiple formats.

One of the key interventions in this podcast, as well as among all the podcasts in this chapter in general, is the emphasis on telling stories of disabled people of color *by* disabled people of color. Organizations—from the Harriet Tubman Collective to Sins Invalid—have worked to challenge the dominance of white voices within disability activism, which often suppress people of color who face significantly different experiences of disability from white folks. Black people are more likely to experience disabilities, as a result of the long-lasting effects of systemic racism. Their disabilities are less likely to be accommodated, and more often met with carcerality, police violence, disbelief, and dismissal. Disability should be considered intersectional, as always entwined with gender, sexuality, race, class, and geography, but stereotypical stories about disability often present it as an individual condition, disconnected from the kinds of structural inequities associated with other categories of identity. The work by Patty Berne and others, organized under the framework of disability justice,[10] pushes to empower queer and disabled folks of color as leaders against ableism, capitalism, and patriarchy. This framework recognizes that all social-justice movements must account for disability, or else they will be at risk of reproducing ableist harm. Similarly, all disability activism must be invested in these other struggles, or else it will be fated to reproduce these systems of oppression.

Methods

As a white podcast listener, I focus on podcasters of color telling their own stories, in order to support the disability-justice movement, and I strive to highlight the people doing important work to bring these issues to light. In Christopher Bell's "Introducing a White Disability Studies," he offers a trenchant critique of the white center that appears in many prominent works in disability studies, which often assumes "the disabled community is a monolithic one, struggling against the same oppressors, striving for identical degrees of dignity, recognition and cultural representation."[11] I hope my case studies throughout this book honor a variety of perspectives about disability in general, and I organize this chapter around podcasters of color in particular, in order to directly confront this white center that tends to dominate both disability studies and media studies. Indeed, the history of media practices and disability studies are much more complex and diverse than dominant narratives often portray, and I hope this chapter can one day be part of a more encompassing history, where many subcultures and communities can offer a wide range of approaches to disability justice.

I sought to examine these podcasts on three fronts. First, as an avid podcaster listener, I dwell on the particular compositions of these three podcasters. I listened to all of the episodes of each podcast (up until December 1, 2020): Power Not Pity (10 episodes), Disability Visibility (91 episodes), and Reid My Mind (130 episodes). I took notes on common themes and compositional strategies. All three podcasters know one another, appearing as guests on one another's podcasts, but each of them runs their own podcast independently. I assigned episodes to my classes, where we analyzed their form and content, and I spent time with a few episodes to engage in a close reading of them.

Second, I reflected on the craft of podcast creation. I once aspired to a career in radio journalism, leading me to intern at the National Public Radio headquarters in Washington DC. By working with Susan Stamberg, Bob Mondello, Neta Ulaby, and others, I had the benefit of learning the craft of creating audio stories, as well as the creative process that goes into their conceptualization. In my teaching career, I have also made countless audio lectures for students, culling together sound clips, scholarly insights of others, and my own words, and I spent the entire year of 2020 transforming all kinds of would-be in-person content in digital audio, including conversations with others in an interview format.

Finally, I have taught students in multiple classes how to use digital audio workstations to craft their own sound stories. These stories emphasized connections between music and social justice in their local communities, requiring students to transform field recordings into compelling narratives. The act of teaching podcast creation helped expand my awareness of the many ways people might approach podcast creation, which entail the same kinds of artistic questions musicians often consider. So I recognize the skills required to organize recordings into a cohesive narrative, taking listeners on a particular journey of discovery that also responsibly covers difficult content.

I include a case study on podcasting in order to challenge the visual connotations of spectacular listening as well. Spectacle may imply a *visual* striking scene, just as podcast may imply an exclusively auditory media practice. By positioning podcasts as multisensory, I aim to contribute to my broader argument that spectacular listening involves modes of listening far beyond the ears and the mind. I also approach podcasting as a multidimensional art, which centers around audio but extends to many different format and media. Podcasting may seem to be primarily audio form of media, but these three podcasts offer podcasting as multisensory, in a way that challenges characteristics of normal listening that I describe in my introduction to this book.

Much like all of the other case studies in this book, all of these podcasts circulate others' art forms as a component of a new artistic practice, and I chose all three podcasts because they so often centralize media reception as a subject. Power Not Pity was established in 2017, emerging out of what Bri calls a "fierce desire to change the way disabled people of color are seen in mass media." With a website that offers an extensive self-description as a "Black, Jamaican-American, queer, non-binary, disabled alien-prince from The Bronx," Bri has worked with record labels and music venues, turning to podcasting after a diagnosis of Multiple Sclerosis. A love for music shines throughout the episodes of the podcast. They open with sound composition combining harmonies and protest chants, which echo the words "power not pity." The episodes feature a range of artists and musicians in particular, many of whom share friendships with Bri and whose sonic art appears in the

Figure 4.1 Power Not Pity. Podcast Thumbnail.

i. The thumbnail for Power Not Pity displays a circle with those words written around the perimeter. Inside of the circle appears a person with a cape in a wheelchair with flames blowing behind the figure.

Figure 4.2 Reid My Mind. Podcast Thumbnail.

i. The thumbnail for Reid My Mind displays a green radio on the right. On the left, three symbols appear. The top symbol displays the word "Read" with an "i" replacing the "a." The word "my" appears below this with a mind underneath.

episodes. Episodes include expansive topics with titles such as: "Awakening Our Powers feat. Ade Raphael," "Infinite Lives feat. Eman Rimawi," and "Is God Inaccessible feat. Zaynab Shahar."

Reid My Mind comes from Thomas Reid, whose website describes the podcast in this way: "Stories and profiles of compelling people impacted by all degrees of blindness and disability. Plus, Reid explores his own experiences in his unique way of pairing his words with music and sound design."[12] Reid is a Black man who became blind as a result of cancer, ultimately deciding to launch an advocacy organization and pursue podcasting. The podcast is sometimes referred to as "Reid My Mind Radio,"

Figure 4.3 Disability Visibility. Podcast Thumbnail.
i. The thumbnail for Disability Visibility depicts Alice Wong's face with red headphones, sunglasses, lipstick, and a bi-pap machine on her nose. Below read the words: "Politics, Culture, Media: Hosting by Alice Wong."

again revealing an ambiguity of the radio-podcast divide given that the podcast has the word radio in its title. The podcast started in 2014, beginning with an episode that documents Reid at a Stevie Wonder concert with his family, and subsequent episodes feature his recurring interests in audio production, sound design, and popular music. Episodes include: "Music On My Mind," "On the Mic with Roy Samuelson," and "Black on Audio Description."

Finally, Disability Visibility began in 2017 under the direction of Alice Wong, emerging out of an online project by the same name that began in 2014. Wong created the podcast in order to affirm that "disabled narratives matter and that they belong to us." She describes herself as a disabled activist, media maker, and consultant, and her podcasts frequently feature artists. Her episodes tend to frame particular cultural arenas by focusing on one or two guests with a distinct topic, such as "Disabled Artists," "Storytelling," "Disabled Comedians," "Black Deaf Filmmakers," "Film Criticism," and "Disabled Musicians." All of these podcasts feature quite a range of material, but all offer a reflection on disabled artmaking as a core theme, something that they feature as a subject of conversations and as a practice enacted through podcasting.

Listening as Exchange

Accessible listening involves honoring the importance of listening itself, as a profound exercise in the exchange of perspectives and a specific practice of recognizing how these exchanges occur through bodily abilities in a certain situation. All three podcasts attend to both of these dynamics—listening in general and listening in particular. In this section, I explore examples of both approaches to listening, in order to reveal how listening is both a feature and a subject of this work.

Disability Visibility presents a model of listening to others that honors a flexible approach to time. Often called "crip time,"[13] this non-normative approach to time embraces pacing that suits the particular abilities of folks, who might require different amounts of time to participate in various tasks. Crip time emerged as a rejection of the many aspects of disability that tend to be measured in time, from the practical time required for a particular task to developmental stages of people as they age and grow.

On episode eleven of Disability Visibility called "Crip Bodies and Crip Aging," Alice Wong speaks with Leroy Moore. He's the founder of Krip Hop Nation, a hip-hop collective featuring musicians with disabilities and an educational network that promotes disability workshops. The two are talking about listening to one's elders.

> WONG: It is a huge achievement just to survive and get to the ages that we are. I don't think that's really valued or celebrated, and our culture doesn't appreciate the wisdom of our elders. What are your thoughts about aging and disability?
>
> MOORE: Yeah. I think in this society, in this world we live in with capitalism, [we] don't really take into account our elders. It's such a shame. When I was younger, in my teens and 20s, I used to work at this summer camp for people with disabilities, and every session was different. The last session was elders, and I had a really good chance . . . I had a chance in my life when I was younger to really sit down and listen to older people that had CP, you know? And now, I look back on it. It's like, wow. Those times was like gold. Because I think we don't take the time, especially now, with the Internet, we don't really take the time to really listen to our elders and take in that knowledge.

Moore reflects on the importance of listening to elders as a practice in self-discovery, where wisdom can be passed down from elders in a community.

This conversation echoes my conclusion to Chapter 3, which considers questions of lineage and ancestry in music criticism. So the conversation between Wong and Moore offers an expansive perspective on listening to others, which translates knowledge about disability—Cerebral Palsy in particular—through generations.

An important part of this conversation is the presence of disabled voices—not just in the metaphorical sense. Both Wong and Moore have non-normative voices that represent a type of vocal variation often excluded from the hyper-efficient editing mode of many mainstream podcasts and radio. While at NPR, I remember how people would train their voices to sound a particular way on the radio, involving a specific fast-paced cadence, non-accented pronunciations,[14] and efficient scrips for information delivery. In distinction, Wong's podcast models an alternative way of sounding. With a high-pitched voice, Wong speaks slowly with the sounds of a bi-bap machine punctuating her speech every few words. Her sentences are careful and unhurried. Moore speaks slowly as well, affecting pronunciation of particular syllables. Both speak from a position of expertise and wisdom on the podcast, challenging ableist assumptions that link speech with intellect (assumptions that stigmatize both neurodivergence and speech differences). Their dialogue comes together in a way that challenges the more conventional cadence of podcasting.

Wong's podcast offers a deliberate approach to what Alison Kafer calls "reimagining our notions of what can and should happen in time."[15] Wong's many guests speak and listen in a wide variety. Her guests use ASL interpreters, augmentative and alternative communication devices, and many other modes of communication. In an essay, Wong directly acknowledges her vocal style as an intervention into ableist media practices in an essay:

> Radio can be a familiar friend, source of knowledge, a marker of time and place. But as a cultural institution, what constitutes a "good voice" in radio reflects and transmits cultural norms and structures. By accepting the default "good voice" as one that is able-bodied, one that is pleasant, clear, articulate and devoid of any markers of disability, you erase disabled people . . . How do disabled people take these instruments and make them ours by cripping them with our culture?[16]

In his work on radio, Bill Kirkpatrick describes how non-disabled voices are ubiquitous in radio (Diane Rhem being the notable exception), as a result of

124　SPECTACULAR LISTENING

a "capitalist logic" and "listener-centered approach to speaker selection" that operates on the assumption that disabled voices are less pleasing or engaging. Indeed, Wong continues, in the same essay, to explore her own thoughts about her voice:

> [T]he Bi-Pap pushes breaths of air into a person's lungs at a set rate and volume; these breaths enter the body through a tube and mask. It is a life-saver and something I'll use for the rest of my life. Two years ago, I needed to start using the Bi-Pap during most of the day, which called for a lot of changes and adjustments . . . As I attend meetings and events, I noticed a difference in the way people relate to me. I have to repeat myself be-cause people can't understand me. If a breath is coming in right in the middle of speech, I have to pause, creating unnatural and awkward speech patterns . . . A big part of my identity, ego, and self-image is centered on my voice and writing. I had to confront my discomfort and accept my new sound and body that has become increasingly cyborg-like as time goes on. To paraphrase a beloved poem in the disability community by Laura Hershey, a woman who also used a Bi-Pap, I continually work on regaining a sense of pride by practicing.

While Wong opens up about her self-consciousness at times about her own voice, her podcasting practice opens up a space with a wide variety of voices, creating a domain where vocal variation can be typical. These non-normative voices may seem remarkable in mainstream radio or podcasting, but they ap-pear quite commonplace and unremarkable in Disability Visibility. Wong's podcast affirms that people want to listen to conversations that sound like their own, in all the varieties of ways people engage with one another.

And she offers many possibilities for how someone might listen. While transcripts have increasingly become an accessibility strategy for podcasts in recent years, Disability Visibility goes far beyond this offering. For example, the podcast episodes are hosted on the *Disability Visibility Project* website for free. The site offers hyperlinks to additional reading materials, summaries of episodes, five possible ways of subscribing, keywords, two formats for transcripts, and the option to play in a new window, embed, or download the file.

Wong's podcast exemplifies diverse strategies for listening as a form of ex-change in a specific sense, and all three of these podcasts also honor the act of listening as a more abstract practice. Power Not Pity exemplifies the way that these podcasts prioritize a more abstract approach to listening, which values an exchange of perspectives and the way someone might be changed by hearing others. At the end of one of Bri's episodes, Bri asks a recurring question of all of the guests: "What's your disabled superpower?" In this instance, Bri asks Lilac Vylette Maldonado, who identifies as a sick and disabled, neurodivergent, two-spirit, Chicanx femme. Lilac's answer to the question is:

> I want to be remembered as somebody who embodied radical love. And I think that one of the most important facets of radical love is radical vulnerability. I think that for me, as somebody who has oftentimes felt very vulnerable in public, I think that it's shown me that vulnerability is not a status of weakness. It is actually a, you know, a conduit for strength.

Lilac suggests a definition of vulnerability that may be empowering. The quote recalls the acts of performers in Chapter 1, who render themselves vulnerable onstage as an act of empowerment. Listening can open up that state of vulnerability, enabling people to be receptive to influence from others in a moment of exchanging perspectives.

Power Not Pity centers themes of self-awareness and growth, creating conversational contexts in which listening can enable self-care. In another episode (Episode 10), Bri responds to a guest in saying: "Our Black and brown disabled ancestors have a way of burying knowledge inside of us and it is only waiting to be watered by self-awareness." This framing acknowledges how listening can involve embodied, subconscious forms of knowledge, which can be enacted and enhanced through listening. Listening, in other words, can provide access to latent feelings or forms of understanding that can be activated.

In various ways, these podcasts celebrate the practice of receptivity to others' perspectives, in acts that involve attention to the specific conduits through which we listen and the abstract acts through which generational knowledge can be exchanged. They foreground an accessibility that goes both ways. Accessibility implies someone being able to access another perspective or a conversation, and accessibility also implies someone giving oneself up to be accessed by others, through the act of sharing and revealing aspects of an interior experience.

126 SPECTACULAR LISTENING

Listening Technologies

One of the core themes of these podcasts, which recurs in various discussions, is how central technology can be to the act of listening. Because disabled people are alienated or oppressed by the technological assumptions built into many communal places, the hosts spend time talking about how technologies can be used to gain access to public places, services, and conversations. These technologies can involve high-tech hacks of new technologies, but they also include the widespread adoption of relatively conventional technologies. In this section, I emphasize how these podcasts center access through technologies as listening devices.

The affordances of contemporary media platforms come from many inventions by disabled innovators—from tech wearables to SMS text messaging. As Reid puts it when he was interviewed on Bri's podcast, "Blind folks were doing podcasting in a sense for like years passing around audio cassettes, you know what I'm saying?" Reid's comment reflects a similar sentiment raised by Amy Cohen Efron in Chapter 2, who points to video tapes as a predecessor to contemporary d/Deaf TikTok practices.

One example of how specific technological innovations inform contemporary media practices comes from the story of variable playback speed, a common feature associated with podcast listening. Spinelli and Dann describe the ability to customize listening speeds of podcasts as a particularly appealing feature that distinguishes them from traditional radio. For example, on Spotify, a user may play a podcast at 0.5x, 0.8x, 1x, 1.2x, 1.5x, 2s, or 3x the original speed. The variable playback rate, which does not affect the pitch of the podcast, represents an innovation catalyzed by blind speed-readers in the early twentieth century. Mara Mills and Jonathan Sterne give an account of this history offered by Harvey Lauer.[17] They describe the use of what we today call audio books in blind education, which translated written text into sound recordings. Unlike reading a book with ink-based text, these talking books tended to be played on turntables with fixed speeds, such that blind readers could not determine how slow or fast to engage with a text. Through a series of life-long experiments and the eventual discovery that variable playback speed could be possible without pitch shifting, Lauer and others eventually became part of the long history of variable playback speed that informs these podcast listening options today.

The practice of adapting technologies is something featured on these podcasts, in a way that valorizes creativity as a disabled practice. In one of

ACCESSIBLE LISTENING 127

Reid's episodes called "I Do It My Way," he describes how much he relies upon translation as part of his compositional techniques. He gives an audio tour of his process of composing episodes at home, using the digital audio workstation Reaper. He makes use of screen readers, which render digital text and icons as audible words. We hear snippets of this process in the podcast, coming to understand how he listens as part of his creative process. He describes using Skype as a preferable way to get good audio quality. He accounts for how various rooms shape his recordings, giving listeners a comparison of audio quality in his computer area versus his closet, and he also describes the editing process of using one earbud plugged in to his computer as he puts finishing touches on an episode. The whole process documents a dense web of listening technologies, physical spaces, and bodily interactions with media, which constitute his compositional approach.

The idea of disabled listeners as hackers can honor a history of innovation, recognizing the many creative solutions that stem from the need for more accessible spaces. In episode 3 of Disability Visibility, Jessie Lorenz tells Wong: "Technology allows us to hack our disabilities." The executive director of the Independent Living Resource Center San Francisco, Lorenz, who is blind, described using Aira smart glasses to Wong. These sunglasses connect with her phone, enabling her to tap a button and receive live assistance from a sighted person who can direct her movements in public. For example, the person can describe where an Uber is located, how to find a walking path, a grocery story item, or the activity happening in a new place. She pays an expensive $89/100 minutes. She tells a story of going to the National Archives with the glasses, where she used an assistant named Drew on the Aira phone to read through documents at the archives. As Lorenz describes her listening to Wong, podcast listeners listen to their conversation, understanding how listening can have an inherent interdependency that links technologies and people through a chain of communication.

While these examples represent creative technological hacks and usages, the high-tech "solutions" to disability problems can often play upon deeply ableist ideas that celebrate a technologically utopian future without any bodily differences. Jillian Weise writes:

There is a cyborg hierarchy. They like us best with bionic arms and legs. They like us Deaf with hearing aids, though they prefer cochlear implants. It would be an affront to ask the Hearing to learn sign language. Instead they wish for us to lose our language, abandon our culture, and consider

128 SPECTACULAR LISTENING

> ourselves cured. They like exoskeletons, which none of us use. They don't count as cyborgs those of us who wear pacemakers or go on dialysis. Nor do they count those of us kept alive by machines, those of us made ambulatory by wheelchairs, those of us on biologics or antidepressants. They want us shiny and metallic in their image.[18]

She points to fantasies of technological intervention that erase disability or render disability as a sort of fetishized superhuman power. Weise recognizes that technologies can provide assistance and yet they can also yield new forms of oppression, both through their affordances and through the kinds of imaginative post-disability society that they attempt to produce.

Universal design offers one alternative to these high-tech forms of ableism. In one episode of Disability Visibility called "Assistive Technology," Alice Wong and Lateef McLeod discuss the need to break away from high-tech solutions and move toward the implementation of assistive technology in common consumer devices not exclusively meant for folks with disabilities. Wong interviews McLeod, a poet and doctoral student in anthropology and social change at California Institute of Integral Studies. He lists the assistive technologies that he uses in everyday life: "The assistive technologies that I cannot live without are my power wheelchair, because that is how I get around, and the Proloquo2Go and Proloquo4Text apps on iPad and my iPhone . . . and of course I cannot live without my laptop." He describes how these devices, many of them under the broad umbrella of augmentative and alternative communication, enable "nonverbal communication for people with speech disabilities, using symbols, letters, and words on low-tech and high-tech devices." The two go on to discuss the often prohibitively expensive AAC devices, which many cannot afford. Alternatively, the push for universal design—design that maximizes participants with a variety of bodies and abilities—has put many apps and functionalities into devices like iPads and iPhones, which can be much cheaper to obtain and use. They both talk about a desire for these AAC devices to be better integrated with phones and laptops. Accessible listening can be a way of thinking about what universal design means for podcasting, simply in terms of creating podcast media that speaks—literally and figuratively—to the broadest group of listeners.[19]

Many low-tech solutions can offer opportunities to practice accessible listening. The use of Google docs, PDFs, and various forms of captioning can offer a more significant impact on access than some of the high-tech ideas that often circulate as (ableist) solutions to disability. On Disability Visibility, Reid was featured as a guest, and he describes his emerging awareness about transcriptions. He recounts doing an episode with Lainey Fiengold, a disability rights lawyer and pioneer in digital accessibility. Reid says:

> I actually did a story on Lainey, Lainey Feingold. She's a great advocate and a great help for accessibility, and during that, she was just really cool about it—she was like, "Hey, so, when this is done, just let me know because I wanna make sure that it's transcribed." And at that time, I wasn't transcribing. She was willing to have someone transcribe it. She was gonna pay for it. And I sat with that for a while, while I was producing that episode. It really hit me. She's walking that walk, you know? That's the right thing to do. That is absolutely the right thing to do because how can I be out here talking about, "Hey, this is inaccessible! And this should be accessible for the blind community," but meanwhile, I'm not making my own stuff accessible for another community? So, I said hey, let me start it.

Honest about his learning process, Reid recognizes the need to translate things into a format that may not be preferable to him but affirms his desire to include listeners with a wide range of listening modalities.

All three podcasts dwell on the idea that all listening involves technological assistance. These technologies may include spaces, architectures, electronics, and networks. Wong puts this succinctly in episode 3: "I think the lines between technology and assistive technology is really blurry, right? Everybody who has an iPhone can use Siri, and Siri is a form of assistive technology for a lot of people with disabilities. So, I think that the lines are blurry, and when more people think of it as a standard feature, it could only help everyone."

Accessibility through technologies can take many forms—running the gamut between high-tech hacks and low-tech solutions. In all cases, technology offers an important realm in which power dynamics play out, determining who can access information and in what way. These podcasts centralize technology as a core part of a listening practice. The hosts emphasize how listening technologies not only assist disabled listeners but offer a fundamental foundation for all forms of listening.

Much of the scholarship on listening within music studies explores listening as an abstract technique that occurs independent of technologies and other people. Music analyses may examine a particular pop song without any reference to how that song might be different depending on how something

130 SPECTACULAR LISTENING

listens and in what format. These podcast hosts draw attention to the ways that technologies matter, in terms of format, circulation, reception, sharing, and ultimately understanding.

Listening Through Others

People not only listen *to* other bodies, but they also listen *through* other bodies. My two previous sections dwell on listening in podcast exchanges, as well as the role of technology in making listening accessible. In this final section, I focus on listening through other bodies, in the sense that podcast hosts become avatars for the listening of others.

A recurring topic across many disability-focused podcasts is how people consume media, which entails questions of how media representations match up against experiences of disability in real lives. In Leroy Moore's book *Black Disabled Ancestors*, he tells a story from the vantage point of 2020 that could easily be today:

> We must realize in 2020 that disabled people have ancestors that left knowledge, art, music, culture, politics, and a lot of pain for us to pick up, build on, and to tell the harsh truth. I noticed in my late teens in the early 1980s that what creates a solid foundation of self is knowing your history, but that is easy to say and hard to do, especially in the 1980s for a Black disabled teenager before the Americans with Disabilities Act, Disability Studies and Disability Arts/Culture. This solid self-empowerment foundation started when I was watching TV back in 1979 and, for the first time, saw a Black disabled man on TV. I screamed to my mother from the living room, "Mom, I'm on TV!" My mom came into the living room, then she started laughing. "No, that is Porgy!" . . . That started my home education about being Black and disabled.[20]

The story reveals how media narratives—in this instance a musical—enact narratives of disability and ableism, creating a self-conception of disability for consumers at home.[21]

The DIY nature of podcast creation offers a sharp contrast to the limited media representations of generations past, which have been vastly diversified through social media. In episode 9 of Power Not Pity, Bri interviews Reid, asking him about why he gravitated toward podcasting. Reid responds:

ACCESSIBLE LISTENING 131

REID: Audio was something I was interested in I guess as a teenager, you know growing up in the 80s like that and in the 70s with hip-hop emerging and all. I had dreams of being a DJ and MC. I was a tabletop MC, you know, and I was the beat maker the lunch room and all that, right? . . . I think I came back to audio when I lost my sight . . . I just really got into it. I just really got into the whole the aspect of writing, you know, um, because that's the way I like to tell my stories . . .

BRI: B: I mean, you've got that that kind of like hip-hop Spirit right? Like always about the culture and always about like for us, you know for Us by us and I love that spirit because that's what drives me too.

Reid presents podcasting as a logical extension of his musical impulses. Interestingly, he traces his musical background to the practice of DJing, a musical practice that revolves around curating the work of other artists in a way that transforms them into new compositions.[22] DJs, in other words, very much turn listening into a performative act, using a listening device (the turntable) as a musical instrument.

On Reid's podcast, examples abound of detailed discussions that might otherwise never find a place in more conventional media channels. For example, one of the prominent themes on Reid My Mind is audio description, which enables blind folks to follow along with a film either at home or in a theater. In one podcast, he talks about Black Panther and the Black community's excitement about the film's mostly Black cast. "The vibe of this movie was unapologetically Black," he says on the episode. As he goes to the film with his family and proceeds to listen to the audio description during the film with headphones, he hears a voice that he describes as a white British man, providing audio description for the entire film. The voice totally diminishes the experience for Reid. Other factors add onto this lackluster situation, such as when the audio description fails to recount the credits to give him a full sense of the cast that motivated him wanting to see the movie in the first place.

Over the course of a few episodes, Reid describes the prominence of less-than-desirable audio description in many films, which often gets made by third-party companies outside of the artistic direction of the director. So they rarely feel like part of the aesthetic package of the film. He goes on to describe how he must constantly contend with the whiteness of these audio descriptions and glitchy technology that fails to effectively work with a movie.

132 SPECTACULAR LISTENING

Reid imagines a world of mass media that could be otherwise. He suggests more Black folks writing and recording audio descriptions. He considers expanding the temporal limitations of the movie for blind viewers. For example, he imagines audio description that could familiarize blind audiences with characters' voices or context before the film actually begins (as is the standard with plays and musicals), and he explores these ideas by bringing in podcast guests who work in audio description, in order to think through these dynamics. Reid's example reveals how listening to a film relies upon others, whose own artistic interpretations script the artistic interpretations of listeners.

Throughout this book, I give numerous examples of listening through others, in which listening becomes a social act that relies on the persuasive translations of others. Reaction videos, which I analyze in Chapter 3, are an entire genre comprised of people reacting to media, which then scripts and influences subsequent reactions. Air guitar competitions, from Chapter 1, revolve around theatrical re-stagings of guitar solos, which convince audience members to listen to music in particular ways. Podcasting is perhaps more subtle, but it nonetheless involves an audience listening to someone listen to someone or something.

While the case studies in this book and specific examples in this chapter may seem sui generis and/or particularly pertinent to online performance genres, the act of listening through others is a quite common facet of off-line musical practices as well. For example, in his book *Music and Autism*, Michael Bakan describes the Artism Ensemble, which features neurodiverse children (many of whom with Autism spectrum disorder diagnoses) who perform with musicians and their parents.[23] Bakan describes interviewing a member of the Artism ensemble who, despite being a creative music maker in previous ensembles, stimmed while the group was making music together. The Autistic Self Advocacy Network defines stimming: "We might do the same movement over and over again. This is called 'stimming,' and it helps us regulate our senses."[24] When Bakan asked the girl why she wasn't making music, she responded:

> I have characters in my head. I think about them a *ton*, like probably more than I think about my own life. That's fine with me because they kind of relate to me . . . And what was happening was, they were all musicians, the people in my head, and so I was imagining them playing the instruments, like I had one on the *zheng* and one on the *djembe*, and everything.

ACCESSIBLE LISTENING **133**

Thus stimming was connected to conjuring this musical group in her head. She later describes the ways that these performers were proxies for her own embodied relationship to music. Bakan writes: "[She] has shown that her decision to not play instruments early on in Artism, to instead stim or listen silently while jamming with the 'band of brothers' in her head, was just that a decision . . . a choice determined by her preference." In other words, listening through proxies can be a particularly enjoyable way to engage with music.

Indeed, in a wide range of examples, people listen with and through others. In concerts, people may turn from the group on a stage in order to engage with other listeners in a live audience. People may listen to music in the car and conjure images of performers in their heads. People may pantomime popular music parts, as they listen with headphones. All of these everyday examples are instances in which people listen through other bodies.

From a certain vantage point, podcasting can be conceived as a vast network of people who listen to one another. All three podcasts in this chapter place an emphasis on building a broad coalition. Describing a desire to create podcasts that can acknowledge underrepresented perspectives, Bri says:

> I hope to eventually create a network for podcasters with disabilities just so that people can find us more immediately and connect with us in yet another safe space. I would love to have a podcasting conference for disabled people. If we have a conference for all of us who are making new media and trying to put our voices and our experiences out there on the map, then we should definitely have a venue for our voices, to amplify our voices.

While Bri focuses on the work to be done, the three podcasts in this chapter represent 231 episodes (and counting) that document people with disabilities telling their stories, essentially creating the kind of media that Moore wanted as a youth.

The network created by these podcasters differs from the one on musical.ly in Chapter 2, in terms of the decentralized nature of podcasting. The community forged by people on musical.ly existed as part of a single company, which then became acquired by another company. Thus the musical.ly community became susceptible to dramatic changes, suppression of content, and changing affordances. By contrast, podcasting is not centralized as property of a single company. Podcasts can be distributed in many formats and platforms. Podcasts can also be made using a wide variety of software and hardware, as opposed to musical.ly or TikTok videos that must be made in the apps themselves. While

134 SPECTACULAR LISTENING

large podcasting companies have begun to form conglomerates within the podcasting industry, the podcasting practice remains quite diverse, enabling DIY content that offers a wide range of ideologies, identities, and approaches. The definition of podcasting even remains in flux.

While podcasting may seem to offer a vast array of networks for diverse perspectives, media scholars have been critical of kinds of egalitarianism attached to online networks. Benjamin Peters reminds us: "A network is not a map."[25] His work untangles the functioning of networks from the abstract representations of them, which often present networks as decentralized, egalitarian spaces. The messaging from social-media companies for digital platforms can often present them as empowering platforms for lofty ideals, such as democracy, togetherness, and freedom of expression, but these platforms can often represent extremely nebulous and complex dynamics of power. As I discuss in my conclusion with the sharing imperative, these platforms can often present sharing of information as empowering, when in fact this sharing can be deeply disempowering and coercive. Building on the works of dana boyd and others, ethnomusicologist Kyra Gaunt theorizes "context collapse" to explain how the online dance practices of Black girls on YouTube can often spread in ways that "reduce spatial, temporal, and social boundaries for both the viewer and subscribers," obscuring the context that make Black artistic practices so significant in the first place.[26] In other words, the networked nature of online sociality can increase exposure to harm for historically oppressed groups in digital subcultures, as media circulates beyond the cultural context of its initial creation. The fact that the podcasters in this chapter frequently interact and appear on each others' podcasts, as well as those in a much broader network, helps preserve this context and essential fabric for holding a community together. They reveal how a healthy network can require maintenance and upkeep.

The podcasters in this chapter demonstrate an inherent interdependency on others in the act of listening, which can enhance a sense of collaboration among participants but also expose people to risks. In other words, the podcasters who share their perspectives do so for the benefit of listeners but also at the risk of rendering oneself vulnerable to potential ableist replies or misrepresentations. Indeed, accessibility to a network can be a liability for all participants, just as much as it can be an enabling feature of an egalitarian community. By attending to listening as social and shared, these three podcasters reveal that people never listen individually but always listen in ways informed by others' listenings.

Podcasting as Accessible

While researching podcasts for this chapter, I found myself confronted with the similarities between physical and digital spaces, particularly in terms of accessibility. One conversation with Kalyn Heffernan stuck with me. A rapper, educator, and activist, Kalyn performs under the name Wheelchair Sports Camp. The group is part of Leeroy Moore's Krip Hop organization, which supports anti-ableist, disability-centered hip hop. Kalyn's music also appears as a theme song in the Disability Visibility podcast, and her website describes her work in this way:

> Fronted by the wheelchair using, rap heavy, beat-making, freedom fighting producer, educator, foul mouthed, queer rebel rouser Kalyn, the band is a combination of live and electronic instruments with a more noisy, jazzy, experimental, combination to the traditional hip-hop group. Raised by the DIY (Do It Yourself) spirit of experimental independence, the band has since relied on interdependence in order to stretch into theatre, performance art, public television, politics, prison tours, permanent installations, and more to come.

Kalyn and I spoke about the DIY spirit that informs the music, particularly how the music comes from alternative spaces for disabled artists in the Denver area. She reflected on these DIY spaces in a pretty critical way: "I'm a DIY punker. I came up in a lot of inaccessible places . . . So there are spots that my band came up in and now I'm like 'fuck those places.' I could get in because I'm small and because I have people to lift me. Not everyone can get into those places. So I'm advocating for safe places." She went on to express a sense of deep conflict rooted in a desire to spread her message by performing everywhere, while nonetheless feeling like performing in inaccessible places represents a tacit endorsement of those places.

Her description of these DIY places in Colorado, famous for its underground music scenes in makeshift locations, struck a contrast with the kinds of accessible spaces described beautifully by s.e. smith in an essay on "crip space":

> I am spellbound. I am also overwhelmed, feeling something swell in my throat as I look out across the crowd, to the wheelchair and scooter users at the front of the ranked seating, the ASL interpreter in crisp black next to

the stage. Canes dangle from seat backs and a gilded prosthetic leg gleams under the safety lights. A blind woman in the row below me turns a tiny model of the stage over in her hands, tracing her fingers along with it in time to the audio description.[27]

Such a space offers a model of centering disability, rather than treating disability accommodations as an added feature to a pre-existing space.

These two examples—DIY spaces and crip spaces—call to mind two core challenges of accessible listening. One challenge is abandoning ableist structures that exclude certain listeners through a rejection of the mainstream. DIY spaces often operate with an ethos of subcultural rejection of mainstream strictures. In order to foster accessible listening, we have to directly challenge the narrowness of listening, in a way that can be transgressive and counter-hegemonic. In his book *Extraordinary Measures*, Joseph Straus describes *disablist hearing* as an alternative to normative ideas people often attach to musical listening. Straus writes of music theory: "Each theory imagines—effectively calls into being—a suitable listener."[28] Accessible listening involves challenging the theory that undergirds this suitable listener, opening up space for an inclusive collection of listeners who listen differently and together. The impulse to listen against the grain appears throughout these podcasts, as they challenge some of the conventions and assumptions of mainstream audio media.

The second challenge of accessible listening involves consciously curating multiple access points to listening. Accessibility as a practice protects the ways people might access sounds through various senses and contexts. In a rejection of normal listening, we must also celebrate the many alternative forms of listening that can give people access to sonic media. In *Top 40 Democracy*, Eric Weisbard argues that pop music on the radio offers multiple access points to modernity, and he traces a history of how music formats enable people to gain entry into questions of identity and collective belonging, through finding rival mainstreams in popular music.[29] His ideas offer a framework for not only radio formats but more granular approaches as well, including individual songs that can be radically different depending on the particular format and delivery mechanisms through which one accesses it. The podcasts in this chapter imagine ways that musical listening could become more accessible, by honoring the multiple senses, media, and formats that enable listening.

In my Introduction, I define *normal listening* as the dominant regime of listening in the United States, consisting of three characteristics: ear-based listening, a concept of sound as a bounded object, and a celebration of meaningful listening as something that may be verbalized. The model of listening we receive from these three podcasts cut against all three of these values. They present listening as something that happens through a dependence on other people and devices. They challenge the idea that sound should be a bounded object for analysis, instead offering podcasts in a variety of formats that expand the boundaries of the "work" of itself. And third, they challenge normative conceptions of voice and verbalized explanations as the most sophisticated way to demonstrate understanding of something.

The practice of accessible listening could be developed in a much more expansive way, encompassing podcasting infrastructures, industries, web content accessibility guidelines of platforms, recording technologies, software, advertisements, and many other domains. As I demonstrate throughout this book, I approach listening as an abstract and expansive engagement with sound, and I would suggest that an even broader approach to listening could inform future scholarship on these other areas.

Perhaps one critique of my theory of listening throughout this book might be: are these practices really listening? To pose this more specifically, someone might ask: would someone reading a transcript still be listening? These podcasts, in their various subjects and approaches, demonstrate how these questions can stem from a much deeper sense that certain sensory perceptions are truer, deeper, or better than others. For example, some may suggest that music is fundamentally composed of frequencies perceived through the ears, and auditory perception remains the principal way people should perceive music. However, listening involves a much more complex interaction between our own bodies and senses, as well as collaboration among the many technologies that make listening possible.

These three podcasts call upon us to listen to listening. In the *Race of Sound*, Nina Sun Eidsheim describes Jimmy Scott, a singer who navigated many stereotypes about Blackness, masculinity, and disability. She writes of his artistry in this way: "That is, if we listen to our own listening to Scott, he offers us the opportunity to confront the *habitus* of that listening, that choir of voices to which we compare every new voice."[30] Eidsheim argues that great artists often invent new material by leveraging expectations of listeners, in ways that may call attention to the listening act itself.

138 SPECTACULAR LISTENING

Our sensory possibilities determine how we listen. We listen through avatars and machines. We listen through other people. The strength of Reid My Mind, Power Not Pity, and Disability Visibility comes from their ability to dwell on the profound and peculiar aspects of listening. They confront an inherited and socialized habitus of listening, and they honor the way disability can inform listening in a way that can add depth and dimensions to the experience of sound media.

Conclusion

When Spectacular Becomes Standard

What happens when spectacular listening becomes standard? In my introduction to this book, I juxtapose two broad listening regimes—normal listening and spectacular listening. Normal listening occupies a dominant, privileged, and powerful position in our contemporary musical cultures. Normal listening is enshrined in our music halls and music institutions. With an emphasis on private contemplation, masterful consumption, and ear-based analysis of sounds, normal listening is implicit in our textbooks, music reviews, and everyday language. Normal listening is default and also ableist. Normal listening is so ubiquitous as to be almost unremarkable.

Contemporary digital cultures bring forth alternatives, challenging the dominance of normal listening. Each of my case studies offers a version of spectacular listening, where people translate private reception into a public display of interpretation. Spectacular listening emphasizes porous boundaries between sounds and the body, where play can be as meaningful as serious critical analysis. Spectacular listening offers the idea that embodied reactions to media can be the most convincing demonstration of musical understanding. In my survey of these different case studies, I offer a few possible examples of listening as an expressive practice, which are constituted in a wide variety of networks, formats, and locations.

Despite their seemingly niche status as subcultures, these examples also seem to be growing in popularity. In the course of writing this book, podcasting has become a major industry. TikTok has emerged as the most popular global amateur music practice, stemming from its origins as musical. ly. Reaction videos, once a specific video genre on YouTube, are now prevalent in the affordances of many apps, and reactivity, as an affective bodily response to media, has become quite commonplace as a way to express ideas about popular media. Think of clicks, likes, emojis, videos responses, and countless other ways for listeners to input their feelings about sharable media without using words. Finally, pantomiming to popular music—central to US

Spectacular Listening. Byrd McDaniel, Oxford University Press. © Oxford University Press 2024.
DOI: 10.1093/oso/9780197620458.003.0006

140   SPECTACULAR LISTENING

Air Guitar—is now a widespread phenomenon in a way that entwines dance, humor, and gesture. One can hardly go in a public place without seeing people filming videos of themselves in sync with popular media, in order to post the videos online.

The once marginal status of these practices make them robust—if not somewhat unconventional—sites for disability activism. In all of my case studies, I highlight how creators with disabilities found opportunity in these performance genres, leveraging listening into an activist opportunity. I define activism broadly and expansively. Some of my case studies explicitly aim for disability activism in a formal sense, such as Chapters 3 and 4. In Chapters 1 and 2, my case studies emphasize disability in a more subtle way, creating affinities, alliances, and common understandings around bodily differences. All of these examples represent ways that creators with disabilities have creatively imagined new modes of listening, which offer greater inclusive possibilities than normal listening.

So I return to my question: what happens when spectacular listening becomes the standard approach to listening online? In this conclusion, I consider what broader values are attached to spectacular listening, particularly the ways that spectacular listening can usher in a set of ethical questions about new listening norms. I organize my thoughts into three categories: the sharing imperative, syncing out loud, and marginal practices. These areas represent some of the broader considerations of spectacular listening as an increasingly popular practice. My conclusion offers opportunities for future scholarship, which might consider some of the consequences and new questions that emerge when spectacular listening becomes a more standard and recognizable approach to listening.

The Sharing Imperative

Digital platforms demand sharing. At the time of writing this book, major debates are taking place about privacy, surveillance, personal data, and digital rights, and these debates will exist as long as digital cultures do. Indeed, they stem from longstanding historical debates about power in public and private spaces. Many of these contemporary debates pertain to questions about the design and use of platforms, particularly how they generate data for financial gain. In my case studies here, I reveal how performance practices appear to mirror what is happening behind the scenes in platform

CONCLUSION 141

design—the translation of listening into something visible, measurable, and ultimately sharable.

Digital worlds are driven by user attention and engagement. In Nick Seaver's work on algorithmic traps, he describes the rise of contemporary platform design, as the creators of digital platforms find ways to "hook" users.[1] Relying on a wide variety of input systems and sources of data, major media companies have come to embrace captivation metrics, which seek to measure a user's attention or "engagement" on a platform. In other words, the infrastructures of platforms have become all-encompassing systems for gathering information based on user activity, which occurs through deliberate user actions (likes, clicks, taps) and data collection without user knowledge. Users on these online platforms engage in a relationship with digital platforms that is premised on consensual and nonconsensual sharing.

While data collection may feel disempowering or frightening, many people take great joy in sharing information online, in a way that can feel empowering and validating. Tara McPherson suggests that digital worlds can be characterized by a sense of liveness and user control in interactions with media:

> This liveness foregrounds volition and mobility, creating a liveness on demand. Thus, unlike television which parades its presence before us, the Web structures a *sense of causality* in relation to liveness, a liveness which we navigate and move through, often structuring a feeling that our own desire drives the movement. The Web is about presence but an unstable presence: it's in process, in motion.[2]

In short, digital platforms and digital worlds give us a sense of live interactivity, as we click, search, like, follow, move, scale, and rearrange objects on screens. They create incentives for us to share updates about our lives, locations, and habits. These platforms reward our participation, and they create a sense of interaction that can feel personally empowering. In Chapter 2, I offer examples of these forms of thrilling interactivity online, as people curate videos of themselves as joyful music consumers.

The rise of spectacular listening does not seem so unsurprising, given the proliferation of incentives to share our activity online. Spectacular listening documents the act of listening to music, creating elaborate opportunities to theatricalize listening abilities. Spectacular listening stems from and

142 SPECTACULAR LISTENING

contributes to the idea that sharing is inherently rewarding, valuable, and empowering. These spectacular acts of listening are user-generated performance genres that mirror some of the more subtle platform designs that require and encourage sharing.

I spoke to one musician who offered a candid explanation of how sharing can generate personal power and profit. A member of band Social Repose, Richie is a white man who lives near Las Vegas with over 1.06 million subscribers as of December 2019. He shoots videos in what he calls "gothy battle armor," which consists of a war bonnet, studs, animatronic wings, blackout lenses, and face paint. He labels his reaction videos by emphasizing his "goth" status, though he admits this is kind of a gimmick. His reactions include videos, such as "Goth Reacts to Die Antwoord," "Goth Reacts to K-Pop," "Goth Reacts to Billie Eilish—xanny (music video)," and "Goth Reacts to Poppy—BLOODMONEY (Official Music Video)." Generating reactions among viewers is part of the business model for creators like Richie. He recognizes reactions as a feedback loop. He described it this way:

> It's an endless cycle of "I'm going to talk about this because you talked about this . . ." I told my fans to make reaction videos to this video. And people would react to those reactions. Which ultimately always trickles back to you. It's a great marketing tool. You want people to talk about you, whether it's negative or not. Generally, the worst thing in the world for entertainers is to be forgotten.

Even his subscribers will try to get him to react to their reactions to him, in what I call chain reactions in Chapter 3. He tells me:

> People want the attention from you. You're verified and all that. It's a weird thing. You should never respond to petty comment. The best course of action is to ignore it. You're validating it . . . I think engagement is important and hate comments are still engagement. You don't want people to go on your page and be all hate. But you're polarizing, so people care. Which is ultimately kind of a win . . . As long as the hate is petty and not real, then it's ok.

He seems to have accepted that this kind of animosity is useful for keeping attention on his channel, despite the drawbacks. Richie embraces edgy content as a way to shock viewers, recognizing that generating powerful responses

CONCLUSION 143

from his viewers can be "ultimately kind of a win," so long as it does not generate any directly threatening response.

Richie's description of these videos emphasizes engagement, in the same ways that platform designers seek to engineer engagement. He recognizes reaction videos as a key to revenue as a result of the way that they generate attention from users. He understands how attention can be good or bad and yet always profitable.

Richie's comments also relate to my discussion at the conclusion of Chapter 1, in terms of how vulnerability can also reflect a tolerance for hostility that reflects privilege. Many air guitarists take a similar approach. In other words, such an embrace of transgressive content, not to mention the vaguely Indigenous attire from his war bonnet cosplay, reveals the white male privilege of being able to provoke others without fear of a direct threat to one's wellbeing. In ways that evoke bell hooks' "Eating the Other,"[3] reaction videos can empower people to profit from their consumption of marginalized identities. Provocative posturing certainly evokes a kind of confidence that can reveal a sense of invincibility.

Provocations can be a great way to generate engagement through a pursuit of frictions. Reaction videos come from people who often seek to emphasize the conflict between media and their bodies. These frictions can reveal structures of oppression, but they can be a will to power. Some creators use these frictions to diminish the art itself, instead asserting the power of the creator to intervene in a chain of circulation.

I interviewed one YouTube creator who reflected on the consequences of creating connections and provocations with viewers. The person had a fan show up unexpectedly at their home, following a tongue-and-check invitation they mentioned on a video that they called an "ill-advised joke." The fan showed up at the creator's house, documenting the encounter on social media, and the creator abruptly sent the fan away. The creator seemed genuinely triggered by this encounter, resulting in them taking many life-changing safety precautions thereafter to prevent this from happening again. Making matters worse, the fan later committed acts of self harm and blamed the creator, resulting in a series of reactions online from audiences on both people's social media feeds. The whole encounter and ensuing fallout was made highly visible online.

This story reveals a few things. First, the blame that many users online placed on the creator reinforces widespread misconceptions about self-harm. The fan's psychological struggles were compounded by a society that

Figure C.1 Social Repose. "BILLIE EILISH REACTED TO MY COVER II Billie Eilish Watches Fan Covers on YouTube | Glamour." Screenshot by the author on July 17, 2022.

i. Richie appears in black body armor with black animatronic wings, white face paint, black lipstick, and a black headdress. Richie reacts to Billie Eilish reacting to his cover of her song, in a perfect encapsulation of chain reactions.

ostracizes neurodivergence and places the onus on individuals to deal with their impairments, instead of making society more accommodating to those who need relational forms of support. Second, the grossly predatory nature of reactions to these events reveals how many creators on YouTube—not unlike their for-profit cable TV news counterparts—work to turn trauma into profit, under the guise of some altruistic motive to bring awareness to an issue. Finally, the episode reveals how creators must navigate complicated boundaries with their subscribers, who come to see them not as actors or media pundits but more so as friends, allies, and confidants. Data breaches may call to mind leaked passwords, but this story reminds us that they involve physical confrontations.

While this episode might have seemed to create a desire to increase boundaries between people, the conflict actually produced a desire to share more. Both the creator and the fan felt the need to document the encounter in a series of successive videos, and these videos reverberated across social-media platforms, as others shared their reactions. Following the encounter, a series of competing reactions from both people sought to frame what happened.

The sharing imperative can leave people feeling like they need to constantly labor to translate an experience to others, in order to render their emotions legible to audiences for validation. Wendy Chun calls this the "epistemology of outing," which is "a form of knowledge based on the forced exposure of open secrets."[4] Both people seemed to want to explain the narrative, and yet both had to explain the narrative through constantly re-living the episode in a public way.

Reactions, as a performance genre, stem from a broader digital landscape, in which platforms seek to push people together under the auspice of empowering global networks or communities. In her analysis of social-media platforms, José van Dijck says we should really refer to these platforms as "connective media," since they take human input and direct that input via sociotechnical functions that generate behavioral and profiling data.[5] In other words, they generate data via forcing connectivity, even though they couch this activity in the rhetorical of friendship and communalism. She writes:

> From the technological inscription of online sociality we drive that connectivity is a quantifiable value, also known as the popularity principle: the more contacts you have and make, the more valuable you become, because more people think you are popular and hence you want to connect with you.

The compounding effects of connectivity can occur through creating content that people like and relate to, and this process can also occur through creating shocking media that generates relationships born out of conflict. If reactivity is the way people generate connections online, then what kinds of relationships does it reward?

I think of reactivity as a quality of relationships online that can be an implicit part of platforms, as well as a conscious approach to others that can sometimes seek to spark attention through conflict. People are encouraged to be reactive; people also cultivate a reactive engagement with others. In my research on reaction videos, I frequently encountered people who would say that their reactions are not something that they can control. They would suggest reactions are involuntary responses to popular music, and they would suggest that a video's virality is also something out of their control. These

146 SPECTACULAR LISTENING

modes of reactivity, though, can be rehearsed by listeners and steered by platforms. Even if one reacts spontaneously to a piece of popular music, the person's reaction comes from acculturated ways of responding to music in the moment. People can be primed to listen reactively. Online platforms incentivize listeners to react in strong ways to popular media, by rewarding them for inputting their responses in bold, attention-grabbing ways. So the fact that performance genres have emerged that prioritize a reactive approach to popular media seems somewhat expected.

The *sharing imperative* is a way of naming the expectation that valuable forms of media reception always translate into measurable responses. In musical terms, if someone truly listens to the music, then listening will evoke almost an involuntary response that communicates receptivity to music's power. Alternatively, if one doesn't move in response to music, then the music must not resonate with them. Many digital platforms empower people to share listenings with others. They enable the need and desire to make one's listening legible to people and platforms.

The sharing imperative brings forth many troubling assumptions. One may be the idea that the antidote for misinformation is always more information. This assumption can lead to the need to constantly narrate, re-live, and ultimately react to media, as a way of justifying the effect media has on the body. Another assumption would be the idea that reactions are honest representations of how one feels, rather than curated performances. People use reactions to their advantage. This can empower activist communities, but it can also empower profiteering individuals, who want to show off a virtuosic individualism.

My case studies in this book tend to dwell on instances of spectacular listening that involve empowering acts of listening. However, spectacular listening can also be leveraged by people for performances that promote ableist, racist, sexist, and other oppressive ends, by creating reactive contexts with significant collateral damage. Spectacular listening can be symptomatic of an emphasis on sharing, which does not serve everyone equally or equitably.

Syncing Out Loud

Many performance genres in this book share a common feature: they involve people syncing their bodies with pre-recorded media. Such a technique appears most prevalent in Chapters 1 and 2, where performers create artistic

CONCLUSION 147

practices out of synchronizing their bodies with music clips. In my earlier work, I theorized this as "syncing out loud," in order to acknowledge the appeal of syncing the body with popular music.[6]

In my preliminary research for this book, I surveyed a wide range of digital music performance genres, and I found that many involve a combination of musical scripts and embodied performances. Whether in the form of app-based karaoke, lip syncing, or dance, people sought ways to film their bodies in sync with popular music, in order to create interesting juxtapositions and tensions.

Syncing out loud highlights diffuse yet prevalent approaches to listening in the twenty-first century, which use sound as a pre-text or a script for new performances. Video games are a particularly prominent field of practice for these scripts,[7] but the syncing feeling also pertains to many other online activities. Whereas syncing bodies and sounds can occur in many types of listening, *out loud* emphasizes the impulse to amplify aspects of the listening experience for others, by using the body as a conduit and resonator for music recordings. The *out loud* component connects back to the idea in the previous section, in which all forms of listening should be made visible, audible, and ultimately sharable.

One way to think about the prevalence of syncing out loud in our contemporary media landscape would be to imagine the many historical precedents that played with creative juxtapositions between moving images and sound. Since the initial development of recording technologies, people have sought creative ways to sync bodies with pre-recorded sounds, and in the late twentieth and early twenty-first centuries, the syncing impulse has become increasingly corporatized, commodified, and conventionalized.

From TV shows (*Sing Along with Mitch*, *Lip Service*, *America's Got Talent*, and *Lip Sync Battle*) to apps (*Smule*, *musical.ly*, and *Dubsmash*) to live performance formats (karaoke, air-band competitions, breakdancing, and drag shows), to video games (*PaRappa the Rapper*, *Dance Dance Revolution*, *Rock Band*, and *Guitar Hero*), the phenomenon of syncing one's body with pre-recorded popular music has transformed amateur music-making. Karen Collins refers to this as "kinesonic synchresis," which aligns bodily motion with sonic production.[8] Despite the public outcry when the occasional syncing scandal arises, large-scale live music has increasingly incorporated the (often unacknowledged) assistance of pre-recorded sounds, which ensure that Broadway shows, Super Bowl halftime performances, and national anthems at major political events will not be marred by microphone mishaps or human error.

148 SPECTACULAR LISTENING

Syncing has also become part of our mundane listening experiences. Syncing points to the way our technologies hail us as subjects, calling on us to react and respond to sonic prompts in our homes, cars, offices, and public spaces. Running apps can sync our heartbeats or running pace with the play-back speed of music recordings, keeping bodily motion and musical tempo in sync. Music streaming services (e.g., Spotify or YouTube) organize lis-tening into commodifiable information, by syncing our listening history and selling our habits via digital databases. These smart technologies demand we make our listening intelligible to our devices.

As a performance practice, syncing out loud can be a creative argument for an alignment between body and sound. Scholars have written about how the body can serve as a kind of living archive—a reservoir of embodied memories and cultural knowledge in opposition to the written record.[9] In her work on Civil War reenactors, Rebecca Schneider asks:

> Might a live act even "document" a precedent live act, rendering it, in some way, ongoing, even preserved? An action repeated again and again and again, however fractured or partial or incomplete, has a kind of staying power—persists through time—and even, in a sense, serves as a fleshy kind of "document" of its own recurrence.[10]

Think of Shreddy Boop (Chapter 1) combing through album covers as a child and then, in her air guitar routine in 2018, re-creating the act of Jimi Hendrix lighting his guitar on fire at Monterrey Pop Festival. Her performance does not simply draw attention to rock history; she embodies this legacy. She extends and heightens this history through using her own body as a conduit to circulate and extend the meaningful media of her childhood.

While syncing out loud might imply a precise synchrony between moving image and sound, this mode of listening can also enable creative expression rooted in purposeful out-of-syncness. Performers may desire to create forms of expression that challenge oppressive ideas of timeli-ness. The activists with disabilities throughout my case studies also relish opportunities be out of sync, drawing attention to a transgression of tem-poral constraints.

As I argue in Chapter 4, time can manifest power relations on and in the body in profound ways. Addressing the power of normative time, Ellen Samuels writes:

CONCLUSION 149

> When disabled folks talk about crip time, sometimes we just mean that we're late all the time—maybe because we need more sleep than nondisabled people, maybe because the accessible gate in the train station was locked. But other times, when we talk about crip time, we mean something more beautiful and forgiving.[11]

Samuels goes on to elaborate on crip time as an opportunity to reorient priorities around a more "forgiving" time that accommodates different forms of social synchronies and asynchronies.

A more forgiving time does not simply mean an extension of typical timeframes but rather a reimagining of cycles of life. Jack Halberstam theorizes queer time as emergent through a unique relationship to normative time frames, an "outcome of strange temporalities, imaginative life schedules, and eccentric economic practices."[12] Alison Kafer asks: "Can we crip queer time?" She elaborates:

> We can then understand the flexibility of crip time as being not only an accommodation to those who need "more" time but also, and perhaps especially, a challenge to normative and normalizing expectations of pace and scheduling. Rather than bend disabled bodies and minds to meet the clock, crip time bends the clock to meet disabled bodies and minds.[13]

The solution she offers, in other words, is that of bending time—of controlling time in an effort to personalize and customize time for communities excluded by typical time frames.

Many of my case studies exemplify bending time to be out-of-sync or synchronized differently, and one example helps drive this point home. In April of 2021, Alice Wong announced the final episode of her podcast—episode 100. In ways that complement the aesthetic approach in the pacing of her content in individual episodes, she describes the pacing of the podcast episode releases, emphasizing a value system that revolves around deliberate action rather than hurried output, and she credits podcasting as enabling this approach. In "Episode 100" she says:

> And I think another thing that I was very intentional was really building in as much flexibility as possible. And this is why, for some people who are listening, people who were former guests probably wonder, why did it

take four months for my episode to come out?! And that's because I work very much in advance, and I take my time. Because I'm working with audio producers. I'm making sure that I have my text transcript. I have all these little elements that I wanna put together, and I have the luxury of not being a fancy-shmancy kind of podcast on a network or on a radio. Because, you know, I have control over my schedule and my workflow. And I think that's a luxury, but it's also interesting that it's very much this sense of I don't want to always be under this pressure for myself, because I don't think good work would come out of pressuring myself and pushing myself. And I think that's just something that learned out of my own lived experience.

Wong bends the practice. She expresses a separation from the "fancy-shmancy" formalized podcasting that has become generic on mainstream platforms, embracing a more DIY aesthetic that encompasses flexible time.

Figure C.2 Ford Foundation. "(Audio Described) Political participation & disability, ft Alice Wong, #CripTheVote."

i. In an audio-described YouTube video, Alice Wong speaks in a Ford Foundation video, saying: "Disabled people have a voice whether it's an actual literal voice or not." This quote appears on the left side of the screen, while Wong appears on the right side of the screen in a blue-black shirt with arms folded.

CONCLUSION   151

Spectacular listening can communicate *within* time *about* time. Part of the appeal of the podcasting can be the ability to reference time as a subject, while doing things in time that evoke timeliness and liveness. Wong's emphasis on time as a subject of her work mirrors the way the podcast itself plays within time. In *Coming of Age in Second Life*, Boellstorff points out that people sometimes experience lag in digital realms "not as a delay *in* time, but as a delay *of* time."[14] In other words, people do not experience lag as a type of waiting (e.g., waiting for the bus in the actual world) but rather as a suspension of time itself, as a result of their immersion in various digital worlds. His work reminds us not only that the immersive flow of media can create opportunities for playing with the experience of time that involve slowing down or speeding up, but also that media can invite us to consider time itself.

As artistic sound production, podcasting creates an opportunity for flexible and forgiving approaches to time, which are themselves part of the artistry. In this respect, podcasters are very much like musicians, whose artistry revolves around playing with and in time. Musicians sculpt time, and musical time can model the kinds of coalitions that form around different experiences of time. A wide range of expressions communicate approaches to time that are part of an individual style or genre. Jazz drummers might play "in the pocket," and blues players might "swing notes." Classical musicians might play with tempo rubato, and rock musicians might groove. All of these terms describe a relationship to rhythm and time, and they gesture to broader theories of collaboration.

I hope my theory of spectacular listening enables us to imagine how people might listen musically, in ways that shape a relationship through time. Listeners might listen in the pocket. They might swing notes or lyrics. They might listen at 1.5x the original speed. They might groove. They might film reaction videos days after their initial listening. They may need a year to process.

The strange synchronies in spectacular listening performances can enable people to translate ideas about time to the public. Spectacular listening can show off an ability to synchronize with music, in a way that champions normative bodies and musical abilities. Spectacular listening can also play with these expectations in ways that advance a challenge to normative, ableist time.

Scholars theorizing both crip and queer time have come to a similar conclusion that a solution can be found in the acceptance and embrace of a collective, counter-normative time. Universal time can be normative, oppressive, and hegemonic. Individual time can be isolating and atomizing,

152 SPECTACULAR LISTENING

while serving neoliberal projects that separate communities into personal interests. The third way is a collective time that exists as a shared cultural space or experiential domain, which resists normative time and simultaneously creates a community where members are capable of being in-sync with one another in their own communal social rhythm.

Marginal Practices

In this book, I focus on cultural practices that may be marginal, both in the sense of participants who may be historically oppressed and in the sense of musical approaches that may be deemed unmusical. By focusing on listeners as creative participants in musical acts, I cut against some typical distinctions within music studies, particularly those between art versus Art, artist versus Artist, listener versus performer. Admittedly I focus primarily on performance genres that create artistry through unconventional means. I call podcasters artists, aligning them with musicians. I present reaction videos as a performance practice, and I elevate air guitarists as one might do for guitarists. My goal is to be generous with musical values, in order to challenge the specialized ways that people think of musicking.[15]

I am skeptical of institutions that confer prestige on the Arts and yet remain largely disconnected from the creative works of amateurs across our digital and physical landscapes. I think of music scholars who intimately know works of the past and works of elsewhere, but they do not know the contemporary music of their own lived communities. I think of institutions that direct resources to "sophisticated" and "complex" art, while serving as gatekeepers for musical values. I think of the institutions that praise experimental practices and yet only protect arts that appeal to people with a particular class and educational status.

Protecting the boundaries of the Arts simply creates categories of creativity, which extends creativity to select few while creating the idea that all others belong at the uncreative side of the spectrum. By focusing on listening as a creative act throughout this book, I hope to depict a fluid relationship between listeners and performers. Listeners are fundamental to music's meaning. Creativity is co-constitutive, produced by listeners, performers, and everyone and all devices in between.

Listening is also specific and not an abstract act, and the ability to listen reveals major disparities in our social worlds. How do music institutions

CONCLUSION 153

protect the listening of those marginalized by racist structures of systemic violence? And how does normal listening protect a white, European idea of listening, which always reproduces a sonic color line?[16] The possessive investment in normal listening endures as a feature of white supremacy,[17] and challenging these listening norms involves grappling with a deeper fabric of injustice that undergirds ideas of pleasure and public spaces.

While I dwell on case studies that offer, at times, an optimistic view of listening possibilities, these performances occur in a society that polices listening according to deeply oppressive racist, sexist, and ableist systems. In the *Sonic Color Line*, Jennifer Lynn Stoever describes a cultural context in which whiteness represents itself as "inaudible," while policing the sound practices of people of color.[18] Will Cheng demonstrates how this dynamic operates in the "Loud Music Trial" of Jordan Russell Davis, a teenager from Florida whose life was taken by a white man who confronted Davis about listening to music too loudly.[19] Showing how systemic forces inform a specific encounter between Dunn and Davis, Cheng describes how the pleasure of Davis came to be a target of violence, as a result of the excess associated with Black listening.[20] The Black Lives Matter movement has been a powerful force for addressing racism, police violence, and incarceration, and disability activists have worked hard to ensure the movement includes disabled Black activists as well. In the words of the Harriet Tubman Collective, "True liberation of all Black people cannot be achieved without the intentional centering of Black Disabled/Deaf narratives and leadership."[21]

In 2020, the US Air Guitar found itself connected to a particular instance of policing people of color, which caused the community to mobilize in a way that took me by surprise. According to the *Washington Post* and *Alabama Appleseed Center for Law and Justice*, the story begins in Pickens County, Alabama, where Eboni and Sean stopped for gas as they were driving from Mississippi to North Carolina.[22] They planned to help Sean's grandmother rebuild her house after a hurricane. Sean is a disabled veteran, who has a traumatic brain injury compounded with post-traumatic stress disorder as a result of his time in Iraq. He earned a purple heart for his service. Sean requires a caregiver to help him with cognitive problems, depression, sleep regulation, and other tasks—a role Eboni took on as his partner. After finding many medications ineffectual, Sean began using medically prescribed marijuana to help cope with these impairments.

A police officer who sat Highway 82 observed this couple from across the road. His arrest report describes what he saw: ". . . observed a Black male

154 SPECTACULAR LISTENING

get out of the passenger side vehicle. They were pulled up at a pump and the Black male began playing air guitar, dancing, and shaking his head. He was laughing and joking around and looking at the driver while doing all this." The officer called for backup and approached the car, citing loud music that violated the town's noise ordinance. Sean tried to show his medical marijuana card, in order to explain the smell, but the officer claimed the county—a dry county where even some alcohol can be illegal—does not honor the card, since he got the prescription in Arizona. The *Washington Post* summarized what happened next: "The worst-case scenario was far more severe than Worsley could have ever imagined: a years-long legal fight that plunged him into homelessness, cost him thousands of dollars in legal fees and recently concluded in a 60-month prison sentence."

Awareness about this case found its way to the US Air Guitar community during the summer of 2020, when the pandemic was ravaging the world and the United States. During this time, the organizers of US Air Guitar cancelled competitions all over the United States, eventually moving the competition online. But they also began drawing attention to Sean's case, raising money to help with legal fees and drawing attention to the Worsley's cause. During nationals, they found a way to coordinate a phone call from the Pickens County Jail in Carrollton, Alabama, thanks to Eboni. They spoke with Sean on the phone, who told them to keep "rocking out, out there, while I stay strong in here." They donated money and offered to volunteer to help in various ways. Over time, Sean's case gained publicity and a public outcry emerged. The publicity eventually helped free Sean, and he is now back at home with his wife.

From a certain vantage point, Sean's situation reveals the deep systemic structures that shape listening, where transgressive acts of listening can yield extremely variable consequences. In my discussions with air guitarists, they reflected on the privilege of being able to stage their listening as a form of free transgression, while anti-Black racism and ableism prevents many from doing so outside of the community. The situation also called upon them to reflect on racism and sexism within the air guitar community.

I also saw many radical acts of inclusion among the US Air Guitar community, which speaks to its ability to mobilize as a marginal practice. Throughout my time working with the air guitar community, I saw this mobilization happen many times. People in the community experienced all kinds of economic, social, and personal challenges, and they would be met with support through a quasi-mutual-aid system. The self-proclaimed outcast nature of the community made it particularly adaptable to include new

Figure C.3 Marquina in Oulu. Photo credit: author.
i. Marquina performs in Oulu, Finland, as part of the Air Guitar World Championships. She appears in a tank top with leather pants. Her arms trace a large air guitar. Her purple hair flies in the air.

members. After all, you do not need to possess any musical skills to be in the community. The weirdness of air guitar is one of its signature values; anyone can join as they are. I describe this lure toward air guitar in Chapter 1. A marginal art form can act in a way that institutions cannot.

Air guitar can also be adaptable to new situations. Marquina Iliev-Piselli offers one such example. An air guitarist, Marquina found herself with HER2-positive breast cancer, an especially aggressive form of cancer. As a result, she embraced activism, by creating the Glam Chemo Project and the Breast Cancer Women's Empowerment Project, a body-painting and photography shoot for women being treated at the Weill Cornell Breast Center. The project was a body-positive affirmation. The Glam Chemo project brought together air guitar, glam, and cancer treatment in a profound way. She created a series of photos that glamorize her body in a time of powerlessness. She described it to me this way:

> I might not be able to get off the couch right now. But I will. And I will again. And I will again. So it was more for myself. When I was in my house

156 SPECTACULAR LISTENING

and I look in the mirror, I don't see anyone I recognize. And somehow seeing photos of me looking confident helps me. I don't think that project is for everyone . . . There's a lot of pressure to be a fighter and warrior. Not everyone wins . . . and it's ok. It's more than ok. (sighs) We're not always strong . . . I always like performing. I was a dancer. There aren't many opportunities to dance as an adult. Like I would have to travel over and hour and half to class and hour and half back. It's not possible as an adult to have that kind of time . . . I think [air guitarists are] all working within the same parameter. We're imagining different versions of ourselves.

Marquina beautifully describes the way air guitar enables people to find alternative version of themselves, which can awaken imaginative modes of optimistic enjoyment but also be a particular resource at times when one's self-conception proves frustrating or brings anguish.

The seemingly superficial nature of air guitar and the other case studies in this book may seem to be at odds with the more serious politics that I attribute to them, but I want to emphasize that sites of play can be critical areas of political intervention. Along similar lines, extremely serious musical performances that promote seemingly serious political objectives can also be extremely ineffective in producing any sort of political mobilization. Serious artistry with loudly proclaimed progressive values can actually conceal deeply conservative and oppressive operations. In other words, the aesthetic sensibility of musical performance should not be confused for the political output that it generates. By focusing on practices that may seem superficial or silly on the surface, I hope I have shown how they also embody radical potential.

My four case studies often evoke serious performance genres while poking at them. For example, lip syncing suggests singing without involving the production of sounds with vocal cords. Many of the performance genres in this project could easily become more formalized traditions in music institutions, and some already operate in this way. College students can take courses on podcasting. I could imagine a class on air guitar. Reactivity can be a key facet of marketing and user experience research, as people learn to measure user feedback and engagement. And yet all of the performance genres here remain somewhat untamed, informal, and wild.

I hope that these practices continue to exist in productive friction with formal musical practices—that they do not become typical or lose their sense of playful irony. In *Undercommons*, Fred Moten and Stefano Harney question what role academia plays in shaping knowledge and the professionalization

Figure C.4 Air guitarists play "Free Bird." Photo credit: author.
i. Air guitarists collectively take the stage to perform the solo to "Free Bird" by Lynyrd Skynyrd, as is customary at the end of live competitions. A group of people appear in a messy combination of bodies, face paint, costumes, and motion.

of its many inhabitants, and they gesture to a relationship that can embody healthy antagonisms and subversive challenges to institutional structures.[23] I outline some of the musical dimensions of the problems in higher education in my introduction, and I hope that these listening performances in this book can reflect back to higher-ed institutions a distorted version of their own values, in a way that can be transformative of the kinds of hierarchies and virtuosities that institutions often protect.

Performing Listening

So what happens if and when spectacular listening becomes standard? I offer the concept of the sharing imperative to highlight the potential consequences of this emergent mode of listening, where sharing can exacerbate tensions and empower creators to profit from their conspicuous consumption. My focus on syncing out loud reveals the appeal of being in- and out-of-sync with recordings, which has consequences for the ways we imagine time and power. And I emphasize the marginality of the performance genres in my four case studies, in order to suggest what might be gained and lost by the elevation of these acts into serious and institutionalized art forms. Their marginal status may make them particularly useful to those from marginalized identities.

158 SPECTACULAR LISTENING

I want to leave you, my readers, with two productive questions, which I hope might influence the kinds of conversations scholars have in media studies, music studies, and disability studies in the future.

Question one: *what is the theory of disability in this analysis?* I want to emphasize the insufficiency of any analysis of platforms, film, music, media, and networks that does not account for bodily variation, instead assuming all users share universal bodily norms. By "theory of disability," I do not simply mean disability as an abstract concept. I am referring to the assumptions about universally shared bodily norms that operate in our conversations and embodied experiences of music. At the time of writing this book, I continue to see incredibly insightful scholarship completely bracket disability as outside of the concerns of the author, and this happens even in contexts in which the subject is the body, activism, and/or identity. We must consider ableism alongside other forms of oppression. We should name disability and actively impose disability in conversations about difference and sameness.

Question two: *what is the theory of listening in this practice?* This question deserves a place during any musical discussion, whether the topic is live music, composition, aesthetics, virtuosity, sound art, or digital audio workstation software. As I hope I have shown throughout this work, a theory of listening haunts any musical topic, and the assumption that listening should be straightforward—normal—often conceals a set of extremely exclusive values about musical value and listeners.

Spectacular listening offers a way of thinking about listening beyond the zones of the body that orient dominant ideas of listening today. Mara Mills writes:

> Sound waves transfer between media (air, water, solid), and can be experienced by sensory domains beyond the ear. Vibrations, visual recordings, and speech gestures are all possible components of an acoustic event. The ear itself is a composite organ, which hears by mechanical and electrical means.[24]

My case studies reveal cultivated practices that proceed under the assumption that listening is, by default, multimodal.

Throughout this book, I have extended this idea to a broad constellation of performance genres, in which people use various mechanical, electrical, bodily, technological, digital, physical, and social means to share and extend their listening. Listening becomes a multi-dimensional event, which always exists relationally with others.

People listen in incredibly varied ways. People communicate listening in varied ways as well. My examples in this book represent one way to explain the potential of spectacular listening, although many listening subcultures could provide additional case studies. By leveraging listening as an expressive practice, the performers in this project emphasize how normal listening does not fit many bodies and fails to fully encompass the messiness of listening itself. When we elevate listening as a spectacular performance, we can amplify the values that we attach to this musical activity. Spectacular listening can highlight the strangeness of listening, as well as the potential to use that strangeness in service of disability possibilities.

Notes

Preface

1. Benjamin W. Mann, "Survival, Disability Rights, and Solidarity: Advancing Cyberprotest Rhetoric through Disability March," *Disability Studies Quarterly* 38, no. 1 (2018). doi: https://doi.org/10.18061/dsq.v38i1
2. Alexis Toliver, Patricia Berne, Kylie Brooks, Neal Carter, Patrick Cokley, Candace Coleman, Dustin Gibson, Timotheus Gordon Jr., Keri Gray, Christopher DeAngelo Huff, Cyree Jarelle Johnson, Lorrell D. Kilpatrick, Carolyn Lazard, Talila A. Lewis, Leroy F. Moore Jr., Vilissa Thompson, and Heather Watkins, Harriet Tubman Collective, "Disability Solidarity: Completing the 'Vision for Black Lives,'" Harvard Kennedy School Journal of African American Public Policy, 2017.
3. Keah Brown, "Nurturing Black Disabled Joy," in *Disability Visibility: First-Person Stories from the Twenty-First Century*, ed. Alice Wong (Vintage Books, 2020), 118.
4. The "spoon theory" comes from Christine Miserandino and refers to a theory of chronic illness, in which people have limited energy to complete tasks throughout the day. See: Christine Miserandino, "The Spoon Theory," https://butyoudontlooksick.com/articles/written-by-christine/the-spoon-theory/, accessed July 17, 2022.
5. Ableism was a particularly strong feature of political attacks during this time, which often used disability stigma. See: Byrd McDaniel and Paul Renfro, "'This Is Not Normal'": Ability, Gender, and Age in the Resistance to Trumpism," *Disability Studies Quarterly* 39, no. 2 (2019), https://doi.org/10.18061/dsq.v39i2.6453.
6. See the creative discussion of platforms in: Nancy Baym, *Playing to the Crowd: Musicians, Audiences, and the Intimate Work of Connection* (New York: New York University Press, 2018).
7. Ellen Samuels, *Fantasies of Identification: Disability, Gender, Race* (New York: New York University Press, 2014).
8. Idris Elba, "This morning . . .," Twitter, March 16, 2020, https://twitter.com/idrise lba/status/1239617034901524481?ref_src=twsrc%5Etfw%7Ctwcamp%5Etwe etembed%7Ctwterm%5E1239617034901524481%7Ctwgr%5E&ref_url= https%3A%2F%2Fwww.cnn.com%2F2020%2F03%2F16%2Fentertainment%2Fid ris-elba-coronavirus-trnd%2Findex.html, accessed July 22, 2022. Sydney Bucksbaum, "Tom Hanks and Rita Wilson Test Positive for Coronavirus," March 11, 2020, https://ew.com/celebrity/tom-hanks-rita-wilson-test-positive-coronavirus/, accessed July 22, 2022. Brooke_Baldwin, "Hi Friends—I've . . .," Instagram, April 3, 2020, https://www.instagram.com/p/B-hqAEDFOKZ/, accessed July 22, 2022.

162 NOTES

9. Paul Renfro, "Coronavirus Is Different from AIDS," *Washington Post*, April 6, 2020, https://www.washingtonpost.com/outlook/2020/04/06/coronavirus-is-different-aids/, accessed July 22, 2020.

10. Amanda Perelli, Dan Whateley, and Sydney Bradley, "How the Coronavirus Is Changing the Influencer Business, According to Marketers and Top Creators on Instagram and YouTube," *Insider*, September 1, 2020, https://www.businessinsider.com/how-coronavirus-is-changing-influencer-marketing-creator-industry-2020-3, accessed July 22, 2022.

11. Sarah Perez, "Report: WhatsApp Has Seen a 40% Increase in Usage Due to COVID-19 Pandemic," TechCrunch, March 26, 2020, https://techcrunch.com/2020/03/26/report-whatsapp-has-seen-a-40-increase-in-usage-due-to-covid-19-pandemic/, accessed July 22, 2022.

12. Patrick Shanley, "Twitch Breaks Various Viewership Records Amid Coronavirus Quarantine," Hollywood Reporter, April 1, 2020, https://www.hollywoodreporter.com/news/general-news/twitch-breaks-viewership-records-coronavirus-quarantine-1287894/, accessed July 22, 2022.

13. UHG IT'S JOE, "We tested positive for Coronavirus (COVID-19)," YouTube.com, March 27, 2020, https://www.youtube.com/watch?v=iq2y5hzpbPQ, accessed July 22, 2022.

14. YouTube Creators, "Coronavirus and YouTube: Answering Creator Questions," YouTube, March 20, 2020, https://www.youtube.com/watch?v=i352PxWf_3M, accessed July 22, 2022.

15. Sarah Perez, "YouTube Will Now Allow Creators to Monetize Videos about Coronavirus and COVID-19," March 11, 2020, https://techcrunch.com/2020/03/11/youtube-will-now-allow-creators-to-monetize-videos-about-coronavirus-and-covid-19/, accessed July 22, 2022.

16. Paul Bond, "Ratings Skyrocket for Cable News Amid Wall-to-Wall Coronavirus Coverage," Newsweek.com, March 23, 2020, https://www.newsweek.com/ratings-skyrocket-cable-news-amid-wall-wall-coronavirus-coverage-1493836, accessed July 22, 2022. Joe Concha, "Fox News Prime-Time Lineup Delivers Highest Ratings in 24-Year History," TheHill.com, February 25, 2020, https://thehill.com/homenews/media/484592-fox-news-primetime-lineup-delivers-highest-ratings-in-network-history/, accessed July 22, 2022. Michael M. Grynbaum, "Trump's Briefings Are a Ratings Hit: Should Networks Cover Them Live?," *New York Times*, March 25, 2020, https://www.nytimes.com/2020/03/25/business/media/trump-coronavirus-briefings-ratings.html, accessed July 22, 2022.

17. Laura Bradley, "How Influencers Are Milking the Coronavirus for Clout—and Money," *The Daily Beast*, March 22, 2020, updated June 23, https://www.thedailybeast.com/how-influencers-are-milking-the-coronavirus-for-clout-and-money, accessed July 22, 2022.

18. Kati Chitrakorn, "Fashion Influencers Find New Opportunities during Covid-19," *Vogue Business*, April 1, 2020, https://www.voguebusiness.com/companies/fashion-influencers-find-new-opportunities-during-covid-19, accessed July 22, 2022.

NOTES 163

19. Flora Tsapovsky, "Could the Coronavirus Kill Influencer Culture?," Wired, April 14, 2020, https://www.wired.com/story/coronavirus-covid-19-influencers/, accessed July 22, 2022.
20. National ADAPT, "National ADAPT Advocates for Disability Justice during Pandemic," September 30, 2021, https://nlihc.org/resource/national-adapt-advocates-disability-justice-during-pandemic, accessed July 22, 2022.
21. The "auditory gaze" is an idea that comes from multiple sources. See: Jonathan Sterne, *The Audible Past: Cultural Origins of Sound Reproduction* (Durham, NC: Duke University Press, 2003). Alan Beck, "Point-of-Listening in Radio Plays," Sound Journal [Online], 1998.
22. Eli Clare, *Exile and Pride* (Durham, NC, and London: Duke University Press, 2015), p. xxi.

Introduction

1. Wendy Hui Kyong Chun, *Updating to Remain the Same Habitual New Media* (Cambridge, MA: MIT Press, 2016). Nick Seaver, "Captivating Algorithms: Recommender Systems as Traps," *Journal of Material Culture* 24, no. 4 (2019): 421–436.
2. Jean-Luc Nancy, *Listening*, trans. Charlotte Mandell (Fordham University Press, 2007).
3. Pauline Oliveros, "Auralizing the Sonosphere: A Vocabulary for Inner Sound and Sounding," *Sounding the Margins: Collected Writings 1992–2009*, ed. Lawton Hall (Kingston, NY: Deep Listening Publications, 2010).
4. Joseph Straus, *Extraordinary Measures: Disability in Music* (New York: Oxford University Press, 2011), 177.
5. Lennard Davis, *Enforcing Normalcy: Disability, Deafness, and the Body* (New York: Verso, 1996 [1995]), 3–16.
6. Ellen Samuels, *Fantasies of Identification: Disability, Gender, Race* (New York: New York University Press, 2014).
7. David Mitchell and Sharon L. Snyder, *Narrative Prosthesis: Disability and the Dependencies of Discourse* (Ann Arbor: University of Michigan Press, 2014).
8. Douglas Baynton, "Disability and the Justification of Inequality in American History," in *The New Disability History: American Perspectives*, ed. Paul Longmore and Lauri Umansky (New York: New York University Press, 2001).
9. Lennard Davis, "Normalcy, Power, and Culture," in *The Disability Studies Reader*, ed. Lennard Davis (New York: Taylor and Francis, 2013a). Robert McRuer, *Crip Theory: Cultural Signs of Queerness and Disability* (New York: New York University Press, 2006). Fiona Kumari Campbell, *Contours of Ableism: The Production of Disability and Abledness* (Basingstoke: Palgrave Macmillan, 2009).
10. Fiona Kumari Campbell, "Inciting Legal Fictions: Disability's Date with Ontology and the Ableist Body of the Law," *Griffith Law Review* 10 (2001): 42–62.

164 NOTES

11. Tom Shakespeare, "The Social Model of Disability," in *Disability Studies Reader*, ed. Lennard Davis (New York: Taylor and Francis, 2013 [2006]), 214–222.

12. A full history of disability studies as a field can be found: Daniel Blackie and Alexia Moncrieff, "State of the Field: Disability History," *History* 107, no. 376 (2022).

13. Alison Kafer, *Feminist, Queer, Crip* (Bloomington: Indiana University Press, 2013).

14. Rosemarie Garland-Thomson, *Extraordinary Bodies: Figuring Physical Disability in American Culture and Literature* (New York: Columbia University Press, 1997), 22.

15. Patty Berne, Mia Mingus, Stacy Milbern, Leroy Moore, Eli Clare, and Sebastian Margaret, "10 Principles of Disability Justice," SinsInvalid.org, 2015, https://www.sins invalid.org/blog/10-principles-of-disability-justice.

16. Alison Kafer, *Feminist, Queer, Crip* (Bloomington: Indiana University Press, 2013), 11.

17. Lydia Brown, "The Significance of Semantics: Person-First Language: Why It Matters," Autistic Choya. Accessed July 7, 2022. https://www.autistichoya.com/2011/08/signi ficance-of-semantics-person-first.html. Republished as "Identity-First Language," Autistic Self-Advocacy Network, accessed July 7, 2022, https://autisticadvocacy.org/ about-asan/identity-first-language/.

18. Merri Lisa Johnson and Robert McRuer, "Cripistemologies: Introduction," *Journal of Literary & Cultural Disability Studies* 8, no. 2 (2014): 127–147.

19. Marcel Maus, "Techniques of the Body," *Economy and Society* 2, no. 1 (1934): 70–88.

20. Jean-Luc Nancy, *Listening*, trans. Charlotte Mandell (New York: Fordham University Press, 2007).

21. Judith Becker, *Deep Listeners: Music, Emotion, and Trancing* (Bloomington: Indiana University Press, 2004), 71.

22. My approach to listening takes inspiration from Straus 2011 (cited above) and Blake Howe's theorization of the "normal performing body." See: "Disabling Music Performance," in *Oxford Handbook of Music and Disability Studies*, ed. Blake Howe, Stephanie Jensen-Moulton, Neil Lerner, and Joseph Straus (New York: Oxford University Press, 2004).

23. Jonathan Sterne, *The Audible Past: Cultural Origins of Sound Reproduction* (Durham, NC: Duke University Press, 2003), 95.

24. Veit Erlmann, *Reason and Resonance: A History of Modern Aurality* (New York: Zone Books, 2010), 10.

25. Theodore Gracyk, *Listening to Popular Music: Or, How I Learned to Stop Worrying and Love Led Zeppelin* (Ann Arbor: University of Michigan Press, 2010 [2007]), 139–140.

26. Ibid., 139–140.

27. Theodor W. Adorno, *Introduction to the Sociology of Music*, trans. E. B. Ashton (New York: Seabury Press, 1976 [1962]), 4.

28. Rose Subotnik, *Deconstructive Variations: Music and Reason in Western Society* (Minneapolis: University of Minnesota Press, 1996).

29. Ibid., 161–162.

30. Andrew Dell'Antonio, *Beyond Structural Listening?: Postmodern Modes of Hearing* (Oakland: University of California Press, 2004), 3.

31. Hillel Schwartz, "The Indefensible Ear: A History," in *The Auditory Culture Reader*, ed. Michael Bull and Les Back (New York: Berg, 2003), 493.

NOTES   165

32. Dylan Robinson, *Hungry Listening: Resonant Theory for Indigenous Sound Studies* (Minneapolis: University of Minnesota Press, 2020).

33. Jennifer Lynn Stoever, *The Sonic Color Line: Race and the Cultural Politics of Listening* (New York: New York University Press, 2016), 13.

34. H-Dirksen L. Bauman and Joseph L. Murray, *Deaf Gain: Raising the Stakes for Human Diversity* (Minneapolis: University of Minnesota Press, 2014). See also Jonathan Sterne, *The Audible Past: Cultural Origins of Sound Reproduction* (Durham, NC: Duke University Press, 2003), 37–40.

35. Jeannette Dibernardo Jones, "Music-Making in Deaf Culture," in *Oxford Handbook of Music and Disability Studies*, ed. Blake Howe, Stephanie Jensen-Moulton, Neil William Lerner, and Joseph Nathan Straus (New York: Oxford University Press, 2016), 67.

36. Emily Thompson, *The Soundscape of Modernity: Architectural Acoustics and the Culture of Listening in America, 1900–1933* (Cambridge, MA: MIT University Press, 2002), 2.

37. Michael Bull, *Sound Moves: iPod Culture and Urban Experience* (London: Routledge, 2007). Arild Bergh, Tia DeNora, and Maia Bergh, "Forever and Ever: Mobile Music in the Life of Young Teens," in *Oxford Handbook of Music and Mobility Studies*, ed. Sumanth Gopinath and Jason Stanvek (New York: Oxford University Press, 2014). Wayne Marshall, "Treble Culture," in *Oxford Handbook of Music and Mobility Studies*, ed. Sumanth Gopinath and Jason Stanyek (New York: Oxford University Press, 2014).

38. Perceptual coding points to a neurotypical bias in the encoding of musical details, since people have different responses to sensory stimuli. For example, the Autistic Self Advocacy Network website draws attention the different sensory experiences of people with Autism, characterized at times by "hearing loud sounds as soft and soft sounds as loud, or synesthesia." Autisticadvocacy.org. See: Jonathan Sterne, *MP3: The Meaning of a Format* (Durham, NC: Duke University Press).

39. Hillel Schwartz, Making Noise: From Babel to the Big Bang and Beyond (New York: Zone Books, 2011), 22.

40. Dylan Robinson, *Hungry Listening: Resonant Theory for Indigenous Sound Studies* (Minneapolis: University of Minnesota Press, 2020), 50.

41. Joseph Straus, *Extraordinary Measures: Disability in Music* (New York: Oxford University Press, 2011), 177.

42. Moretoki, "Another Car Ride with Motoki," YouTube.com, published July 25, 2016, accessed March 4, 2022.

43. Mark Katz, *Capturing Sound: How Technology Has Changed Music* (Berkeley: University of California Press, 2010), 66–67.

44. Timothy Taylor, "The Commodification of Music at the Dawn of the Era of 'Mechanical Music,'" *Ethnomusicology* 51, no. 2 (2007): 285.

45. David Goodman, "Distracted Listening: On Not Making Sound Choices in the 1930s," in *Sound in the Age of Mechanical Reproduction*, ed. David Suisman and Susan Strasser (Philadelphia: University of Pennsylvania Press, 2010).

46. Carol Langley, "Borrowed Voice: The Art of Lip-Synching in Sydney Drag," *Australasian Drama Studies* 48 (2006): 5–17.

166 NOTES

47. Philip Auslander, *Liveness: Performance and Mediatized Culture* (New York: Routledge, 2008 [1999]).

48. Casey Lum, *In Search of a Voice: Karaoke and the Construction of Identity in Chinese America* (Lawrence: Erlbaum Associates, 1996). Shūhei Hosokawa and Tōru Mitsui, *Karaoke Around the World: Global Singing, Local Technology* (New York: Routledge, 1998).

49. Henry Jenkins, *Convergence Culture: Where Old and New Media Collide* (New York: NYU Press, 2008). Lawrence Lessig, *Remix: Making Art and Commerce Thrive in the Hybrid Economy* (New York: Penguin, 2008). Aram Sinnreich, *Mashed Up: Technology and the Rise of Configurable Culture* (University of Massachusetts Press, 2010).

50. José van Dijck, *The Culture of Connectivity: A Critical History of Social Media* (New York: Oxford University Press, 2013), 4–6.

51. Deborah Kapchan, "Body," in *Keywords in Sound*, by David Novak and Matt Sakakeeny (Durham, NC: Duke University Press, 2015).

52. Tobin Siebers, *Disability Theory* (Ann Arbor: University of Michigan Press, 2008), 105.

53. Jack Halberstam, *The Queer Art of Failure* (Durham, NC: Duke University Press, 2011), 116.

54. Fred Moten and Stefano Harney, *The Undercommons* (New York: Minor Compositions, 2013).

55. The work of Paula Clare Harper, Kate Galloway, and Kaleb Goldschmitt has done much to illuminate how core questions in the fields of ethnomusicology and musicology have found their way into digital media platforms, resulting in the need to take these platforms as series sites of inquiry. See for example: Kate Galloway, K. E. Goldschmitt, and Paula Harper, Eds. *Twentieth-Century Music* 19(3) (2022): 363–368. K. E. Goldschmitt, Kate Galloway, and Paula Harper, eds., *American Music Special Issue: Platforms, Labor, and Community in Online Listening* 38(2) (2020): 125–130.

56. See for example: Katherine Meizel, *Idolized: Music, Media, and Identity in American Idol* (Bloomington: Indiana University Press, 2011). In addition, the subfield of ludomusicology draws upon ideas of play that come from a range of interdisciplinary sources. Two notable examples have influenced my own work: Johan Huizinga, *Homo Ludens: A Study of the Play Element in Culture* (Boston: Random House, [1938] 1950) and Brian Sutton-Smith, *The Ambiguity of Play* (Cambridge, MA: Harvard University Press, 1997).

57. Wendy Hui Kyong Chun, *Updating to Remain the Same Habitual New Media* (Cambridge, MA: MIT Press, 2016). José van Dijck, *The Culture of Connectivity: A Critical History of Social Media* (New York: Oxford University Press, 2007, 2013). Jean Burgess and Joshua Green, *YouTube: Online Video and Participatory Culture* (Malden: Polity Press, 2009). Tomie Hahn, *Sensational Knowledge: Embodying Culture through Japanese Dance* (Middletown, CT: Wesleyan University Press, 2007). Deborah Wong, *Speak It Louder: Asian Americans Making Music* (New York: Routledge, 2004).

58. Tom Boellstorff, *Coming of Age in Second Life: An Anthropologist Explores the Virtually Human* (Princeton, NJ: Princeton University Press, 2008), 60–86. See also: Tom

NOTES 167

Boellstorff, T. L. Taylor, Bonnie Nardi, and Celia Pearce, *Ethnography and Virtual Worlds: A Handbook of Method* (Princeton, NJ: Princeton University Press, 2012).

59. Kiri Miller, *Playable Bodies: Dance Games and Intimate Media* (New York: Oxford University Press, 2017), 21–23.

60. Ibid., 208.

61. Kyra Gaunt, *The Games Black Girls Play: Learning the Ropes from Double-Dutch to Hip Hop* (New York: New York University Press, 2006), 60.

62. George McKay, *Shakin' All Over: Popular Music and Disability* (Ann Arbor: University of Michigan Press, 2013).

63. Neil Lerner and Joseph Straus, *Sounding Off: Theorizing Disability in Music* (New York: Routledge, 2006).

64. William Cheng, *Just Vibrations: The Purpose of Sounding Good* (Ann Arbor: University of Michigan Press, 2016).

65. Dan Cavicchi, *Listening and Longing: Music Lovers in the Age of Barnum* (Middletown, CT: Wesleyan University Press, 2011).

66. Joseph Straus, "Normalizing the Abnormal: Disability in Music and Music Theory," *Journal of the American Musicological Society* 59, no. 1 (2006): 113–184. Nina Sum Eidsheim, *Sensing Sound: Singing and Listening as Vibrational Practice* (Durham, NC: Duke University Press, 2015). Jessica Holmes, "Expert Listening Beyond the Limits of Hearing: Music and Deafness," *Journal of the American Musicological Society* 70, no. 1 (2017): 171–220.

67. Mara Mills, "Hearing Aids and the History of Electronics Miniaturization," *IEEE Annals of the History of Computing* 33, no. 2 (2011): 24–45. Katie Ellis and Mike Kent, *Disability and New Media* (New York: Palgrave Macmillan, 2011); *Disability and Social Media: Global Perspectives* (New York and London: Routledge, 2017).

68. Mack Hagood, *Hush: Media and Sonic Self-Control* (Durham, NC: Duke University Press, 2019).

69. Michael Bakan, "Toward an Ethnographic Model of Disability in the Ethnomusicology of Autism," in *Oxford Handbook of Music and Disability Studies*, ed. Blake Howe, Stephanie Jensen- Mouton, Neil William Lerner, and Joseph Nathan Straus (New York: Oxford University Press, 2016). See also: Michael Bakan, and Mara Chasar, Graeme Gibson, Elizabeth J. Grace, Zena Hamelson, Dotan Nitzberg, Gordon Peterson, Maureen Pytlik, Donald Rindale, Amy Sequenzia, and Addison Silar, *Music and Autism: Speaking for Ourselves* (New York: Oxford University Press, 2020).

Chapter 1

1. See for example: April White, "An Electrifying History of Air Guitar," *Smithsonian Magazine*, July 2019; Byrd McDaniel, "How Air Guitar Became a Serious Sport," *The Conversation*, April 29, 2019, https://theconversation.com/how-air-guitar-became-a-serious-sport-113154.

2. Michael Bakan, "'Don't Go Changing to Try and Please Me': Combating Essentialism through Ethnography in the Ethnomusicology of Autism," *Ethnomusicology* 59, no. 1 (2015): 116–144. See also Alison Kafer, *Feminist, Queer, Crip* (Bloomington: Indiana University Press, 2013), 14.

3. For a full history of popular music pantomime see: Byrd McDaniel, "Air Apparent: Amplifying the History of Air Guitar, Air Bands, and Air Guitar in the Twentieth Century," *American Quarterly* 70, no. 4 (2018): 419–445. A more detailed history of the US Air Guitar Championships can be found here: Sydney Hutchinson, "Putting Some Air on Their Chests: Masculinity and Movement in Competitive Air Guitar," *The World of Music* 3, no. 2 (2014): 79–104.

4. Jim Higgins, "Guitar Wizards Take to 'Air' Contest," *The Milwaukee Sentinel*, July 16, 1982, 4.

5. Robert Walser, *Running with the Devil: Power, Gender, and Madness in Heavy Metal Music* (Middletown: Wesleyan University Press, 1993).

6. John McKenna and Michael Moffitt, *The Complete Air Guitar Handbook* (New York: Pocket Books, 1983), 7.

7. In a similar vein, George McKay articulates the way punk music opened up subcultures for new representations of stigmatized disabilities. He analyzes "punk and post-punk enfreakment" that championed "staring, sneering, spiky-haired, hunched, pierced, swearing, and spit-covered" figures, as well as bands like "the Epileptics, the Subhumans, and the Happy Spastics (all UK), another Subhumans (Canada), Disability, and the Cripples (both U.S.)." George McKay, *Shakin' All Over: Popular Music and Disability* (Ann Arbor: University of Michigan Press, 2013), 11.

8. Byrd McDaniel, "Out of Thin Air: Configurability, Choreography, and the Air Guitar World Championships," *Ethnomusicology* 61, no. 3 (Fall 2017): 419–445. .

9. Sydney Hutchinson, "Asian Fury: A Tale of Race, Rock, and Air Guitar," *Ethnomusicology* 60, no. 3 (2016): 411–433.

10. VICE News, "Why I Love Being a Ferocious Air Guitar God," August 1, 2017, https://video.vice.com/en_ca/video/why-i-love-being-a-ferocious-air-guitar-god/5960050e6152bceb15df8840.

11. Jeffrey A. Brune and Daniel J. Wilson, *Disability and Passing: Blurring the Lines of Identity* (Philadelphia: Temple University Press, 2013).

12. Joan Riviere, "Womanliness as a Masquerade," *The International Journal of Psychoanalysis* 10 (1929): 303–313.

13. Tobin Siebers, *Disability Theory* (Ann Arbor: University of Michigan Press, 2008), 10.

14. Tara Rodgers interviewed the composer Pamela Z in her book *Pink Noise*. Pamela Z offers interesting insight into the gendered aspects of using one's body to convey altered states. Pamela Z says: "Historically, women are socialized to use our bodies as a way of communicating with the world. And men are kind of uncomfortable with their bodies. Not in terms of doing physical things, or showing their strength—but basically, for them, they like to manipulate tools. Women tend to be placed in a position where they're expected to use their body in this public way. Like in the old tradition of jazz ensembles, you'd always have an entire ensemble of men, and then the front person would be this pretty woman. She was supposed to wear a really attractive gown, and what was she using as her instrument, but part of her body. So

NOTES 169

somehow it's more acceptable for a woman to do something that seems like losing her mind, being wild and being crazy with her body or her voice, either as a dancer or a singer. While a man can be really wild and crazy, but he has to do it with a tool. He's got to buffer himself with something—a guitar or a saxophone—it can't be coming right out of his face, because that somehow seems like losing control. This is stereotyping, but it's sort of analysis of why that is the stereotype." Her statement conveys why stigmatized forms of disability can be read differently in men and women. Air guitar is an interesting instance of this dynamic, given that it offers a tool but one that is wholly conjured by the body. p. 223. See: "Pamela Z" in Tara Rodgers, Pink Noise: Women on Electronic Music and Sound (Durham: Duke University Press, 2010), 223.

15. For gendered aspects of disability in musical performance, see: Alex Lubet, *Music, Disability, and Society* (Philadelphia: Temple University Press, 2011), 160.

Chapter 2

1. Susan M. Schweik, *The Ugly Laws: Disability in Public* (New York University Press, 2009), 1–3.

2. Lateef McLeod, "I Am Too Pretty for Some 'Ugly Laws,'" *New York Times*, August 15, 2018, accessed December 12, 2022, https://www.nytimes.com/2018/08/15/opinion/10-poets-with-disabilities.html

3. This list of suppressed content was first reported by Netzpolitik here: Chris Köver and Markus Reuter, "TikTok Curbed Reach for People with Disabilities," Netzpolitik. org, February 12, 2019, https://netzpolitik.org/2019/discrimination-tiktok-curbed-reach-for-people-with-disabilities/#netzpolitik-pw . Then the Intercept obtained additional documents, reported here: Sam Biddle, Paulo Victor Ribeiro, and Tatiana Dias, "Invisible Censorship: TikTok Told Moderators to Suppress Posts by 'Ugly' People and the Poor to Attract New Users," *The Intercept*, March 16, 2020, https://theintercept.com/2020/03/16/tiktok-app-moderators-users-discrimination/. My list combines characteristics from both of these sources.

4. Todd Spangler, "Musical.ly Launches Major Update to Video App, Which May Help Broaden Its Audience," *Variety*, August 23, 2016, https://variety.com/2017/digital/news/musical-ly-app-upgrade-content-related-videos-1202535239/.

5. I define "affordances" as what something allows one to do. My definition stems from the work of Gibson in: James Gibson, "The Theory of Affordances," *The Ecological Approach to Visual Perception*, (Boston: Houghton Mifflin, 1979).

6. José van Dijck, *The Culture of Connectivity: A Critical History of Social Media* (New York: Oxford University Press, 2013), 21.

7. Burcu Simsek, Crystal Abidin, and Megan Lindsay Brown, "Musical.ly and Microcelebrity Among Girls," in *Microcelebrity Around the Globe: Approaches to Cultures of Internet Fame*, ed. Crystal Abidin and Megan Lindsay Brown (Bingley, UK: Emerald Publishing Limited, 2018). Todd Spangler, "Musical.ly Launches Major Update to Video App, Which May Help Broaden Its Audience," *Variety*, 2017,

170 NOTES

accessed December 12, 2022, https://variety.com/2017/digital/news/musical-ly-app-upgrade-content-related-videos-1202535239/.

8. Carol Langley, "Borrowed Voice: The Art of Lip-Synching in Sydney Drag," *Australasian Drama Studies* 48 (2006): 5–17. Stephen Farrier, "That Lip-Synching Feeling: Drag Performance as Digging the Past," in *Queer Dramaturgies: International Perspectives on Where Performance Leads Queer*, ed. Alyson Campbell and Stephen Farrier (London: Palgrave Macmillan, 2016). Philip Auslander, *Liveness: Performance and Mediatized Culture* (New York: Routledge, 2008 [1999]), 73–127.

9. Nick Walker, "Neuroqueer: An Introduction," *Neurocosmopolitanism: Dr. Nick Walker's Notes on Neurodiversity, Autism, and Self-Liberation*, 2015, https://neuroqueer.com/neuroqueer-an-introduction/. See also: Nick Walker, *Neuroqueer Heresis: Notes on the Neurodiversity Paradigm, Autistic Empowerment, and Postnormal Possibilities* (Fort Worth, TX: Autonomous Press, 2021).

10. José Muñoz, "Feeling Brown, Feeling Down," *Signs: Journal of Women in Culture and Society* 31, no. 3 (2006): 679.

11. Melia Robinson, "This Teen Went from Getting Bullied in School to Being a Musical. ly Star with Millions of Fans," *Business Insider*, August 11, 2016, https://www.businessinsider.com/musically-star-kaylee-halko-2016-8.

12. Kate Galloway theorizes many forms of play that involve animals as digital stand ins and interlocutors for human desires. See: Kate Galloway, "Sensing, Sharing, and Listening to Musicking Animals across the Sonic Environments of Social Media," *Twentieth-Century Music* 19 (2022): 363–368.

13. Mara Mills and Jonathan Sterne, "Dismediation: Three Propositions and Six Tactics (Afterword)," in *Disability Media Studies: Media, Popular Culture, and the Meanings of Disability*, ed. Elizabeth Ellcessor and Bill Kirkpatrick (New York City: New York University Press, 2017), 365–378.

14. Sara Hendren, *What Can a Body Do?* (New York City: Riverhead Books, 2020).

15. Gerard Goggin, *Cell Phone Culture: Mobile Technology in Everyday Life* (London and New York: Routledge, 2006). Mara Mills, "Hearing Aids and the History of Electronics Miniaturization," *Media, Culture, and Communication* 33, no. 2 (2011): 24–44.

16. Many music cultures pass down embodied knowledge in ways that can be both conscious and stated, as well as subconscious and embodied. Tomie Hahn's "sensational knowledge" offers a useful concept on how this works in Japanese Dance: Tomie Hahn, *Sensational Knowledge: Embodying Culture through Japanese Dance* (Middletown, CT: Wesleyan University Press, 2007).

17. Jill Walker Rettberg, "Hand Signs for Lip-Syncing: The Emergence of a Gestural Language on Musical.ly as a Video-Based Equivalent to Emoji," *Social Media + Society* 3, no. 4 (2017): 1–11.

18. H-Dirksen L. Bauman and Joseph L. Murray, "Introduction," in *Deaf Gain: Raising the Stakes for Human Diversity*, ed. H-Dirksen L Bauman and Joseph J Murray (Minneapolis: University of Minnesota Press, 2014).

19. Anabel Maler, "Musical Expression Among Deaf and Hearing Song Signers," in *Oxford Handbook of Music and Disability Studies*, ed. Blake Howe, Stephanie Jensen-Moulton, Neil Lerner, and Joseph Straus (New York: Oxford University Press, 2016). Jeannette Dibernardo Jones, "Music-Making in Deaf Culture," in *Oxford Handbook*

of Music and Disability Studies, ed. Blake Howe, Stephanie Jensen-Moulton, Neil William Lerner, and Joseph Nathan Straus (New York: Oxford University Press, 2016).

20. In "The Black Beat Made Visible," Thomas DeFrantz theorizes "corporeal orature," which "aligns movement with speech to describe the ability of black social dance to incite action" via "performative gestures that cite contexts beyond dance." This is, in a sense, signifyin' in literal and expansive ways. Thomas DeFrantz, "The Black Beat Made Visible," in *Of the Presence of the Body: Essays on Dance and Performance Theory*, ed. André Lepecki (Middletown, CT: Wesleyan University Press, 2004), 67. Henry Louis Gates, *The Signifying Monkey: A Theory of African-American Literary Criticism* (New York: Oxford University Press, 1989).

21. Katherine Meizel, *Multivocality: Singing on the Borders of Identity* (Oxford: Oxford University Press, 2020), 91, 114.

Chapter 3

1. Joe Coscarelli, "The Only Music Critic Who Matters (if You're Under 25)," *New York Times*, September 30, 2020. Section AR, p. 9. Accessed October 29, 2020.

2. For critiques of this variety of criticism, see: Kelefa Sanneh, "The Rap Against Rockism," *New York Times*, October 31, 2004, http://www.nytimes.com/2004/10/31/arts/music/the-rap-against-rockism.html. Daphne Brooks, "The Write to Rock: Racial Mythologies, Feminist History, and the Pleasures of Rock Music Criticism," *Women and Music: A Journal of Gender and Culture* 12 (2008): 54–62.

3. Alison Kafer, *Feminist, Queer, Crip* (Bloomington: Indiana University Press, 2013).

4. Tom Shakespeare, "The Social Model of Disability," in *Disability Studies Reader*, ed. Lennard Davis (New York: Taylor and Francis, 2013 [2006]), 214–222.

5. Robert McRuer, *Crip Theory: Cultural Signs of Queerness and Disability* (New York: New York University Press, 2006).

6. Maria Eriksson, Rasmus Fleischer, Anna Johansson, Patrick Vonderau, and Pelle Snickars, *Spotify Teardown: Inside the Black Box of Streaming Music* (Cambridge, MA: MIT Press, 2019).

7. The English-language term for this would be a picture-in-picture, and this editing technique is extremely influential in Japan, called a waipu (not to be confused with a wipe, an English media production term noting something else). See: Alice Gordenker, *Japan Times*, October 18, 2011, https://www.japantimes.co.jp/news/2011/10/18/reference/annoying-tv-pop-ups/.

8. "React," Fine Brothers Properties, Inc., *USPTO*, https://uspto.report/TM/86689364.

9. Natalie Robehmed and Madeline Berg, "Highest-Paid YouTube Stars 2018: Markiplier, Jake Paul, PewDiePie and More," *Forbes.com*, December 3, 2018, https://www.forbes.com/sites/natalierobehmed/2018/12/03/highest-paid-youtube-stars-2018-markiplier-jake-paul-pewdiepie-and-more/?sh=7f8f2995909a. Chris Stokel-Walker, *YouTubers: How YouTube Shook Up TV and Created a New Generation of Stars* (Croydon, UK: Canbury Press, 2019), 14.

172 NOTES

10. Jean Burgess and Joshua Green, *YouTube: Online Video and Participatory Culture* (Malden, MA: Polity Press, 2009).

11. Chris Stokel-Walker, *YouTubers: How YouTube Shook Up TV and Created a New Generation of Stars* (Croydon, UK: Canbury Press, 2019), 59.

12. "YouTube Top Lists" (n.d.), Kworb.net, https://kworb.net/youtube/topvideos.html.

13. Theresa Senft, "Microcelebrity and the Branded Self," In *A Companion to New Media Dynamics*, Eds. John Hartley, Jean Burgess, Axel Bruns (Hoboken, NJ: Blackwell Publishing Limited, 2013).

14. Melissa Click, *Anti-Fandom* (New York: New York University Press, 2019), 8, 14.

15. Heather Warren-Crow, "Screaming like a Girl: Viral Video and the Work of Reaction," *Feminist Media Studies* 16, no. 6 (2016): 1113–1117.

16. Nancy Baym, *Playing to the Crowd: Musicians, Audiences, and the Intimate Work of Connection*, (New York: New York University Press, 2018), 19.

17. Byrd McDaniel, "Popular Music Reaction Videos: Reactivity, Creator Labor, and the Performance of Listening Online," 23, no. 6 (2020): 1624–1641.

18. Evelyn from the Internetz, "Beyoncé Played My #Lemonade Video On Tour & You Can #StayMad | @EVEEEEEZY," May 23, 2016. YouTube.com. https://www.youtube.com/watch?v=Qy4NVh4JSK0. Accessed October 23, 2023.

19. Evelyn, along with all the creators in this chapter, must grapple with the fact that viral videos often work to turn affective reactions into viral content that circulate far beyond their initial contexts. Lauren Michele Jackson writes about how reactions often become reaction GIFs that align Black bodies with excessive emotions, enabling white people who circulate them to engage in "the act of inhabiting a black persona. . . . in a minstrel-like tradition" Lauren Michele Jackson, "We Need to Talk About Digital Blackface in Reaction GIFs," *Teen Vogue*, August 2, 2017, https://www.teenvogue.com/story/digital-blackface-reaction-gifs.

20. Elizabeth Ellcessor, *Restricted Access: Media, Disability, and the Politics of Participation* (New York: New York University Press, 2016).

21. "Disability Impacts ALL of US," *Center for Disease Control*, https://www.cdc.gov/ncbddd/disabilityandhealth/infographic-disability-impacts-all.html.

22. bell hooks, "Eating the Other: Desire and Resistance," in *Black Looks: Race and Representation* (Boston: South End Press, 1992), 21–39.

23. Merri Lisa Johnson and Robert McRuer, "Cripistemologies: Introduction," *Journal of Literary & Cultural Disability Studies* 8, no. 2 (2014): 136.

24. I use identity-first language throughout this chapter to refer to Autism. For a full explanation of why identity-first language offers an affirmative way to describe Autism, see: Lydia Brown, "Identity-First Language," Autistic Self-Advocacy Network, accessed July 7, 2022, https://autisticadvocacy.org/about-asan/identity-first-language/.

25. Lydia X. Z. Brown, "We Can't Address Disability Without Addressing Race. Here's Why," *Learn Play Thrive*, June 18, 2020, https://www.learnplaythrive.com/single-post/Racism.

26. William Cheng, "Staging Overcoming: Narratives of Disability and Meritocracy in Reality Singing Competitions," *Journal of the Society for American Music* 11, no. 2 (2017): 189.

NOTES   173

27. Joseph Straus, *Extraordinary Measures: Disability in Music* (New York: Oxford University Press, 2011), 17.

28. Rosemarie Garland-Thomson, *Staring: How We Look* (New York: Oxford University Press, 2009), 188.

29. Eds. Ann Powers and Evelyn McDonnell, *Rock She Wrote: Women Write about Rock, Pop, and Rap* (Lanham, MD: Cooper Square Press, 1999). Daphne Brooks, "The Write to Rock: Racial Mythologies, Feminist History, and the Pleasures of Rock Music Criticism," *Women and Music: A Journal of Gender and Culture* 12 (2008): 62.

Chapter 4

1. John Blacking, *How Musical Is Man?* (Seattle: University of Washington Press, 1977).

2. Peter Szendy, *Listen: A History of Our Ears* (New York: Fordham University Press, 2008), 5, 102.

3. For a full list of all episodes mentioned in this chapter, see: M. Bri, "Power Not Pity," Powernotpity.com. Thomas Reid, "Reid My Mind," https://reidmymind.com/. Alice Wong, "Disability Visibility: Podcast," https://disabilityvisibilityproject.com/podcast-2/.

4. Martin Spinelli and Lance Dann, *Podcasting: The Audio Media Revolution* (New York: Bloomsbury Publishing Inc., 2019), 7–8.

5. David Goodman, "Distracted Listening: On Not Making Sound Choices in the 1930s," in *Sound in the Age of Mechanical Reproduction*, ed. David Suisman and Susan Strasser (Philadelphia: University of Pennsylvania Press, 2010), 15–46.

6. Allison McCracken, "'God's Gift to Us Girls': Crooning, Gender, and the Re-Creation of American Popular Song," *American Music* 17, no. 4 (1999), 365–395.

7. Andrew J. Bottomley, *Sound Streams: A Cultural History of Radio-Internet Convergence* (Ann Arbor: University of Michigan Press, 2020).

8. For a more general discussion of the persuasive dimensions of podcast listening, see: Byrd McDaniel, "All Songs Considered: The Persuasive Listening of Music Podcasts," *Twenty-First Century Music* 19, no. 3 (2022): 411–426, published by Cambridge University Press, https://doi.org/10.1017/S1478572222000275.

9. Alan Beck, "Point-of-Listening in Radio Plays," Sound Journal [Online], 1998.

10. Patty Berne, "Disability Justice - a working draft by Patty Berne," *SinsInvalid*, 2015, https://www.sinsinvalid.org/blog/disability-justice-a-working-draft-by-patty-berne.

11. Chris Bell, "Introducing *White* Disability Studies: A Modest Proposal," in *The Disability Studies Reader*, 2nd ed., ed. Lennard J. Davis (New York: Routledge, 2006), 276.

12. Thomas Reid, "Reid My Mind," *Reid My Mind*, reidmymind.com. Accessed October 24, 2023.

13. Ellen Samuels, "Six Ways of Looking at Crip Time," *Disability Studies Quarterly* 37, no. 3 (2017).

14. At least, they preferred particular accents over others.

174   NOTES

15. Alison Kafer, *Feminist, Queer, Crip* (Bloomington: Indiana University Press, 2013), 27.
16. Alice Wong, "Diversifying Radio with Disabled Voices," Transom.org, 2016, https://transom.org/2016/alice-wong/. Accessed July 17, 2022.
17. Mara Mills and Jonathan Sterne, "Aural Speed-Reading: Some Historical Bookmarks," *PMLA* 135, no. 2 (2020).
18. Jillian Weise, "Common Cyborg," in *Disability Visibility: First-Person Stories from the Twenty-First Century*, ed. Alice Wong (New York: Vintage Books, 2020), 65.
19. Lateef also hosts a podcast along with Leroy Moore, Keith Jones, and Ottis Smith called Black Disabled Men Talk.
20. Leroy F. Moore, *Black Disabled Ancestors* (independently published, 2020), 5.
21. For a full discussion of discourse and narrative, see: David Mitchell and Sharon L. Snyder, *Narrative Prosthesis: Disability and the Dependencies of Discourse* (Ann Arbor: University of Michigan Press, 2014).
22. Joseph Schloss, *Making Beats: The Art of Sample-Based Hip-Hop* (Middletown, CT: Wesleyan University Press, 2004).
23. Michael Bakan, Mara Chasar, Graeme Gibson, Elizabeth J. Grace, Zena Hamelson, Dotan Nitzberg, Gordon Peterson, Maureen Pytlik, Donald Rindale, Amy Sequenzia, and Addison Silar, *Music and Autism: Speaking for Ourselves* (New York: Oxford University Press, 2020), 26–29.
24. "About Autism," accessed July 7, 2022, https://autisticadvocacy.org/about-asan/about-autism/.
25. Benjamin Peters, "A Network Is Not a Network," in *Your Computer Is On Fire*, ed. Thomas S. Mullaney, Benjamin Peters, Mar Hicks, and Kavita Philip, (Cambridge: The MIT Press, 2021), 71–90.
26. Kyra D. Gaunt, "YouTube, Twerking and You: Context Collapse and the Handheld Co-Presence of Black Girls and Miley Cyrus," *Journal of Popular Music Studies* 27, no. 3: 244–273. See also: David Novak's discussion of feedback. David Novak, *Japanoise: Music at the Edge of Circulation* (Durham, NC: Duke University Press, 2013).
27. s.e. smith, "The Beauty of Spaces Created for and by Disabled People," in *Disability Visibility: First-Person Stories from the Twenty-First Century*, ed. Alice Wong (New York City: Vintage Books, 271–276.
28. Joseph Straus, *Extraordinary Measures: Disability in Music* (New York: Oxford University Press, 2011), 151.
29. Eric Weisbard, *Top 40 Democracy: The Rival Mainstreams of American Music* (Chicago: University of Chicago Press).
30. Nina Sun Eidsheim, *The Race of Sound: Listening, Timbre, and Vocality in African American Music* (Durham, NC: Duke University Press, 2019), 113. In Hungry Listening, Dylan Robinson similarly writes about Indigenous perspectives on listening and composition, particularly how "the act of listening should attend to the relationship between the listener and the listened-to." Dylan Robinson, *Hungry Listening: Resonant Theory for Indigenous Sound Studies*, (Minneapolis: University of Minnesota Press, 2020), 15.

Conclusion

1. Nick Seaver, "Captivating Algorithms: Recommender Systems as Traps," *Journal of Material Culture* 24, no. 4 (2019): 421–436.
2. Tara McPherson, "Reload: Liveness, Mobility and the Web," in *The Visual Culture Reader*, 2nd ed., ed. Nicholas Mirzoeff (New York: Routledge, 2002), 462.
3. bell hooks, *Black Looks: Race and Representation* (Brooklyn: South End Press, 1992), 21–39.
4. Wendy Hui Kyong, Chun, *Updating to Remain the Same Habitual New Media* (Cambridge, MA: MIT Press, 2016) 141.
5. José van Dijck, *The Culture of Connectivity: A Critical History of Social Media* (New York: Oxford University Press, 2013), 14, 16.
6. Byrd McDaniel, "Syncing Out Loud: Listening Norms in the 21st Century" (PhD diss., 2019).
7. Kiri Miller, *Playing Along: Digital Games, YouTube, and Virtual Performance* (New York: Oxford University Press, 2012); *Playable Bodies: Dance Games and Intimate Media* (New York: Oxford University Press, 2017).
8. Karen Collins, *Playing with Sound: A Theory of Interacting with Sound and Music in Video Games* (Cambridge, MA: MIT Press, 2013).
9. Tomie Hahn, *Sensational Knowledge: Embodying Culture through Japanese Dance* (Middletown, CT: Wesleyan University Press, 2007). Diana Taylor, *The Archive and the Repertoire: Performing Cultural Memory in the Americas* (Durham, NC: Duke University Press, 2003).
10. Rebecca Schneider, *Performing Remains: Art and War in Times of Theatrical Reenactment* (New York: Routledge, 2011).
11. Ellen Samuels, "Six Ways of Looking at Crip Time," *Disability Studies Quarterly* 37, no. 3 (2017).
12. Jack Halberstam, *In a Queer Time and Place: Transgender Bodies, Subcultural Lives* (New York: NYU Press, 2005), 1.
13. Alison Kafer, *Feminist, Queer, Crip* (Bloomington: Indiana University Press, 2013), 27.
14. Tom Boellstorff, *Coming of Age in Second Life: An Anthropologist Explores the Virtually Human* (Princeton, NJ: Princeton University Press, 2008), 106.
15. Christopher Small, *Musicking: The Meanings of Performing and Listening* (Middletown, CT: Wesleyan University Press, 1998).
16. Jennifer Lynn Stoever, *The Sonic Color Line: Race & the Cultural Politics of Listening* (New York: New York University Press, 2016).
17. See George Lipsitz's influential discussion of the possessive investment in whiteness in: George Lipsitz, *The Possessive Investment in Whiteness: How White People Profit from Identity Politics* (Philadelphia: Temple University Press, 2006).
18. Stoever 2016.
19. William Cheng, *Loving Music Till It Hurts* (Oxford: Oxford University Press, 2020).
20. See also: Tricia Rose, *Black Noise: Rap Music and Black Culture in Contemporary America* (Middletown, CT: Wesleyan University Press, 2004 [1994]).

176　NOTES

21. Alexis Toliver, Patricia Berne, Kylie Brooks, Neal Carter, Patrick Cokley, Candace Coleman, Dustin Gibson, Timotheus Gordon Jr., Keri Gray, Christopher DeAngelo Huff, Cyree Jarelle Johnson, Lorrell D. Kilpatrick, Carolyn Lazard, Talila A. Lewis, Leroy F. Moore Jr., Vilissa Thompson, and Heather Watkins, "Disability Solidarity: Completing the 'Vision for Black Lives,'" Harriet Tubman Collective, Harvard Kennedy School Journal of African American Public Policy, 2017.

22. Teo Armus, "A Disabled Black Veteran Drove through Alabama with Medical Marijuana: Now He Faces Five Years in Prison," *Washington Post*, July 14, 2020, https://www.washingtonpost.com/nation/2020/07/14/alabama-veteran-marijuana-prison/.

   Leah Nelson, "This Veteran's Day, Sean Worsley is finally home with his wife. May Alabama learn from the mistake of imprisoning this decorated Iraq War hero in the name of 'law and order.'" *Alabama Appleseed*. November 9, 2020. https://alabamaap pleseed.org/alabama-prisons/this-veterans-day-sean-worsley-is-finally-home-with-his-wife-may-alabama-learn-from-the-mistake-of-imprisoning-this-decora ted-iraq-war-hero-in-the-name-of-law-and-order/

23. Fred Moten and Stefano Harney, *The Undercommons* (New York: Minor Compositions, 2013).

24. Mara Mills, "Deafness," in *Keywords in Sound*, ed. David Novak and Matt Sakakeeny (Durham, NC: Duke University Press, 2015), 52.

Bibliography

Adorno, Theodor W. *Introduction to the Sociology of Music*. Translated by E.B. Ashton. New York: Seabury Press, 1976. Original publication: 1962.

Ariel. "Musical.ly Tutorial Part #2 Making Duets!:) | Baby Ariel." YouTube.com. Published October 14, 2015. Accessed June 23, 2023. https://www.youtube.com/watch?v=BbWQ aI91RfY.

Auslander, Philip. *Liveness: Performance and Mediatized Culture*. New York: Routledge, 2008 [1999].

Autistic Self Advocacy Network. 2011. "Identity-First Language." Autisticadvocacy.org. https://autisticadvocacy.org/about-asan/identity-first-language/. Accessed October 23, 2023.

Armus, Teo. "A Disabled Black Veteran Drove through Alabama with Medical Marijuana: Now He Faces Five Years in Prison." 2020. https://www.washingtonpost.com/nation/2020/07/14/alabama-veteran-marijuana-prison/.

Bakan, Michael. "'Don't Go Changing to Try and Please Me': Combating Essentialism through Ethnography in the Ethnomusicology of Autism." *Ethnomusicology* 59, no. 1 (2015): 116–144.

Bakan, Michael. "Toward an Ethnographic Model of Disability in the Ethnomusicology of Autism." In *Oxford Handbook of Music and Disability Studies*, edited by Blake Howe, Stephanie Jensen- Mouton, Neil William Lerner, and Joseph Nathan Straus, 15–37. New York: Oxford University Press, 2016.

Bakan, Michael, and Mara Chasar, Graeme Gibson, Elizabeth J. Grace, Zena Hamelson, Dotan Nitzberg, Gordon Peterson, Maureen Pytlik, Donald Rindale, Amy Sequenzia, and Addison Silar. *Music and Autism: Speaking for Ourselves*. New York: Oxford University Press, 2020.

Bauman, H-Dirksen L. and Joseph L. Murray. *Deaf Gain: Raising the Stakes for Human Diversity*. Edited by H-Dirksen L Bauman and Joseph J Murray. Minneapolis: University of Minnesota Press, 2014.

Baym, Nancy. *Playing to the Crowd: Musicians, Audiences, and the Intimate Work of Connection*. New York: New York University Press, 2018.

Baynton, Douglas. "Disability and the Justification of Inequality in American History." In *The New Disability History: American Perspectives*, edited by Paul Longmore and Lauri Umansky, 33–57. New York: New York University Press, 2001.

Beck, Alan. "Point-of-Listening in Radio Plays." Sound Journal [Online]. 1998. https:kent. ac.uk/arts/soundjournal/beck981.htm.

Becker, Judith. *Deep Listeners: Music, Emotion, and Trancing*. Bloomington: Indiana University Press, 2004.

Bell, Chris. "Introducing *White* Disability Studies: A Modest Proposal." In *The Disability Studies Reader*. 2nd edition, edited by Lennard J. Davis, 275–282. New York: Routledge, 2006.

BIBLIOGRAPHY

Bergh, Arild, Tia DeNora, and Maia Bergh. "Forever and Ever: Mobile Music in the Life of Young Teens." In *Oxford Handbook of Music and Mobility Studies*, edited by Sumanth Gopinath and Jason Stanyek, 317–334. New York: Oxford University Press, 2014.

Berne, Patty. "Disability Justice—a working draft by Patty Berne." *SinsInvalid*. 2015. https://www.sinsinvalid.org/blog/disability-justice-a-working-draft-by-patty-berne. Accessed October 25, 2023.

Berne, Patty, Mia Mingus, Stacy Milbern, Leroy Moore, Eli Clare, and Sebastian Margaret. "10 Principles of Disability Justice." SinsInvalid.org. 2015. https://www.sinsinvalid.org/blog/10-principles-of-disability-justice. Accessed October 25, 2023.

Biddle, Sam, Paulo Victor Ribeiro, and Tatiana Dias. "Invisible Censorship: TikTok Told Moderators to Suppress Posts by 'Ugly' People and the Poor to Attract New Users." *The Intercept*. 2020. https://theintercept.com/2020/03/16/tiktok-app-moderators-users-discrimination/. Accessed October 23, 2023.

Blackie, Daniel, and Alexia Moncrieff. "State of the Field: Disability History." *History* 107, no. 376 (2022): 729–811.

Blacking, John. *How Musical Is Man?* Seattle: University of Washington Press, 1977.

Boellstorff, Tom. *Coming of Age in Second Life: An Anthropologist Explores the Virtually Human*. Princeton, NJ: Princeton University Press, 2008.

Boellstorff, Tom, T. L. Taylor, Bonnie Nardi, and Celia Pearce. *Ethnography and Virtual Worlds: A Handbook of Method*. Princeton, NJ: Princeton University Press, 2012.

Bond, Paul. "Ratings Skyrocket for Cable News Amid Wall-to-Wall Coronavirus Coverage." Newsweek.com. March 23, 2020. https://www.newsweek.com/ratings-skyrocket-cable-news-amid-wall-wall-coronavirus-coverage-1493836. Accessed July 22, 2022.

Bottomley, Andrew J. *Sound Streams: A Cultural History of Radio-Internet Convergence*. Ann Arbor: University of Michigan Press, 2020.

Bradley, Laura. "How Influencers Are Milking the Coronavirus for Clout—and Money." *The Daily Beast*. March 22, 2020. Updated June 23. https://www.thedailybeast.com/how-influencers-are-milking-the-coronavirus-for-clout-and-money. Accessed July 22, 2022.

Brooke_Baldwin. "Hi Friends—I've . . ." Instagram. April 3, 2020. https://www.instagram.com/p/B-hqAEDFOKZ/. Accessed July 22, 2022.

Brooks, Daphne. "The Write to Rock: Racial Mythologies, Feminist History, and the Pleasures of Rock Music Criticism." *Women and Music: A Journal of Gender and Culture* 12 (2008): 54–62.

Brown, Keah. "Nurturing Black Disabled Joy." In *Disability Visibility: First-Person Stories from the Twenty-First Century*, edited by Alice Wong, 117–120. Vintage Books, 2020.

Brown, Lydia X. Z. 2011. "The Significance of Semantics: Person-First Language: Why It Matters." *Autistic Choya*. Accessed July 7, 2022. https://www.autistichoya.com/2011/08/significance-of-semantics-person-first.html

Brown, Lydia X. Z. "We Can't Address Disability Without Addressing Race. Here's Why." *Learn Play Thrive*. June 18, 2020. https://www.learnplaythrive.com/single-post/Racism. Accessed October 23, 2023.

Brune, Jeffrey A., and Daniel J. Wilson. *Disability and Passing: Blurring the Lines of Identity*. Philadelphia: Temple University Press, 2013.

Bucksbaum, Sydney. "Tom Hanks and Rita Wilson Test Positive for Coronavirus." March 11, 2020. https://ew.com/celebrity/tom-hanks-rita-wilson-test-positive-coronavirus/. Accessed July 22, 2022.

BIBLIOGRAPHY 179

Bull, Michael. *Sound Moves: iPod Culture and Urban Experience*. London: Routledge, 2007.

Burgess, Jean, and Joshua Green. *YouTube: Online Video and Participatory Culture*. Malden, MA: Polity Press, 2009.

Cahill, Keenan. "Teenage Dream (Keenan Cahill)." YouTube.com. August 28, 2010. Accessed June 23, 2023. https://www.youtube.com/watch?v=lm_n3hg-Gbg

Campbell, Fiona Kumari. *Contours of Ableism: The Production of Disability and Abledness*. Basingstoke: Palgrave Macmillan, 2009.

Cheng, William. *Just Vibrations: The Purpose of Sounding Good*. Ann Arbor: University of Michigan Press, 2016.

Cheng, William. *Loving Music Till It Hurts*. Oxford: Oxford University Press, 2020.

Cheng, William. "Staging Overcoming: Narratives of Disability and Meritocracy in Reality Singing Competitions." *Journal of the Society for American Music* 11, no. 2 (2017): 184–214.

Chitrakorn, Kati. "Fashion Influencers Find New Opportunities during Covid-19." *Vogue Business*. April 1, 2020. https://www.voguebusiness.com/companies/fashion-influenc ers-find-new-opportunities-during-covid-19. Accessed July 22, 2022.

Chun, Wendy Hui Kyong. *Updating to Remain the Same Habitual New Media*. Cambridge: MIT Press, 2016.

Clare, Eli. *Exile and Pride: Disability, Queerness, and Liberation*. Durham, NC: Duke University Press, 1999.

Click, Melissa. *Anti-Fandom*. New York: New York University Press, 2019.

Collins, Karen. *Playing with Sound: A Theory of Interacting with Sound and Music in Video Games*. Cambridge, MA: MIT Press, 2013.

Concha, Joe. "Fox News Prime-Time Lineup Delivers Highest Ratings in 24-Year History." TheHill.com. February 25, 2020. https://thehill.com/homenews/media/484592-fox-news-primetime-lineup-delivers-highest-ratings-in-network-history/. Accessed July 22, 2022.

Coscarelli, Joe. "The Only Music Critic Who Matters (if You're Under 25)," *New York Times*, September 30, 2020. Section AR, p. 9. Accessed October 29, 2020.

Davis, Lennard. *Enforcing Normalcy: Disability, Deafness, and the Body*. New York: Verso, 1996 [1995].

Davis, Lennard. "Normalcy, Power, and Culture." In *The Disability Studies Reader*, edited by Lennard Davis, 18–31. New York: Taylor and Francis, 2013.

DeFrantz, Thomas. "The Black Beat Made Visible." In *Of the Presence of the Body: Essays on Dance and Performance Theory*, edited by André Lepecki, 64–81. Middletown, CT: Wesleyan University Press, 2004.

Dell'Antonio, Andrew. *Beyond Structural Listening?: Postmodern Modes of Hearing*. Oakland: University of California Press, 2004.

Dijck, José van. *The Culture of Connectivity: A Critical History of Social Media*. New York: Oxford University Press, 2013.

"Disability Impacts ALL of US." *Center for Disease Control*. https://www.cdc.gov/ncbddd/ disabilityandhealth/infographic-disability-impacts-all.html. Updated May 15, 2023. Accessed October 23, 2023.

Eidsheim, Nina Sum. *The Race of Sound: Listening, Timbre, and Vocality in African American Music*. Durham, NC: Duke University Press, 2019.

Eidsheim, Nina Sum. *Sensing Sound: Singing and Listening as Vibrational Practice*. Durham, NC: Duke University Press, 2015.

180 BIBLIOGRAPHY

Elba, Idris. "This morning . . . " Twitter. March 16, 2020. https://twitter.com/idrise
lba/status/1239617034901524481?ref_src=twsrc%5Etfw%7Ctwcamp%5Etwe
etembed%7Ctwterm%5E1239617034901524481%7Ctwgr%5E&ref_url=
https%3A%2F%2Fwww.cnn.com%2F2020%2F03%2F16%2Fentertainment%2Fidris-
elba-coronavirus-trnd%2Findex.html. Accessed July 22, 2022.

Eliza Caws. "GLITCHY MUSICAL.LY TUTORIAL // Tips and tricks [Eliza Caws]."
YouTube.com. December 1, 2016. Accessed June 23, 2023. https://www.youtube.com/
watch?v=hxtfMVr4uPQ.

Ellcessor, Elizabeth. *Restricted Access: Media, Disability, and the Politics of Participation.*
New York: New York University Press, 2016.

Ellis, Katie, and Mike Kent. *Disability and New Media.* New York: Palgrave Macmillan,
2011.

Ellis, Katie, and Mike Kent. *Disability and Social Media: Global Perspectives.* New York
and London: Routledge, 2017.

Eriksson, Maria, Rasmus Fleischer, Anna Johansson, Patrick Vonderau, and Pelle
Snickars. *Spotify Teardown: Inside the Black Box of Streaming Music.* Cambridge, MA:
MIT Press, 2019.

Erlmann, Veit. *Reason and Resonance: A History of Modern Aurality.* New York: Zone
Books, 2010.

Evelyn from the Internetz, "Beyoncé Played My #Lemonade Video On Tour & You Can
#StayMad | @EVEEEEEZY," May 23, 2016. https://www.youtube.com/watch?v=Qy4N
Vh4JSK0. Accessed October 23, 2023.

Farrier, Stephen. "That Lip-Synching Feeling: Drag Performance as Digging the Past." In
Queer Dramaturgies: International Perspectives on Where Performance Leads Queer,
edited by Alyson Campbell and Stephen Farrier, 192–209. London, UK: Palgrave
Macmillan, 2016.

Ford Foundation. "(Audio Described) Political participation & disability, ft Alice Wong,
#CripTheVote." YouTube.com. January 7, 2022. Accessed June 23, 2023. https://www.
youtube.com/watch?v=hqAZuVUt_N0

Galloway, Kate. "Sensing, Sharing, and Listening to Musicking Animals across the Sonic
Environments of Social Media," *Twentieth-Century Music* 19 (2022): 363–368.

Galloway, Kate, K.E. Goldschmitt, and Paula Harper, eds. *Twentieth-Century Music* 19,
no. 3 (2022): 363–368.

Gibson, James. "The Theory of Affordances." In *The Ecological Approach to Visual
Perception.* Boston: Houghton Mifflin, 1979.

Goldschmitt, K.E., Kate Galloway, and Paula Harper, eds. *American Music Special Issue:
Platforms, Labor, and Community in Online Listening* 38, no. 2 (2020): 125–130.

Garland-Thomson, Rosemarie. *Extraordinary Bodies: Figuring Physical Disability in
American Culture and Literature.* New York: Columbia University Press, 1997.

Garland-Thomson, Rosemarie. *Staring: How We Look.* New York: Oxford University
Press, 2009.

Gates, Henry Louis. *The Signifying Monkey: A Theory of African-American Literary
Criticism.* New York: Oxford University Press, 1989.

Gaunt, Kyra. *The Games Black Girls Play: Learning the Ropes from Double-Dutch to Hip
Hop.* New York: New York University Press, 2006.

Gaunt, Kyra. "YouTube, Twerking & You: Context Collapse and the Handheld Co-
Presence of Black Girls and Miley Cyrus." *Journal of Popular Music Studies* 27, no. 3
(2015): 244–273.

BIBLIOGRAPHY 181

Goggin, Gerard. *Cell Phone Culture: Mobile Technology in Everyday Life*. London and New York: Routledge, 2006.

Goodman, David. "Distracted Listening: On Not Making Sound Choices in the 1930s." In *Sound in the Age of Mechanical Reproduction*, edited by David Suisman and Susan Strasser, 15–46. Philadelphia: University of Pennsylvania Press, 2010.

Gordenker, Alice. *Japan Times*. October 18, 2011. https://www.japantimes.co.jp/news/2011/10/18/reference/annoying-tv-pop-ups/.

Gracyk, Theodore. *Listening to Popular Music: Or, How I Learned to Stop Worrying and Love Led Zeppelin*. Ann Arbor: University of Michigan Press, 2010 [2007].

Grynbaum, Michael M. "Trump's Briefings Are a Ratings Hit: Should Networks Cover Them Live?" March 25, 2020. https://www.nytimes.com/2020/03/25/business/media/trump-coronavirus-briefings-ratings.html. Accessed July 22, 2022.

Hahn, Tomie. *Sensational Knowledge: Embodying Culture through Japanese Dance*. Middletown, CT: Wesleyan University Press, 2007.

Halberstam, Jack. *In a Queer Time and Place: Transgender Bodies, Subcultural Lives*. New York: NYU Press, 2005.

Halberstam, Jack. *The Queer Art of Failure*. Durham, NC: Duke University Press, 2011.

Hagood, Mack. *Hush: Media and Sonic Self-Control*. Durham, NC: Duke University Press, 2019.

Hendren, Sara. *What Can a Body Do?* New York: Riverhead Books, 2020.

Higgins, Jim. "Guitar Wizards Take to 'Air' Contest." *The Milwaukee Sentinel*, July 16, 1982, 4.

Holmes, Jessica. "Expert Listening Beyond the Limits of Hearing: Music and Deafness." *Journal of the American Musicological Society* 70, no. 1 (2017): 171–220.

hooks, bell. *Black Looks: Race and Representation*. Brooklyn: South End Press, 1992.

Hosokawa, Shūhei, and Tōru Mitsui. *Karaoke Around the World: Global Singing, Local Technology*. New York: Routledge, 1998.

Howe, Blake. "Disabling Music Performance." In *Oxford Handbook of Music and Disability Studies*, edited by Blake Howe, Stephanie Jensen-Moulton, Neil Lerner, and Joseph Straus, 191–209. New York: Oxford University Press, 2015.

Huizinga, Johan. *Homo Ludens: A Study of the Play Element in Culture*. Boston: Random House, [1938] 1950.

Hutchinson, Sydney. "Asian Fury: A Tale of Race, Rock, and Air Guitar." *Ethnomusicology* 60, no. 3 (2016): 411–433.

Hutchinson, Sydney. "Putting Some Air on Their Chests: Masculinity and Movement in Competitive Air Guitar." *The World of Music* 3, no. 2 (2014): 79–104.

Jackson, Lauren Michele. "We Need to Talk About Digital Blackface in Reaction GIFs." *Teen Vogue*. August 2, 2017. https://www.teenvogue.com/story/digital-blackface-reaction-gifs. Accessed October 23, 2023.

Jenkins, Henry. *Convergence Culture: Where Old and New Media Collide*. New York: NYU Press, 2008.

Johnson, Merri Lisa, and Robert McRuer. "Cripistemologies: Introduction." *Journal of Literary and Cultural Disability Studies* 8, no. 2 (2014): 136.

Jones, Jeannette Dibernardo. "Music-Making in Deaf Culture." In *Oxford Handbook of Music and Disability Studies*, edited by Blake Howe, Stephanie Jensen-Moulton, Neil William Lerner, and Joseph Nathan Straus, 54–72. New York: Oxford University Press, 2016.

Kafer, Alison. *Feminist, Queer, Crip*. Bloomington: Indiana University Press, 2013.

BIBLIOGRAPHY

Kapchan, Deborah. "Body." In *Keywords in Sound*, by David Novak and Matt Sakakeeny. Durham, NC: Duke University Press, 2015. doi:https://doi.org/10.1215/978082 2375494

Katz, Mark. *Capturing Sound: How Technology Has Changed Music*. Berkeley: University of California Press, 2010.

Köver, Chris, and Markus Reuter. "TikTok Curbed Reach for People with Disabilities." Netzpolitik.org. February 12, 2019. https://netzpolitik.org/2019/discrimination-tik tok-curbed-reach-for-people-with-disabilities/. Accessed October 23, 2023.

Langley, Carol. "Borrowed Voice: The Art of Lip-Synching in Sydney Drag." *Australasian Drama Studies* 48 (2006): 5–17.

Lerner, Neil, and Joseph Straus. *Sounding Off: Theorizing Disability in Music*. New York: Routledge, 2006.

Lessig, Lawrence. *Remix: Making Art and Commerce Thrive in the Hybrid Economy*. New York: Penguin, 2008.

Lipsitz, George. *The Possessive Investment in Whiteness: How White People Profit from Identity Politics*. Philadelphia: Temple University Press, 2006.

Lubet, Alex. *Music, Disability, and Society*. Philadelphia: Temple University Press, 2011.

Lum, Casey. *In Search of a Voice: Karaoke and the Construction of Identity in Chinese America*. Mahwah, New Jersey: Lawrence Erlbaum Associates Inc., 1996.

Maler, Anabel. "Musical Expression Among Deaf and Hearing Song Signers." In *Oxford Handbook of Music and Disability Studies*, edited by Blake Howe, Stephanie Jensen-Moulton, Neil Lerner, and Joseph Straus, 73–91. New York: Oxford University Press, 2016.

Mann, Benjamin W. "Survival, Disability Rights, and Solidarity: Advancing Cyberprotest Rhetoric through Disability March." Disability Studies Quarterly 38, no. 1 (2018).

Marshall, Wayne. "Treble Culture." In Oxford Handbook of Music & Mobility Studies, edited by Sumanth Gopinath and Jason Stanyek, 43–76. New York: Oxford University Press, 2014.

Maus, Marcel. "Techniques of the Body." *Economy and Society* 2, no. 1 (1973 [1934]): 70–88.

McCracken, Allison. " 'God's Gift to Us Girls': Crooning, Gender, and the Re-Creation of American Popular Song," *American Music* 17, no. 4 (1999): 365–395.

McDaniel, Byrd. "Air Apparent: Amplifying the History of Air Guitar, Air Bands, and Air Guitar in the Twentieth Century." *American Quarterly* 70, no. 4 (2018): 807–829.

McDaniel, Byrd. "All Songs Considered: The Persuasive Listening of Music Podcasts." *Twenty-First Century Music* 19, no. 3 (2022): 411–426. Published by Cambridge University Press. https://doi.org/10.1017/S1478572222000275.

McDaniel, Byrd. "How Air Guitar Became a Serious Sport." *The Conversation*. April 29, 2019. https://theconversation.com/how-air-guitar-became-a-serious-sport-113154.

McDaniel, Byrd. "Out of Thin Air: Configurability, Choreography, and the Air Guitar World Championships." *Ethnomusicology* 61, no. 3 (Fall 2017): 419–445.

McDaniel, Byrd. "Popular Music Reaction Videos: Reactivity, Creator Labor, and the Performance of Listening Online." 23, no. 6 (2020): 1624–1641.

McDaniel, Byrd. "Syncing Out Loud: Listening Norms in the 21st Century." Dissertation, Brown University, 2019.

McDaniel, Byrd, and Paul Renfro. " 'This Is Not Normal": Ability, Gender, and Age in the Resistance to Trumpism." *Disability Studies Quarterly* 39, no. 2 (2019). https://doi.org/10.18061/dsq.v39i2.6453.

BIBLIOGRAPHY 183

McKay, George. *Shakin' All Over: Popular Music and Disability*. Ann Arbor: University of Michigan Press, 2013.

McKenna, John, and Michael Moffitt. *The Complete Air Guitar Handbook*. New York: Pocket Books, 1983.

McLeod, Lateef. "I Am Too Pretty for Some 'Ugly Laws.'" *New York Times*, August 15, 2018. Accessed December 12, 2022.

McPherson, Tara. "Reload: Liveness, Mobility and the Web." In *The Visual Culture Reader*, 2nd ed., edited by Nicholas Mirzoeff, 199–208. New York: Routledge, 2002.

McRuer, Robert. *Crip Theory: Cultural Signs of Queerness and Disability*. New York: New York University Press, 2006.

Meizel, Katherine. *Idolized: Music, Media, and Identity in American Idol*. Bloomington: Indiana University Press, 2011.

Meizel, Katherine. *Mutivocality: Singing on the Borders of Identity*. New York: Oxford University Press, 2020.

Miller, Kiri. *Playable Bodies: Dance Games and Intimate Media*. New York: Oxford University Press, 2017.

Miller, Kiri. *Playing Along: Digital Games, YouTube, and Virtual Performance*. New York: Oxford University Press, 2012.

Mills, Mara. "Deafness." In *Keywords in Sound*, edited by David Novak and Matt Sakakeeny. Durham, NC: Duke University Press, 2015. https://doi.org/10.1215/978082 2375494

Mills, Mara. "Hearing Aids and the History of Electronics Miniaturization." *Media, Culture, and Communication* 33, no. 2 (2011): 24–44.

Mills, Mara, and Jonathan Sterne. "Aural Speed-Reading: Some Historical Bookmarks." *PMLA*. 135, no. 2 (2020): 401–411.

Mills, Mara, and Jonathan Sterne. "Dismediation: Three Propositions and Six Tactics (Afterword)." In *Disability Media Studies: Media, Popular Culture, and the Meanings of Disability*, edited by Elizabeth Ellcessor and Bill Kirkpatrick, 365–378. New York: New York University Press, 2017.

Miserandino, Christine. "The Spoon Theory." https://butyoudontlooksick.com/articles/written-by-christine/the-spoon-theory/. Copyright 2023. Accessed July 17, 2022.

Mitchell, David, and Sharon L. Snyder. *Narrative Prosthesis: Disability and the Dependencies of Discourse*. Ann Arbor: University of Michigan Press, 2014.

Leroy F. Moore, *Black Disabled Ancestors*. Independently published, 2020.

Moretoki. "Another Car Ride with Motoki." YouTube.com. July 25, 2016. Accessed March 4, 2022.

Morris, Jeremy Wade. *Selling Digital Music: Formatting Culture*. Oakland: University of California Press, 2015.

Moten, Fred, and Stefano Harney. *The Undercommons*. New York: Minor Compositions, 2013.

Muñoz, José. "Feeling Brown, Feeling Down." *Signs: Journal of Women in Culture and Society*. 31, no. 3 (2006): 679.

Nancy, Jean-Luc. *Listening*. Translated by Charlotte Mandell. New York City, New York: Fordham University Press, 2007.

National ADAPT. "National ADAPT Advocates for Disability Justice during Pandemic." September 30, 2021. https://nlihc.org/resource/national-adapt-advocates-disability-justice-during-pandemic. Accessed July 22, 2022.

184 BIBLIOGRAPHY

Nelson, Leah. "This Veteran's Day, Sean Worsley is finally home with his wife. May Alabama learn from the mistake of imprisoning this decorated Iraq War hero in the name of "law and order." *Alabama Appleseed*. November 9, 2020. https://alabamaappleseed.org/alabama-prisons/this-veterans-day-sean-worsley-is-finally-home-with-his-wife-may-alabama-learn-from-the-mistake-of-imprisoning-this-decorated-iraq-war-hero-in-the-name-of-law-and-order/

Novak, David. *Japanoise: Music at the Edge of Circulation*. Durham, NC: Duke University Press, 2013.

Oliveros, Pauline.. "Auralizing the Sonosphere: A Vocabulary for Inner Sound and Sounding." In *Sounding the Margins: Collected Writings 1992–2009*, edited by Lawton Hall, 22–25. Kingston, NY: Deep Listening Publications, 2010.

Perelli, Amanda, Dan Whateley, and Sydney Bradley. "How the Coronavirus Is Changing the Influencer Business, According to Marketers and Top Creators on Instagram and YouTube." Insider. September 1, 2020. https://www.businessinsider.com/how-coronavirus-is-changing-influencer-marketing-creator-industry-2020-3. Accessed July 22, 2022.

Perez, Sarah. "Report: WhatsApp has seen a 40% increase in usage due to COVID-19 pandemic." TechCrunch. March 26, 2020. https://techcrunch.com/2020/03/26/report-whatsapp-has-seen-a-40-increase-in-usage-due-to-covid-19-pandemic/. Accessed July 22, 2022.

Perez, Sarah. "YouTube Will Now Allow Creators to Monetize Videos about Coronavirus and COVID-19." March 11, 2020. https://techcrunch.com/2020/03/11/youtube-will-now-allow-creators-to-monetize-videos-about-coronavirus-and-covid-19/. Accessed July 22, 2022.

Peters, Benjamin. "A Network is Not a Network." In *Your Computer is On Fire*, edited by Thomas S. Mullaney, Benjamin Peters, Mar Hicks, and Kavita Philip, 71–90. Cambridge, MA: MIT Press, 2021.

Powers, Ann, and Evelyn McDonnell, eds. *Rock She Wrote: Women Write about Rock, Pop, and Rap*. Lanham, MD: Cooper Square Press, 1999.

"React." Fine Brothers Properties, Inc. *USPTO*. 2015. https://uspto.report/TM/86689364.

Thomas Reid, "Reid My Mind," *Reid My Mind*, reidmymind.com. Accessed October 24, 2023.

Renfro, Paul. "Coronavirus Is Different from AIDS." *Washington Post*. April 6, 2020. https://www.washingtonpost.com/outlook/2020/04/06/coronavirus-is-different-aids/. Accessed July 22, 2020.

Rettberg, Jill Walker. "Hand Signs for Lip-syncing: The Emergence of a Gestural Language on Musical.ly as a Video-Based Equivalent to Emoji." *Social Media + Society* 3, no. 4 (2017): 1–11.

Riviere, Joan. "Womanliness as a Masquerade." *The International Journal of Pscyhoanalysis* 10 (1929): 303–313.

Robehmed, Natalie, and Madeline Berg. "Highest-Paid YouTube Stars 2018: Markiplier, Jake Paul, PewDiePie and More." *Forbes.com*. December 3, 2018. https://www.forbes.com/sites/natalierobehmed/2018/12/03/highest-paid-youtube-stars-2018-markiplier-jake-paul-pewdie-pie-and-more/#36315b73909a.

Robinson, Dylan. *Hungry Listening: Resonant Theory for Indigenous Sound Studies*. Minneapolis: University of Minnesota Press, 2020.

Robinson, Melia. "This Teen Went from Getting Bullied in School to Being a Musical.ly Star with Millions of Fans." *Business Insider*. August 11, 2016. https://www.businessinsider.com/musically-star-kaylee-halko-2016-8. Accessed October 23, 2023.

BIBLIOGRAPHY 185

Rodgers, Tara. "Pamela Z." In *Pink Noise: Women on Electronic Music and Sound*, 216–225. Durham: Duke University Press, 2010.

Rose, Tricia. *Black Noise: Rap Music and Black Culture in Contemporary America*. Middletown, CT: Wesleyan University Press, 2004 [1994].

Samuels, Ellen. *Fantasies of Identification: Disability, Gender, Race*. New York: New York University Press, 2014.

Samuels, Ellen. "Six Ways of Looking at Crip Time." *Disability Studies Quarterly* 37, no. 3 (2017).

Sanneh, Kelefa. "The Rap Against Rockism." *New York Times*. October 31, 2004. http://www.nytimes.com/2004/10/31/arts/music/the-rap-against-rockism.html. Section 2, p. 1.

Schloss, Joseph. *Making Beats: The Art of Sample-Based Hip-Hop*. Middletown, CT: Wesleyan University Press, 2004.

Schneider, Rebecca. *Performing Remains: Art and War in Times of Theatrical Reenactment*. New York: Routledge, 2011.

Schwartz, Hillel. "The Indefensible Ear: A History." In *The Auditory Culture Reader*, edited by Michael Bull and Les Back, 487–500. New York: Berg, 2003.

Schwartz, Hillel. *Making Noise: From Babel to the Big Bang & Beyond*. Cambridge, MA: MIT Press, 2011.

Schweik, Susan M. *The Ugly Laws: Disability in Public*. New York: New York University Press, 2009.

Seaver, Nick. "Captivating Algorithms: Recommender Systems as Traps." *Journal of Material Culture* 24, no. 4 (2019): 421–436.

Senft, Theresa. "Microcelebrity and the Branded Self," In *A Companion to New Media Dynamics*, edited by John Hartley, Jean Burgess, and Axel Bruns. Hoboken, NJ: Blackwell Publishing Limited, 2013.

Shaheem Sanchez. "Pills and Automobiles: Chris Brown in (Sign Language)." YouTube.com. September 27, 2017. Accessed June 23, 2023. https://www.youtube.com/watch?v=WkOfEBY23_Y.

Shakespeare, Tom. "The Social Model of Disability." In *Disability Studies Reader*, edited by Lennard Davis, 214–222. New York: Taylor and Francis, 2013 [2006].

Shanley, Patrick. "Twitch Breaks Various Viewership Records Amid Coronavirus Quarantine." Hollywood Reporter. April 1, 2020. https://www.hollywoodreporter.com/news/general-news/twitch-breaks-viewership-records-coronavirus-quarantine-1287894/ Accessed July 22, 2022.

Siebers, Tobin. *Disability Theory*. Ann Arbor: University of Michigan Press, 2008.

Simsek, Burcu, Crystal Abidin, and Megan Lindsay Brown. "musical.ly and Microcelebrity Among Girls." In *Microcelebrity Around the Globe: Approaches to Cultures of Internet Fame*, edited by Crystal Abidin and Megan Lindsay Brown, 47–56. Bingley, UK: Emerald Publishing Limited, 2018.

Sinnreich, Aram. *Mashed Up: Technology and the Rise of Configurable Culture*. Amherst: University of Massachusetts Press, 2010.

Small, Christopher. *Musicking: The Meanings of Performing and Listening*. Middletown, CT: Wesleyan University Press, 1998.

smith, s.e. "The Beauty of Spaces Created for and by Disabled People." In *Disability Visibility: First-Person Stories from the Twenty-First Century*, edited by Alice Wong, 271–276. New York: Vintage Books.

Social Repose. "BILLIE EILISH REACTED TO MY COVER II: Billie Eilish Watches Fan Covers on YouTube | Glamour." Youtube.com. November 16, 2018. Accessed June 23, 2023. https://www.youtube.com/watch?v=Yc82zgKOjM0

186 BIBLIOGRAPHY

Spangler, Todd. "Musical.ly Launches Major Update to Video App, Which May Help Broaden Its Audience." Variety. August 23, 2016. https://variety.com/2017/digital/news/musical-ly-app-upgrade-content-related-videos-1202535239/.

Spinelli, Martin, and Lance Dann. *Podcasting: The Audio Media Revolution*. New York: Bloomsbury Publishing Inc., 2019.

Stephanie Bethany. "An Autistic's Thoughts on Kodi Lee (AGT Golden Buzzer)." YouTube.com. June 13, 2019. Accessed June 23, 2023. https://www.youtube.com/watch?v=E9tKcTjlGa0.

Sterne, Jonathan. *The Audible Past: Cultural Origins of Sound Reproduction*. Durham, NC: Duke University Press, 2003.

Sterne, Jonathan. *MP3: The Meaning of a Format*. Durham, NC: Duke University Press, 2012.

Stoever, Jennifer Lynn. *The Sonic Color Line: Race and the Cultural Politics of Listening*. New York: New York University Press, 2016.

Stokel-Walker, Chris. *YouTubers: How YouTube Shook Up TV and Created a New Generation of Stars*. Croydon, UK: Canbury Press, 2019.

Straus, Joseph. *Extraordinary Measures: Disability in Music*. New York: Oxford University Press, 2011.

Straus, Joseph. "Normalizing the Abnormal: Disability in Music and Music Theory." *Journal of the American Musicological Society* 59, no. 1 (2006): 113–184.

Subotnik, Rose. *Deconstructive Variations: Music and Reason in Western Society*. Minneapolis: University of Minnesota Press, 1996.

Sutton-Smith, Brian. *The Ambiguity of Play*. Cambridge, MA: Harvard University Press, 1997.

Szendy, Peter. *Listen: A History of Our Ears*. New York: Fordham University Press, 2008.

Talent Recap. "AGT Winner Kodi Lee ALL Performances on America's Got Talent EVER!" YouTube.com. August 26, 2021. Accessed June 23, 2023. https://www.youtube.com/watch?v=E9tKcTjlGa0.

Taylor, Diana. *The Archive and the Repertoire: Performing Cultural Memory in the Americas*. Durham, NC: Duke University Press, 2003.

Taylor, Timothy. "The Commodification of Music at the Dawn of the Era of 'Mechanical Music.'" *Ethnomusicology* 51, no. 2 (2007): 285.

theneedledrop. "Danny Brown: XXX ALBUM REVIEW." YouTube.com. August 24, 2011. Accessed June 23, 2023. https://www.youtube.com/watch?v=BbWQaI91RfY

Thompson, Emily. *The Soundscape of Modernity: Architectural Acoustics and the Culture of Listening in America, 1900–1933*. Cambridge, MA: MIT University Press, 2002.

Toliver, Alexis, Patricia Berne, Kylie Brooks, Neal Carter, Patrick Cokley, Candace Coleman, Dustin Gibson, Timotheus Gordon Jr., Keri Gray, Christopher DeAngelo Huff, Cyree Jarelle Johnson, Lorrell D. Kilpatrick, Carolyn Lazard, Talila A. Lewis, Leroy F. Moore Jr., Vilissa Thompson, and Heather Watkins. "Disability Solidarity: Completing the 'Vision for Black Lives.'" Harriet Tubman Collective. Harvard Kennedy School Journal of African American Public Policy. 2017.

Tsapovsky, Flora. "Could the Coronavirus Kill Influencer Culture?" Wired. April 14, 2020. https://www.wired.com/story/coronavirus-covid-19-influencers/. Accessed July 22, 2022.

UHG IT'S JOE. "We Tested Positive for Coronavirus (COVID-19)." YouTube.com. March 27, 2020. https://www.youtube.com/watch?v=iq2y5hzpbPQ. Accessed July 22, 2022.

VICE News. "Why I Love Being a Ferocious Air Guitar God." VICE. August 1, 2017. https://video.vice.com/en_ca/video/why-i-love-being-a-ferocious-air-guitar-god/5960050e6152bceb15df8840.Accessed July 22, 2022.

Walker, Nick. "Neuroqueer: An Introduction." In *Neurocosmopolitanism: Dr. Nick Walker's Notes on Neurodiversity, Autistm, and Self-Liberation*. 2015. https://neuroqueer.com/neuroqueer-an-introduction/.

Walser, Robert. *Running with the Devil: Power, Gender, and Madness in Heavy Metal Music*. Middletown, CT: Wesleyan University Press, 1993.

Warren-Crow, Heather. "Screaming like a Girl: Viral Video and the Work of Reaction." *Feminist Media Studies* 16, no. 6 (2016): 1113–1117.

Weisbard, Eric. *Top 40 Democracy: The Rival Mainstreams of American Music*. Chicago: The University of Chicago Press, 2014.

Weise, Jillian. "Common Cyborg." In *Disability Visibility: First-Person Stories from the Twenty-First Century*, edited by Alice Wong, 63–74. New York: Vintage Books, 2020.

White, April. "An Electrifying History of Air Guitar." *Smithsonian Magazine*. July 2019. https://www.smithsonianmag.com/arts-culture/electrifying-history-air-guitar-180972553/ Accessed October 23, 2023.

Wong, Alice. *Disability Visibility: First-Person Stories from the Twenty-First Century*. New York City, NY: Vintage Books, 2020.

Wong, Alice. "Diversifying Radio with Disabled Voices." Transom.org. 2016. https://transom.org/2016/alice-wong/. Accessed July 17, 2022.

Wong, Deborah. *Speak It Louder: Asian Americans Making Music*. New York: Routledge, 2004.

YouTube Creators. "Coronavirus and YouTube: Answering Creator Questions." March 20, 2020. YouTube. https://www.youtube.com/watch?v=i352PxWf_3M. Accessed July 22, 2022.

"Most viewed music videos of all time." YouTube Top Lists. Kworb.net. (n.d.). https://kworb.net/youtube/topvideos.html. Accessed July 1, 2022.

Index

For the benefit of digital users, indexed terms that span two pages (e.g., 52–53) may, on occasion, appear on only one of those pages.

Figures are indicated by *f* following the page number

ableism
  definition, 4–6
  internalized ableism, 34, 45,
    143–44
  in music reception, 88–90, 96, 101,
    107–8, 110
  as related to audism, 78
  as related to norms, 2–4
  as related to technology, 127–30,
    154, 158
accessibility and inaccessibility
  inaccessibility, 59, 111–12
  platforms, 96
  in reference to sound recordings, 19, 24,
    73, 78–79
  as related disability studies, 5–7
  spaces, 135–38
  theory of, 18–19
  in the workplace, 116–17
  See also accessible listening
accessible listening
  defined, 114, 125
  as exchange, 122–25
  technologies, 126–29
  through others, 130–34
Air Guitar
  Art vs art, 152
  broader history of, 16–17, 30–
    31, 139–40
  as reactive media, 132, 143–48
  U.S. Air Guitar Championships,
    23, 25–44
  vignettes, 1, 7–8, 32–33, 35–42, 43–44,
    48–54, 153–56

  See also disability masquerade;
    Chapter 1
American Sign Language, 11–12, 59–60,
  78–82, 127–28
ancestors, 111–12, 124–25, 130

Bakan, Michael, 22, 29–30, 132–33
Beck, Alan, 116
Becker, Judith, 8–9
Bell, Christopher, 117–18
Blacking, John, 113
Boellstorff, Tom, 20, 151
Bottomly, Andrew, 115–16
Brooks, Daphne, 111
Brown, Lydia X.Z. 100

Campbell, Fiona Kumari, 4–5
chain reactions, 24, 69, 104–10
Cheng, Will, 21, 104–6, 153
Chun, Wendy, 145
Click, Melissa, 94
Collins, Karen, 147
community
  air guitar community, 25–27, 41, 52–54,
    56–57, 151–55
  on digital platforms, 60–61, 67–73, 78–
    83, 101–3
  disability community, 117–18,
    122–29
  in general, 20–24
Coscarelli, Joe, 86

Davis, Lennard, 4
Dell'Antonio, Andrew, 10–11

190 INDEX

digital platforms
  affordances, 64–66, 82, 126–31,
    139–40
  definition, 17
  digital editing, 32, 75, 117–18, 126–
    29, 158
  hashtags, 59–60, 61, 67–71, 82
  network, 5, 128, 129, 132, 133–34, 158
  privacy and sharing, 2, 33–35, 86–
    93, 140–46
  the role of the body, 17–18, 32, 96
  social media, 2, 19, 54, 77, 78–79, 92,
    106, 130, 143
  tutorials, 74–77
  universal design, 128–29
  See also chain reactions; fluent
    circulation
disability
  crip, 6–7, 68, 88–89, 96, 97–98, 112
  defined, 4–7, 29–30, 59, 89, 101
  disability justice, 96, 104, 117–18
  masquerade, 33–35, 54
  prompt for future research, 158
  rights and activism, 5–6, 19, 29–30,
    78–83, 87–88, 96, 111–12, 114, 117,
    140, 158
  See also "crip time" under "time";
    "disability community" under
    "community"
DIY, 65, 130–31, 133–36, 150

Eidsheim, Nina Sun, 137
Ellcessor, Elizabeth, 96
Erlmann, Veit, 10

Feingold, Lainey, 128–29
fluent circulation
  community, 82–85
  definition, 23–24, 60–61
  in relation to musical voice, 81–82
  transitions, 75–77

Garland-Thomson, Rosemarie, 5–6, 109
Gaunt, Kyra, 20–21, 134
Goodman, David, 16–17
Gracyk, Theodor, 10

Halberstam, Jack, 18–19, 149

Harriet Tubman Collective, 117, 153
hooks, bell, 143
Hutchinson, Sydney, 32–33

Jones, Jeanette, 11–12

Kafer, Alison, 6, 123–24, 149
Katz, Mark, 16–17
Kirkpatrick, Bill, 123–24

lip syncing
  connections to air guitar, 32
  history, 65–67, 146–47
  overview, 23–24, 61
  vignettes and notable examples, 15–16,
    65–66, 79–81, 84
  See also Chapter 2
listening
  defined, 2–3, 8–9, 17–18
  listening to listening, 113
  normal listening and listening norms, 3,
    7–15, 137, 139
  prompt for future research, 158
  See also accessible listening; spectacular
    listening
Lorenz, Jessie, 127

marginal practices, 14–15, 18–19, 69, 73,
  88, 114, 143, 152–57
McKay, George, 21
McLeod, Lateef, 58, 128
McPherson, Tara, 141
McRuer, Robert and Merri
  Johnson, 97
Meizel, Katherine, 81–82
memes, 17, 61–66, 70, 82, 86, 94
methods
  air guitar, 28–30
  ethnographic model of disability
    (see Bakan)
  lip syncing, 61–63
  overall, CoP52–CoP63
  podcasts, 117–21
  reaction videos, 89–91
Miller, Kiri, 20–21
Mills, Mara, 158
  and Jonathan Sterne, 73, 126
Moore, Leroy, 122–23, 130–33, 135

INDEX 191

Moten, Fred and Stefano Harney, 156–57
Muñoz, José, 69

Nancy, Jean-Luc, 3
neuro-
    divergent/divergence, 69, 88, 89, 112,
       123, 124–25, 143–44
    diverse/diversity, 112, 132
    queer, 69
    typical, 88, 98–99, 108

Oliveros, Pauline, 3

Peters, Benjamin, 134
podcasting
    as activist network, 133–34
    defined, 16–17, 114–16
    as restored behavior, 20–21
    variable playback speed and time,
       126, 149–51
    See also "DIY"; Chapter 4
Powers, Ann, 111

reactions
    consequences of, 141–43
    as criticism, 111
    history, 13–14, 91–95
    as method, 69, 84
    reaction videos defined, 24, 86–87, 91
    as tactical, 99–100
    See also Chapter 3
Rettberg, Jill, 77
Robinson, Dylan, 11–12, 13–14, 137

Samuels, Ellen, 4, 148–49
Schechner, Richard, 20–21
Schneider, Rebecca, 148
Schwartz, Hillel, 11–12, 13–14
Seaver, Nick, 141

sharing imperative, 24, 56, 93, 134, 140–46
Siebers, Tobin, 18, 34
Sins Invalid, 6, 117
smith, s.e. 135–36
spectacular listening
    characteristics, 16, 139
    defined, 2
    as it relates to ableism, 3–4
    See also "normal listening" under
       "listening"
Spinelli, Martin and Lance Dann, 114–
    15, 126
Sterne, Jonathan, 9–10
    and Mara Mills, 73, 126
Stoever, Jennifer Lynn, 11–12, 153
Stokel-Walker, Chris, 92, 93–94
Straus, Joseph, 3, 14, 21, 107, 136
Subotnik, Rose, 10–11
syncing out loud, 24, 32, 65–66, 146–52
Szendy, Peter, 113

Taylor, Tim, 16–17
Thompson, Emily, 12–13
time
    crip time, 122–24, 151
    evergreen content, 92–95
    filters on social media, 74–75
    reactions in real time, 91–92, 99–
       100, 103
tutorials, 74–77

Van Dijck, 64, 145
vulnerability, 22, 25–28, 40, 42, 52–53,
    54–57, 58–59, 70, 94–95, 101–3,
    124–25, 143

Weisbard, Eric, 136
Weise, Jillian, 127–28
Wheelchair Sports Camp, 135